T0075573

Praise for *Functional Programming in Java, Second Edition*

Functional Programming in Java, Second Edition offers a guided tour of how to apply principles of functional programming to make modern Java code more clear, concise, and reliable. Updated to cover the latest features of Java, each chapter is packed with before-and-after examples that illustrate the utility and power of Java's lambdas and streams.

➤ Brian Goetz, Java Language Architect at Oracle and author of
   Java Concurrency in Practice

I don't have time to read all of the books out there, much less re-read anything. The second edition of Venkat's *Functional Programming in Java* is one that is worth doing so. I was a big fan of the first edition, but the new one builds upon those existing strengths to produce the best introduction to modern Java programming. This includes new chapters on error-handling, functional idioms, and most critically, a discussion on concrete techniques to refactor to a functional style. Get on the Functional Bus and write better software.

➤ Brian Sletten, President, Bosatsu Consulting, Inc., and author of
   WebAssembly: The Definitive Guide

To stay relevant, a developer never stops learning. *Functional Programming in Java, Second Edition* offers Java developers of all levels an opportunity to keep their Java coding skills sharp and up-to-date in such areas as lambda expressions and Stream. You'll be going back to this book often to pick up many best practices, approaches and tips to keep your Java programming skills as sharp as possible.

➤ Sharat Chander, Senior Director, Java SE Product Management

Venkat has a unique story-telling style of writing. It doesn't make any assumptions, and leads the reader very easily from one concept to the next with plenty of code examples, in an intuitive and easy to understand way. If you're new to functional programming, this book provides a great foundation on the topic - helping to grasp syntax as well as the more conceptual topics.

➤ Ian Roughley, VP of Engineering at TrueNorth

This work revitalizes the appreciation of craftsmanship, making it an excellent choice for reading groups and team discussions. Specifically, Chapter 12, "Functional Programming Idioms," should be revisited before embarking on any new project. Venkat's talents for distillation are on full display, gifting the reader with material not available by web search or LLM.

➤ Don Bogardus, Quality Automation Architect at Everee and Vice President, Utah JUG

Functional Programming in Java, Second Edition

Harness the Power of Streams and Lambda Expressions

Venkat Subramaniam

The Pragmatic Bookshelf

Raleigh, North Carolina

Many of the designations used by manufacturers and sellers to distinguish their products are claimed as trademarks. Where those designations appear in this book, and The Pragmatic Programmers, LLC was aware of a trademark claim, the designations have been printed in initial capital letters or in all capitals. The Pragmatic Starter Kit, The Pragmatic Programmer, Pragmatic Programming, Pragmatic Bookshelf, PragProg and the linking *g* device are trademarks of The Pragmatic Programmers, LLC.

Every precaution was taken in the preparation of this book. However, the publisher assumes no responsibility for errors or omissions, or for damages that may result from the use of information (including program listings) contained herein.

For our complete catalog of hands-on, practical, and Pragmatic content for software developers, please visit *https://pragprog.com*.

Sir Charles Antony Richard Hoare's quote is used by permission of the ACM.
Abelson and Sussman's quote is used under Creative Commons license.

The team that produced this book includes:

CEO: Dave Rankin
COO: Janet Furlow
Managing Editor: Tammy Coron
Development Editor: Jacquelyn Carter
Indexing: Potomac Indexing, LLC
Layout: Gilson Graphics
Founders: Andy Hunt and Dave Thomas

For sales, volume licensing, and support, please contact *support@pragprog.com*.

For international rights, please contact *rights@pragprog.com*.

Copyright © 2023 The Pragmatic Programmers, LLC.

All rights reserved. No part of this publication may be reproduced, stored in a retrieval system, or transmitted, in any form, or by any means, electronic, mechanical, photocopying, recording, or otherwise, without the prior consent of the publisher.

ISBN-13: 978-1-68050-979-3
Book version: P1.0—July 2023

To perseverance.

Contents

Foreword to the First Edition

Venkat Subramaniam would never be described as a "waterfall" sort of guy. So, when he mentioned that he was starting on a Java 8 book—long before the design of Java 8 was settled—I was not at all surprised. It was clear this was going to be an "agile" book project.

Despite having to more than occasionally rework the text as the language and library features evolved, Venkat had a secret advantage—he knew where we were going. The Java 8 design was heavily influenced by the core principles of functional programming: functions as values, immutability, and statelessness. We didn't do this because functional programming is trendy or cool; we did it because programs that are expressed as stateless transformations on immutable data, rather than as modifications of mutable data structures, tend to be easier to read and maintain, to be less error-prone, and to parallelize more gracefully.

The new features introduced in Java 8 were designed together to facilitate development of more expressive and parallel-friendly libraries. Lambda expressions reduce the syntactic overhead of encoding behavior as data; default methods allow existing libraries to evolve over time, enabling core JDK classes such as Collections to take advantage of lambda expressions; the java.util.stream package leverages these language features to offer rich aggregate operations on collections, arrays, and other data sources in a declarative, expressive, and parallel-friendly manner. All of this adds up to more powerful and performant code, as well as a more pleasant programming experience.

This book not only provides lots of examples of how to use these new features, but offers readers a peek into the underlying principles behind their design, and *why* they result in better code. Let Venkat be your guide to this new and improved Java—you're in for a treat.

Brian Goetz
Java Language Architect, Oracle Corporation
September 2013

Acknowledgments

To say that the past few years have been challenging would be a gross understatement. Every single person in this world has been affected to various degrees, some a lot more than others. Nevertheless, it has rather been a test of perseverance. Taking up the project to update this book to the second edition, while writing yet another new book, in the middle of so many uncertainties and changes, was hard. But here we are, thanks in large part to the support of some amazing people.

I first want to convey my sincere thanks to the Java language team members at Oracle for their continued hard work toward the functional capabilities of Java. The improvements to the JDK over the more recent releases of Java have enriched our ability, as programmers, to use the functional facilities of Java.

My sincere thanks to Brian Goetz, Brian Sletten, José Esteves de Souza Neto, and Ian Roughley for taking the time to review the second edition and for providing valuable feedback. I want to express my gratitude to Brian Goetz for taking the time to provide extensive feedback and helping me make several improvements to various parts of the book. Any errors that may be in the book are solely mine.

I'd like to express my thanks to Joe Horvath and Nicholas Dierauf for being early readers and for reporting errors in the book's errata page. Thank you for your help in improving this book, much appreciated. A huge thanks to David Tonhofer for patiently helping me to improve many things in this book.

This second edition wouldn't have been possible without the aid of many people who helped me with the first edition. Thank you, Kimberly Barnes, Fred Daoud, Raju Gandhi, Marty Hall, Praveen Kumar, Rebecca Parsons, Kirk Pepperdine, Chris Richardson, Ian Roughley, Nate Schutta, Ken Sipe, Dan Sline, and Bruce Take. I am also thankful to Greg Helton, Günter Jantzen, Narayanan Jayaratchagan, Wacek Kusnierczyk, Nabeel Ali Memon, Marc-Daniel Ortega, Arjo Ouwens, Philip Schwarz, Ekaterina Sh, Dan Talpau,

Benjamin Tan, Brian Tarbox, Marco Vermeulen, and Jason Weden for taking the time to report errors in the first edition.

Jackie Carter is the amazing editor for this book, and I am happy to call her a good friend. You made this soooo much fun and a pleasant journey, Jackie. Thank you. The kind folks at The Pragmatic Bookshelf have been amazing yet again and made this so easy. I thank my wife, Kavitha, for giving me her support and patience.

Preface

You're in for a treat. One of the most prominent and widely used languages in the world supports object-oriented, imperative style, and functional style programming. You can mix one of the most powerful tools—the object-oriented paradigm—with the imperative style, as we did in the past, or with the functional style, as you'll learn in this book, to reduce the complexity of code. We can do quite effectively in Java what was previously possible only on the JVM using other languages—this means more power to Java programmers.

I'm thankful to have had the privilege over the past few decades to program with multiple languages: C, C++, Java, C#, F#, Ruby, Groovy, Scala, Clojure, Kotlin, Erlang, Haskell, Elm, JavaScript.... When asked which one's my favorite, my resounding answer has been that it's not the language that excites me, but the way we program.

The science and engineering in programming drew me in, but it's the art in programming that keeps me. Coding has a lot in common with writing—there's more than one way to express our ideas. Java helps us write code using objects, and we can mix that with the functional capabilities to implement our designs and ideas.

The functional programming facilities in Java can make our code more expressive, easier to write, less error-prone, and easier to parallelize than with the imperative style. The functional way has been around for decades and widely used in languages like Lisp, Clojure, Erlang, Smalltalk, Scala, Groovy, and Ruby. It's not only a relatively new way in Java but also a better way.

Since coding is like writing, we can learn a few things from that field. In *On Writing Well [Zin01]*, William Zinsser recommends simplicity, clarity, and brevity. To create better applications, we can start by making the code simpler, clearer, and more concise. We'll explore how the functional style of programming in Java helps us do exactly that throughout this book.

that truly is easier for the team to maintain. You'll learn about the idiomatic styles that work the best in Chapter 12, Functional Programming Idioms, on page 205.

In Chapter 13, Bringing It All Together, on page 217, we'll go over the key concepts and the practices needed to adopt functional programming techniques.

In Appendix 1, Starter Set of Functional Interfaces, on page 225, we'll take a glance at some of the most popular functional interfaces.

A quick overview of the syntax for functional interfaces, lambda expressions, and method/constructor references is in Appendix 2, Syntax Overview, on page 227.

The URLs mentioned throughout this book are gathered together for your convenience in Appendix 3, Web Resources, on page 233.

Java Version Used in This Book

To run most of the examples in this book you need at least Java 8. Some of the examples use features that are present in newer versions of Java.

Using automated scripts, the examples in this book have been tried out with the following version of Java:

```
openjdk version "18.0.1.1" 2022-04-22
OpenJDK Runtime Environment (build 18.0.1.1+2-6)
OpenJDK 64-Bit Server VM (build 18.0.1.1+2-6, mixed mode, sharing)
```

Take a few minutes to download the appropriate version of Java for your system. This will help you follow along with the examples in this book.

How to Read the Code Examples

When writing code in Java, we place classes in packages and executable statements and expressions in methods. To reduce clutter, we'll skip the package names and imports in the code listings. All code in this book belongs to a package:

```
package fpij;
```

Any executable code not listed within a method is part of an undisplayed main() method. When going through the code listings, if you have the urge to look at the full source code, remember it's only a click away on the website for this book.

Online Resources

A number of web resources referenced throughout the book are collected in Appendix 3, Web Resources, on page 233. Here are a couple that will help you get started with this book:

The OpenJDK website[1] for downloading the version of Java used in this book.

This book's page[2] on the Pragmatic Bookshelf website. From there you can download all the example source code for the book. You can also provide feedback by submitting errata entries or posting your comments and questions in the forum. If you're reading the book in PDF form, you can click on the link above a code listing to view or download the specific examples.

Now for some fun with lambda expressions and Stream...

Venkat Subramaniam

June 2023

---

1. https://openjdk.org/projects/jdk/18/
2. http://www.pragprog.com/titles/vsjava2e

CHAPTER 1

Hello, Lambda Expressions!

Java has been evolving at a rapid pace in recent years and Java 8 has become the baseline version in many organizations. We can write object-oriented code in Java with the imperative style or functional style and even mix them within the same application as we see fit. The imperative style has been the most popular and practiced way of writing code in Java. But this style, albeit most familiar to developers, is packed with accidental complexity. Many developers are transitioning to use the functional style of programming in Java, more and more each day. Some of the major reasons are the functional style code's reduced complexity and ease of reading and understanding, once the developers get used to the syntax and the paradigm, of course.

With the functional style, the everyday tasks we perform get simpler, easier, and more expressive. We can quickly write concise, elegant, and expressive code with fewer lines of code and errors. We don't have to figure out what the code is doing, it becomes obvious and easy to understand. The benefit is that we can focus on the domain and the inherent capabilities of the application rather than trying to decipher what the code does. We can also use this to easily enforce policies and implement common design patterns without being drowned in verbose long-winded code. The net result is that we can be more productive in creating and delivering applications faster.

In this book, we'll explore the functional style of programming using direct examples of everyday tasks we do as programmers. Before we take the leap to this elegant style, which is a better way to design and program, let's discuss the reasons to change from the familiar imperative style.

Change the Way You Think

Imperative style—that's what Java has provided us with since its inception. In this style, we tell Java every step of what we want it to do and then we watch it faithfully exercise those steps. That's worked fine, but it's a bit low-level. The code tends to get verbose, and we often wish the language were a tad more intelligent; we could then tell it—declaratively—*what* we want rather than delve into *how* to do it. Thankfully, Java can help us do that. Let's look at a few examples to see the benefits and the differences in style.

The Habitual Way

Let's start on familiar ground to see the two paradigms in action. Here's an imperative way to find if Chicago is in a collection of given cities—remember, the listings in this book only have snippets of code (see How to Read the Code Examples, on page xviii).

introduction/fpij/Cities.java

```java
boolean found = false;
for(String city : cities) {
  if(city.equals("Chicago")) {
    found = true;
    break;
  }
}

System.out.println("Found chicago?:" + found);
```

This imperative version is noisy and low-level; it has several moving parts. We first initialize a smelly boolean flag named found and then walk through each element in the collection. If we find the city we're looking for, then we set the flag and break out of the loop. Finally, we print out the result of our finding.

A Better Way

As observant Java programmers, the minute we set our eyes on this code we'd quickly turn it into something more concise and easier to read, like this:

introduction/fpij/Cities.java

```java
System.out.println("Found chicago?:" + cities.contains("Chicago"));
```

That's one example of declarative style—the contains() method helped us get directly to our business.

Tangible Improvements

That change improved our code in a few ways:

- No messing around with mutable variables
- Iteration steps wrapped under the hood
- Less clutter
- Better clarity; retains our focus

- Less impedance; code closely trails the business intent
- Less error prone
- Easier to understand and maintain

Beyond Simple Cases

That was simple—the declarative function to check if an element is present in a collection has been around in Java for a long time. Now imagine not having to write imperative code for more advanced operations, like parsing files, working with databases, making calls to web services, *programming concurrency*, and so on. Java now makes it possible to write concise, elegant, less error-prone code, not just for simple cases, but throughout our applications.

The Old Way

Let's look at another example. We'll define a collection of prices and try out a few ways to total discounted price values.

```
final List<Integer> prices = Arrays.asList(10, 30, 17, 20, 18, 45, 12);
```

Suppose we're asked to total the prices greater than $20, discounted by 10%. Let's do that in the habitual Java way first.

```
introduction/fpij/DiscountImperative.java
double totalOfDiscountedPrices = 0.0;

for(int price : prices) {
  if(price > 20) {
    totalOfDiscountedPrices += price * 0.9;
  }
}
System.out.println("Total of discounted prices: " + totalOfDiscountedPrices);
```

That's familiar code; we start with a mutable variable to hold the total of the discounted prices. We then loop through the prices, pick each price greater than $20, compute each item's discounted value, and add those to the total. Finally, we print the total value of the discounted prices.

And here's the output from the code.

```
Total of discounted prices: 67.5
```

It worked, but writing it feels dirty. It's no fault of ours; we had to use what was available. But the code is fairly low-level—it suffers from "primitive obsession" and defies the single-responsibility principle (SRP). And the code also violates the single level of abstraction principle (SLAP) since it delves into multiple nested levels of details. It first works with the collection of prices, then for each price it examines the value, and then for each selected value (three levels down in nesting) it computes the products and performs the sum. In addition to having to work with a poor design, those of us working from home have to keep this code away from the eyes of kids aspiring to be programmers, for they may be dismayed and sigh, "That's what you do for a living?"

A Better Way, Again

We can do better—a lot better. Our code can resemble the requirement specification. This will help reduce the gap between the business needs and the code that implements them, further reducing the chances of the requirements being misinterpreted.

Rather than tell Java to create a mutable variable and then to repeatedly assign a value to it, let's talk with it at a higher level of abstraction, as in the next code.

```
introduction/fpij/DiscountFunctional.java
final double totalOfDiscountedPrices =
  prices.stream()
        .filter(price -> price > 20)
        .mapToDouble(price -> price * 0.9)
        .sum();

System.out.println("Total of discounted prices: " + totalOfDiscountedPrices);
```

Let's read that aloud—filter prices greater than $20, map the prices to discounted values, and then add them up. The code flows along with logic in the same way we'd describe the requirements. As a convention in Java, we wrap long lines of code and line up the dots vertically before the method names, as in the previous example.

The code is concise, but we're using a number of new things from modern Java. To start with, we invoke a stream() method on the prices list. This opens the door to a *special* iterator with a wealth of convenience functions, which we'll discuss later.

Instead of explicitly iterating through the prices list, we're using a few special methods, such as filter() and map(). Unlike the methods we were used to in older versions of Java and the Java Development Kit (JDK), these methods take an anonymous function—a lambda expression—as a parameter, within the parentheses (). (We'll soon explore this further.) We invoke the sum() method, which is a special form of the reduce() operation, to compute the total on the result of the mapToDouble() which is a special form of the map() method.

The looping is concealed much like it was under the contains() method. But the map() method (and the filter() method) is more sophisticated. For each price from the prices list that passes through the filter(), the mapToDouble() method invokes the provided lambda expression to transform the given price to a discounted price. The sum() method, which is a reduce operation, adds up the transformed values to provide the final result.

Here's the output from this version of code:

```
Total of discounted prices: 67.5
```

The Improvements

You can see several improvements compared to the habitual way:

- Nicely composed, not cluttered
- Free of low-level operations
- Easier to enhance or change the logic
- Iteration controlled by a library of methods
- Efficient; lazy evaluation of loops
- Easier to parallelize where desired

Later we'll discuss how Java provides these improvements.

Lambdas to the Rescue

Lambdas, which are anonymous functions, are the functional key to relieve us from the hassles of imperative programming. Unlike methods, which belong to a class, lambdas are free-standing functions we can create within methods. By changing the way we program and by making use of lambdas, we can write code that's not only elegant and concise but also less prone to errors; more efficient; and easier to optimize, enhance, and parallelize.

The Big Gains of Functional-Style Code

Functional-style code has a higher signal-to-noise ratio; we write fewer lines of code, but each line or expression achieves more. We gained quite a bit from the functional-style version, compared with the imperative-style version:

- We avoided explicit mutation or reassignment of variables, which are often sources of bugs and result in code that's hard to make concurrent. In the imperative version, we repeatedly set the totalOfDiscountedPrices variable within the loop. In the functional-style version, there is no explicit mutation in our code. Fewer mutations lead to fewer errors in code.

- The functional version can easily be parallelized. If the computation was time-consuming, we can easily run it concurrently for each element in the list. If we parallelized the imperative version, we'd have to worry about concurrent modification of the totalOfDiscountedPrices variable. In the functional version, we gain access to the variable only after it's fully baked, which removes the thread-safety concerns.

- The code is more expressive. Rather than conveying the intent in multiple steps—create an initial dummy value, loop through prices, add discounted values to the variable, and so on—we simply ask the list's map() method to return another list with discounted values and sum them.

- The functional-style version is more concise; it took fewer lines of code than the imperative version to achieve the same result. More concise code means less code to write, less code to read, and less code to maintain—see Does Concise Just Mean Less Code?, on page 7.

- The functional-style version is intuitive—code reads more like how we'd state the problem—and it's easier to understand once we're familiar with the syntax. The map() method applies the given function (which computes the discount) to each element of the collection and produces the resulting collection, as we see in the following figure.

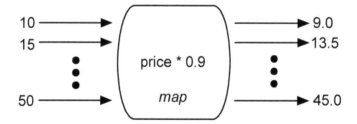

With the support for lambda expressions, we can fully use the power of the functional style of programming in Java. If we embrace this style, we can create more expressive and concise code with less mutability and fewer errors.

One of Java's key strengths has been its support of the object-oriented paradigm. The functional style is not counter to object-oriented programming (OOP). The real paradigm shift is from the imperative to the declarative style of programming. With modern Java, we can now intermix functional and OO styles of programming quite effectively. We can continue to use the OOP style to model domain entities, their states, and their relationships. In addition, we can model the behavior or state transformations, business workflows, and data processing as a series of functions to form a function composition.

> ### Joe asks:
> ## Does Concise Just Mean Less Code?
>
> Concise is short, devoid of noise, and boiled down to its essence to convey the intent effectively. The benefits are far-reaching.
>
> Writing code is like throwing ingredients together; making it concise is like turning that into a sauce. It often takes more effort to write concise code. It's less code to read, but effective code is transparent. A short code listing that's hard to understand or hides details is *terse* rather than *concise*.
>
> Concise code aids design agility and has less ceremony. This means we can quickly try out our design ideas and move forward if they're good, or move on if they turn sour.

Why Code in the Functional Style?

We saw the general benefits of the functional style of programming, but is it worth picking up this new style? Should we expect a marginal improvement, or is it life-altering? Those are genuine questions that we need answered before we commit our time and effort.

Writing Java code isn't that hard; the syntax is simple. We've gotten quite familiar and comfortable with the libraries and their APIs. What really gets us is the effort required to code and maintain the typical enterprise applications that we develop with Java.

We must ensure that fellow programmers have closed the database connections at the right time, that they're not holding on to transactions any longer than needed, that they're handling the exceptions well and at the right level, that they're securing and releasing locks properly...and the list goes on.

Each one of these in isolation may not seem like a big deal. But when combined with the domain's inherent complexities, things get overwhelming, labor-intensive, and hard to maintain.

What if we could encapsulate each of these decisions into tiny pieces of code that can manage the constraints well? Then we wouldn't have to continuously expend time, effort, and energy to enforce policies. That would be a big win—a less cognitive load—so let's see how the functional style can help.

Iteration on Steroids

We write iterations all the time to process a list of objects and to work with sets and maps. The iterators we're used to in Java are familiar and primitive, but not simple. Not only do they take a few lines of code to work with but they're also hard to compose.

How do we iterate and print each element in a collection? We could use a for loop. How do we select some elements from a collection? With the same for loop, but some extra mutable variables have to step in to support the operation. Now after selecting the values, how do we reduce the results to a single value, such as a minimum, a maximum, or an average? More looping, more mutable variables.

That's like having a jack-of-all-iterations, but a master of none. Java now provides specialized internal iterators for various operations: one to simply loop, one to map data values, one to filter out select values, one to reduce, and several convenience functions to pick the min, max, average, and so on. In addition, these operations are easy to compose so we can combine a variety of them to implement the business logic with greater ease and less code. When we're done, the code is easier to understand as it logically flows through the sequence described in the problem. We'll see several examples of this in Chapter 2, Using Collections, on page 19, and throughout the book.

Enforcing Policies

Policies rule enterprise applications. For instance, we may have to ensure an operation has proper security credentials. We may have to ensure that transactions run fast and update audit trails properly. These tasks often turn into mundane service-tier code like the following pseudocode form:

```
Transaction transaction = getFromTransactionFactory();

//... operation to run within the transaction ...

checkProgressAndCommitOrRollbackTransaction();
UpdateAuditTrail();
```

There are two issues with this kind of approach. First, it often leads to duplication of effort and, in turn, increases maintenance costs. Second, it's easy to forget about exceptions that may be thrown in the application code, thus jeopardizing the transaction lifetime and the update of audit trails. We could implement a proper try and finally block, but every time someone touches that code, we'd have to reverify that it's not broken.

Alternatively, we could get rid of the factory and turn this code on its head. Instead of receiving a transaction, we could send the processing code to a well-managed function, like so (in pseudocode):

```
runWithinTransaction((Transaction transaction) -> {
  //... operation to run within the transaction ...
});
```

This is such a small step with huge savings. The policy to check the status and update the audit trails is abstracted and encapsulated within the runWithinTransaction() method. To this method we send a piece of code that needs to run in the context of a transaction. We no longer have to worry about forgetting to perform the steps or about the exceptions being handled well. The policy-enforcing function takes care of all that.

We'll cover how to use lambda expressions to enforce such policies in Chapter 6, Working with Resources, on page 107.

Extending Policies

Policies seem to grow around us—beyond their being enforced, enterprise applications require ways to extend them. Based on some configuration information, we may have to add or remove a series of operations that, in turn, may have to be processed before core logic in a module is executed. This is a common task in Java, but it requires much forethought and design.

The machinery for extensibility is often one or more interfaces. We could carefully design these interfaces and the hierarchy of classes that will implement them. The result may be effective, but this effort possibly leaves a number of interfaces and classes that we have to maintain. The design can easily become heavyweight and hard to maintain, jeopardizing the very goal of extensibility we set out for.

There's an alternative—functional interfaces and lambda expressions, which let us design extensible policies. This way we're not forced to create extra interfaces or conform to a method name, but instead, we can focus on the core behaviors we'd like to provide, as we'll see in Decorating Using Lambda Expressions, on page 95.

Hassle-Free Concurrency

A big application is close to its delivery milestone when a huge performance issue comes to the surface. The team quickly figures out that the bottleneck is in the titanic module of the application, which involves processing large volumes of data. Someone on the team suggests that we can improve performance if we more effectively exploit the available multiple cores. But the excitement from the suggestion is likely short-lived if the titanic module is like typical old-style Java code.

The team quickly realizes that converting the titanic module's code from a sequential to a concurrent version would take substantial effort, create additional complexity, and open doors for many multithreading-related bugs. Isn't there an easier way to get better performance?

What if there is no difference between sequential and concurrent code, and the effort to run it sequentially versus concurrently is merely the flip of a switch to clearly express our intent?

That may seem possible only in Narnia, but it's quite real if we develop our modules with functional purity. The internal iterators and functional style remove the last roadblock to easy parallelism. The JDK library has been designed to make the switch between serial and parallel execution require only a small and explicit but unobtrusive code change, as we'll see in Taking a Leap to Parallelize, on page 163.

Telling the Story

So much is lost in the translation between what the business wants and how the code implements it. The bigger that gap, the greater the chance of errors and the higher the cost of maintenance. If the code reads more like the way the business states the problem, it becomes easier to read, easier to discuss with the business folks, and easier to evolve to meet their changing demands.

For instance, you hear the business say, "Get the prices for all the tickers, find the prices that are less than $500, and total the net asset value of only the stocks that make the cut." Using the new facilities available, we can write something like this:

```
tickers.stream()
  .map(StockUtil::getprice)
  .filter(StockUtil::priceIsLessThan500)
  .sum()
```

There's little chance of losing something in translation here, as there's not much to translate. This is function composition at work, and we'll see more of it in this book, especially in Chapter 9, Composing Functions with Lambda Expressions, on page 155.

Separation of Concerns

A common need in applications is the separation of the core computations from the fine-grained logic the computations depend on. For example, an order-processing system may want to apply different tax computations based on the origin of the transaction. Separating the tax-computation logic from the rest of the processing will help us create more reusable and extensible code.

In OOP we call this *separation of concern* and often use the strategy pattern to solve it. The effort typically involves creating one or more interfaces and a bunch of classes to implement them.

We can achieve the same now but with far less code. And we can try out our design ideas really fast without being bogged down by a hierarchy of code that we have to lay out first. We'll cover how to create this pattern and separate concerns using lightweight functions in Separating Concerns Using Lambda Expressions, on page 85.

Delaying Evaluation

When creating enterprise applications, we may have to interact with web services, make database calls, process XML...the list goes on. There are so many operations that we have to perform, but not all of them are necessary all the time. Avoiding some operations or at least postponing the ones that don't have to be performed yet is one of the easiest ways to improve performance and application start-up or response time.

It's a simple goal, but one that may be hard to implement using a pure OOP approach. We would have to fuss with object references and null checks to postpone the initialization of heavyweight objects, for instance.

Alternatively, we can minimize our effort and make the intent more explicit by using the new Optional class and the functional-style API it provides, as we'll see in Delayed Initialization, on page 121.

Improving Testability

Fewer things tend to break in code that has few moving parts. By nature, functional-style code is more resilient to change and requires relatively less testing effort.

In addition, as we'll see in Chapter 5, Designing with Lambda Expressions, on page 85, and Chapter 6, Working with Resources, on page 107, lambda expressions can stand in as lightweight mocks or stubs and can help create highly expressive exception tests. Lambda expressions can also serve as a great testing aid. A common set of test cases can receive and exercise lambda expressions. The tests can capture the essence of behaviors that need to be tested for regression. At the same time, the lambda expressions being passed in can serve as variations of implementations that need to be exercised.

The automated tests that are part of the JDK itself are great examples of this. These tests show how lambda expressions help parameterize the test cases' key behaviors; for example, they help compose the tests as "make a container for the results" followed by "assert some parameterized postconditions."

We've discussed how the functional style not only helps us write better quality code but also solves elegantly so many of our common application development challenges. That means we can create applications more quickly, with less effort and fewer errors—as long as we follow a few guidelines, as we will discuss next.

Evolution, Not Revolution

To reap the benefits of functional style, we don't have to switch over to another language; we simply have to change the way we use Java.

Languages like C++, Java, and C# started out with support for imperative and object-oriented programming. Now all these languages also embrace the functional style of programming. We've seen examples of these two styles and discussed the benefits we derived from the functional style. Now let's look into some key concepts and practices that will help us adopt the new style.

The Java language team has put in substantial time and effort to bring functional capabilities to the language and the JDK. To reap the benefits, we have to pick up a few new concepts. We can improve our code if we follow some guidelines:

- Be declarative.
- Promote immutability.
- Avoid side effects.
- Prefer expressions over statements.
- Design with higher-order functions.

Let's quickly look at these practices.

Be Declarative

At the core of the familiar imperative style are mutability and command-driven programming. We create variables or objects and modify their state along the way. We also provide detailed commands or instructions to execute, such as create a loop index, increment its value, check if we reached the end, update the nth element of an array, and so on. It made sense for us to program this way in the past due to the nature of the tools and the hardware limitations.

We saw how the declarative use of the contains() method—when used on a collection—was far easier to work with than the imperative style. All the hard work and lower-level details were moved into the library function, and we didn't have to deal with them. We would prefer doing everything this way if it were only easier. Immutability and declarative programming are the essence of the functional style of programming, and Java now makes them quite approachable.

Promote Immutability

Mutable code has many moving parts. The more things change, the easier it is for components to break and for errors to creep in. Code where multiple variables change is hard to understand and difficult to parallelize. Immutability removes all these problems at the root.

Java supports immutability but doesn't enforce it—but we can. We need to change our old habits of mutating objects' states. As much as possible, we must use immutable objects.

When declaring variables, fields, and parameters, lean toward declaring them final, following the sage advice "Treat objects as immutable" from *Effective Java [Blo18]*, by Joshua Bloch.

When creating objects, promote immutable objects such as the String class. When working with collections, create immutable or unmodifiable collections using functions like List.of() or the Collections class's unmodifiableList() method, for example.

By avoiding mutability we can create pure functions—that is, functions with no side effects.

Avoid Side Effects

Imagine writing a piece of code to go out to the Web to fetch a stock price and then update a shared variable. If we have a number of prices to fetch, we're forced to run these time-consuming operations sequentially. If we resort to multithreading, then we have to burden ourselves with threading and synchronization issues to prevent race conditions. The net result is poor application performance and/or lack of sleep trying to manage multiple threads. We can totally eliminate the problems by removing the side effect.

A function with no side effects honors immutability and doesn't change its input or anything in its reach. These functions are easier to understand, have fewer errors, and are easier to optimize. The lack of side effects removes any concerns of race conditions or simultaneous updates. As a result, we can also easily parallelize the execution of such functions, as we'll see in Taking a Leap to Parallelize, on page 163.

Prefer Expressions over Statements

Statements are stubborn and force mutation. Expressions promote immutability and function composition. For example, we first used the for statement to compute the total of the discounted prices. This version promoted mutation and verbose code. By switching over to the more expressive declarative version using the map() and sum() methods, which are expressions, we avoided mutations and were able to chain or compose functions.

It's better to design with expressions and use them more than statements in our code. This will now make the code concise and easier to understand. The code will flow logically, in the same order in which we would state the problem. The concise version is easier to change if the problem changes.

Design with Higher-Order Functions

Unlike some functional programming languages, such as Haskell, that enforce immutability, Java lets us modify variables at will. In that regard, Java is not, and will never be, a pure functional programming language. But we can write code in the functional style in Java by using higher-order functions.

A higher-order function takes the concept of reuse to the next level. Instead of solely relying on objects and classes to promote reuse, with higher-order functions, we can easily reuse small, focused, cohesive, and well-written functions.

In OOP we're used to passing objects to methods, creating objects within methods, and returning objects from within methods. Higher-order functions do to functions what methods do to objects. With higher-order functions, we can do the following:

- Pass functions to functions
- Create functions within functions
- Return functions from functions

We've already seen an example of passing a function to another function, and we'll see examples of creating and returning functions later. Let's look at our "passing a function to a function" example again.

```
prices.stream()
      .filter(price -> price > 20)
      .mapToDouble(price -> price * 0.9)
      .sum();
```

In this example, we're sending a function, price -> price * 0.9, as an argument to mapToDouble. The function being passed is created just in time, at the point of call to the higher-order function mapToDouble. Generally, a function has a body, a name, a parameter list, and a return type. The just-in-time function created here has a parameter list followed by an arrow (->), and then the short body. The type of the parameter may be inferred by the Java compiler here and the return type is implicit. This function is anonymous; it has no name. Rather than referring to these as anonymous functions, we call them *lambda expressions*.

Passing anonymous functions isn't a totally unknown concept in Java; we're used to passing instances of anonymous classes. If our anonymous class had only one method, we still had to go through the ceremony of creating a class, albeit anonymous, and instantiating it. Instead, we can now enjoy a lightweight syntax in Java with lambda expressions. Additionally, we're accustomed to abstracting concepts with objects. Now we can combine that with abstracting behavior using lambda expressions.

It takes some rethinking to design applications with this style of programming. We have to tune our imperative-ingrained minds to think functionally. This may seem a bit difficult at the beginning, but we'll get used to it in no time and can leave those dysfunctional APIs far behind as we move forward.

Let's now switch gears and look at how Java handles lambda expressions. We're used to passing objects to methods, but now we can store functions and pass them around. Let's look at the magic behind how Java accepts a function as an argument.

A Little Sugar to Sweeten

We could implement all the ideas with what was already available in Java, but lambda expressions remove the ceremony and sweeten our efforts by adding a little syntax sugar. This quickly translates into code that's faster to create and makes it easier to express our ideas.

In the past, we've used a number of interfaces that only have single methods: Runnable, Callable, Comparable, and so on. These interfaces are common in the JDK library and often appear where just a single function is expected. All these existing library methods that expect a single-method interface can now accept lightweight functions, thanks to the brilliant syntax sugar provided through functional interfaces.

A functional interface is an interface with one abstract—unimplemented—method. Again, think of single-method interfaces like Runnable, Callable, Comparable, and so on, which all fit that definition. The modern JDK has more of these types of interfaces—Function, Predicate, Consumer, Supplier, and so on (for a summary of the starter set of functional interfaces see Appendix 1, Starter Set of

Functional Interfaces, on page 225). A functional interface may also have zero or more static methods and default methods, which are implemented right within the interface.

We can mark a functional interface with the @FunctionalInterface annotation. The compiler doesn't require this annotation, but it's helpful to explicitly state the purpose that the interface serves. Besides, if we mark an interface with this annotation, the compiler will enforce the rules for the interface to qualify as a functional interface.

If a method takes a functional interface as a parameter, then we can pass any of the following:

- An anonymous inner class, the old-fashioned way (but why would we?)
- A lambda expression, as we did when we called the map() method
- A method or constructor reference (as we'll see later)

The compiler readily accepts a lambda expression or a method/constructor reference as an argument if the method's corresponding parameter is a reference to a functional interface.

When we pass a lambda expression to a method, the compiler will convert the lambda expression to an instance of the appropriate functional interface. This conversion isn't a mere generation of an inner class in place. The synthesized method of this instance conforms to the abstract method of the functional interface that corresponds to the argument. For example, the map() method takes the functional interface Function<T, R> as its parameter. In a call to the map() method, the Java compiler synthesizes it, as the following figure shows.

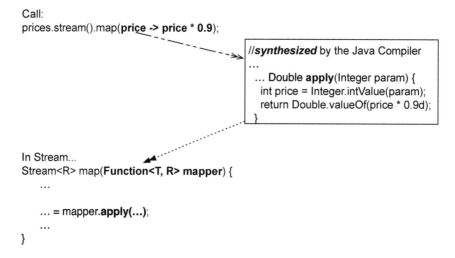

The parameters of the lambda expression must match the parameters of the interface's abstract method. This synthesized method returns the lambda expression's result. If the return type doesn't directly match that of the abstract method, the synthesized method may convert the return value to a proper assignable type.

We took a peek at how lambda expressions are passed as arguments to methods. Let's quickly review what we covered and move on to explore lambda expressions.

Wrapping Up

It's a whole new world in modern Java. We can now program in an elegant and fluent functional style, with higher-order functions. This can lead to concise code that has fewer errors and is easier to understand, maintain, and parallelize. The Java compiler works its magic so we can send lambda expressions or method references where functional interfaces are expected.

We're all set to dive into the fun parts of lambda expressions and the JDK library that's been fine-tuned to work with lambda expressions. In the next chapter we'll start by using lambda expressions in one of the most fundamental programming tasks: working with collections.

CHAPTER 2

Using Collections

We often use collections of numbers, strings, and objects. They're so common-place that removing even a small amount of ceremony from coding collections can reduce code clutter greatly. In this chapter we explore the use of lambda expressions to manipulate collections. We use them to iterate collections, transform them into new collections, extract elements from them, and easily concatenate their elements.

After this chapter, our Java code to manipulate collections will never be the same—it'll be concise, expressive, elegant, and more extensible than ever before.

Iterating through a List

Iterating through a list is a basic operation on a collection, but over the years it's gone through a few significant changes. We'll begin with the old style and evolve an example—enumerating a list of names—to the elegant style.

We can easily create a list of names with the following code:

```
final List<String> friends =
  Arrays.asList("Brian", "Nate", "Neal", "Raju", "Sara", "Scott");
```

To create an immutable list, we may use the more recently introduced function List.of() instead of Arrays.asList().

Here's the habitual, but not so desirable, way to iterate and print each of the elements.

collections/fpij/Iteration.java
```
for(int i = 0; i < friends.size(); i++) {
  System.out.println(friends.get(i));
}
```

I call this style *the self-inflicted wound pattern*—it's verbose and error-prone. We have to stop and wonder, "is it i < or i <=?" This is useful only if we need to manipulate elements at a particular index in the collection, but even then, we can opt to use a functional style that favors immutability, as we will discuss soon.

Java also offers a construct that's a little bit more civilized than the good old for loop.

collections/fpij/Iteration.java
```
for(String name : friends) {
  System.out.println(name);
}
```

Under the hood, this form of iteration uses the Iterator interface and calls into its hasNext() and next() methods.

Both these versions are *external iterators*, which mix *how* we do it with *what* we'd like to achieve. We explicitly control the iteration with them, indicating where to start and where to end; the second version does that under the hood using the Iterator methods. With explicit control, the break and continue statements can also help manage the iteration's flow of control.

The second construct has less ceremony than the first. Its style is better than the first if we don't intend to modify the collection at a particular index. Both of these styles are imperative and we can dispense with them in modern Java.

There are quite a few reasons to favor the change to the functional style:

- The for loops are inherently sequential and difficult to parallelize.

- Such loops are non-polymorphic; we get exactly what we ask for. We passed the collection to for instead of invoking a method (a polymorphic operation) on the collection to perform the task.

- At the design level, the code fails the "Tell, don't ask" principle. We ask for a specific iteration to be performed instead of leaving the details of the iteration to underlying libraries.

It's time to trade in the old imperative style for the more elegant functional-style version of *internal iteration*. With an internal iteration, we willfully turn over most of the *hows* to the underlying library so we can focus on the essential *whats*. The underlying function will take care of managing the iteration. Let's use an internal iterator to enumerate the names.

The Iterable interface has been enhanced with a special method named forEach(), which accepts a parameter of type Consumer. As the name indicates, an instance of Consumer will consume, through its accept() method, what's given to it. Let's use the forEach() method with the all-too-familiar anonymous inner-class syntax.

collections/fpij/Iteration.java

```java
friends.forEach(new Consumer<String>() { //Verbose, please don't do this
  public void accept(final String name) {
    System.out.println(name);
  }
});
```

We invoked the forEach() on the friends collection and passed an anonymous instance of Consumer to it. The forEach() method will invoke the accept() method of the given Consumer for each element in the collection and let it do whatever it wants with it. In this example, we merely print the given value, which is the name.

Let's look at the output from this version, which is the same as the output from the two previous versions:

```
Brian
Nate
Neal
Raju
Sara
Scott
```

We changed just one thing: we traded in the old for loop for the new internal iterator forEach(). As for the benefit, we went from specifying how to iterate to focusing on what we wanted to do for each element. The bad news is the code looks a lot more verbose—so much that it can drain away any excitement about the new style of programming. Thankfully, we can fix that quickly; this is where lambda expressions and the new compiler magic come in. Let's make one change again, replacing the anonymous inner class with a lambda expression.

collections/fpij/Iteration.java

```java
friends.forEach((final String name) -> System.out.println(name));
```

That's a lot better. We look at less code, but watch closely to see what's in there. The forEach() is a higher-order function that accepts a lambda expression or block of code to execute in the context of each element in the list. The variable name is bound to each element of the collection during the call. The underlying library takes control of how the lambda expressions are evaluated. It can decide to perform them lazily, in any order, and exploit parallelism as it sees fit.

This version produces the same output as the previous versions.

The internal-iterator version is more concise than the other ones. But, when we use it, we're able to focus our attention on what we want to achieve for each element rather than how to sequence through the iteration—it's declarative.

This version has a limitation. Once the forEach method starts, unlike in the other two versions, we can't break out of the iteration. (There are facilities to handle this limitation.) As a consequence, this style is useful in the common case where we want to process each element in a collection. Later we'll see alternate functions that give us control over the path of iteration.

The standard syntax for lambda expressions expects the parameters to be enclosed in parentheses, with the type information provided and comma separated. The Java compiler also offers some lenience and can infer the types. Leaving out the type is convenient, requires less effort, and is less noisy. Here's the previous code without the type information.

collections/fpij/Iteration.java
```
friends.forEach((name) -> System.out.println(name));
```

In this case, the Java compiler determines the name parameter is a String type, based on the context. It looks up the signature of the called method, forEach() in this example, and analyzes the functional interface it takes as a parameter. It then looks at that interface's abstract method to determine the expected number of parameters and their types. We can also use type inference if a lambda expression takes multiple parameters, but in that case, we must leave out the type information for all the parameters; we have to specify the type for *none* or for *all* of the parameters in a lambda expression.

The Java compiler treats single-parameter lambda expressions as special: we can leave off the parentheses around the parameter if the parameter's type is inferred.

collections/fpij/Iteration.java
```
friends.forEach(name -> System.out.println(name));
```

There's one caveat: inferred parameters are non-final. In the earlier example, where we explicitly specified the type, we also marked the parameter as final. This prevents us from modifying the parameter within the lambda expression. In general, modifying parameters is in poor taste and leads to errors, so marking them final is a good practice. Unfortunately, when we favor type inference we have to practice extra discipline not to modify the parameter, as the compiler won't protect us.

We've come a long way with this example and reduced the code quite a bit. But there's more. Let's take one last step to tease out another ounce of conciseness.

collections/fpij/Iteration.java
```
friends.forEach(System.out::println);
```

In the preceding code, we used a *method reference*. Java lets us simply replace the body of code with the method name of our choice. We'll dig into this further in the next section, but for now, let's reflect on the wise words of Antoine de Saint-Exupéry: "Perfection is achieved not when there is nothing more to add, but when there is nothing left to take away."

Lambda expressions helped us concisely iterate over a collection. Next, we'll cover how they help remove mutability and make the code even more concise when transforming collections.

Transforming a List

Manipulating a collection to produce another result is as easy as iterating through the elements of a collection. Suppose we're asked to convert a list of names to all capital letters. Let's explore some options to achieve this.

Java's String is immutable, so instances can't be changed. We could create new strings in all caps and replace the appropriate elements in the collection. But the original collection would be lost; also, if the original list is immutable, as it is when created with List.of(), then the list can't change. Another downside is it would be hard to parallelize the computations.

Creating a new list that has the elements in all caps is a better option.

That suggestion may seem naive at first; performance is an obvious concern we all share. Surprisingly, the functional approach often yields better performance than the imperative approach, as we'll see in Performance Concerns, on page 221.

Let's start by creating a new collection of uppercase names from the given collection.

collections/fpij/Transform.java
```
final List<String> uppercaseNames = new ArrayList<>();

for(String name : friends) {
  uppercaseNames.add(name.toUpperCase());
}
```

In this imperative style, we created an empty list and then populated it with all-uppercase names, one element at a time, while iterating through the original list. As a first step to moving toward a functional style, we could use the internal iterator forEach() method from Iterating through a List, on page 19, to replace the for loop, as we see next.

collections/fpij/Transform.java
```
final List<String> uppercaseNames = new ArrayList<>();
friends.forEach(name -> uppercaseNames.add(name.toUpperCase())); //BAD IDEA
System.out.println(uppercaseNames);
```

We used the internal iterator, but that still required the empty list and the effort to add elements to it. Furthermore, we modified a shared mutable variable, the list, from within the lambda expression. That's a bad idea as it makes it unsafe to parallelize this iteration if desired, and such code should be avoided. We can do a lot better.

Using Lambda Expressions and the Stream API

The map() method of the Stream interface can help us avoid mutability and make the code concise. A Stream is much like an iterator on a collection of objects and provides some nice *fluent functions*. Using the methods of this interface, we can compose a sequence of calls so that the code reads and flows in the same way we'd state problems, making it easier to read.

The Stream's map() method can map or transform a sequence of input to a sequence of output—that fits quite well for the task at hand.

collections/fpij/Transform.java
```
friends.stream()
       .map(name -> name.toUpperCase())
       .forEach(name -> System.out.print(name + " "));
System.out.println();
```

The method stream() is available on all collections in the JDK and it wraps the collection into an instance of Stream. The map() method applies the given lambda expression or block of code, within the parenthesis, on each element in the Stream. The map() method is quite unlike the forEach() method, which simply runs the block in the context of each element in the collection. In addition, the map() method collects the result of running the lambda expression and returns the result collection. Finally, we print the elements in this result using the forEach() method. The names in the new collection are in all caps:

```
BRIAN NATE NEAL RAJU SARA SCOTT
```

The map() method is useful to map or transform an input collection into a new output collection. This method will ensure that the same number of elements exists in the input and the output sequence. But the element types in the input don't have to match the element types in the output collection. In this example, both the input and the output are a collection of strings. We could've passed to the map() method a block of code that returned, for example, the number of characters in a given name. In this case, the input would still be a sequence of strings, but the output would be a sequence of numbers, as in the next example.

collections/fpij/Transform.java
```
friends.stream()
        .map(name -> name.length())
        .forEach(count -> System.out.print(count + " "));
```

The result is a count of the number of letters in each name:

```
5 4 4 4 4 5
```

The versions using the lambda expressions have no explicit mutation; they're concise. These versions also didn't need any initial empty collection or garbage variable; that variable quietly receded into the shadows of the underlying implementation.

Using Method References

We can nudge the code to be just a bit more concise by using a feature called *method reference*. The Java compiler will take either a lambda expression or a reference to a method where an implementation of a functional interface is expected. With this feature, a short String::toUpperCase can replace name -> name.toUpperCase(), like so:

collections/fpij/Transform.java
```
friends.stream()
        .map(String::toUpperCase)
        .forEach(name -> System.out.println(name));
```

Java knows to invoke the String class's given method toUpperCase() on the parameter passed into the synthesized method—the implementation of the functional interface's abstract method. That parameter reference is implicit here. In simple situations like the previous example, we can substitute method references for lambda expressions; see When Should We Use Method References?, on page 26.

In the preceding example, the method reference was for an instance method. Method references can also refer to static methods and methods that take parameters. We'll see examples of these later.

> ### ⟍⟋ Joe asks:
> ### When Should We Use Method References?
>
> We'd normally use lambda expressions much more than method references when program-ming in Java. That doesn't mean method references are unimportant or less useful, though. They're nice replacements when the lambda expressions are short and make simple, direct calls to either an instance method or a static method. In other words, if lambda expressions merely pass their parameters through, we can replace them with method references.
>
> These candidate lambda expressions are much like Tom Smykowski, in the movie *Office Space*,[a] whose job is to "take specifications from the customers and bring them down to the software engineers." For this reason, I call the refactoring of lambdas to method references *the office-space pattern*.
>
> In addition to conciseness, by using method references, we gain the ability to use more directly the names already chosen for these methods.
>
> There's quite a bit of compiler magic under the hood when we use method references. The method reference's target object and parameters are derived from the parameters passed to the synthesized method. This makes the code with method references much more concise than the code with lambda expressions. But we can't use this conve-nience if we have to manipulate parameters before sending them as arguments or tinker with the call's results before returning them.
>
> ---
>
> a.   http://en.wikipedia.org/wiki/Office_Space

The Stream API along with lambda expressions helped us enumerate a collec-tion and transform it into a new collection. They can also help us concisely pick an element from a collection, as we'll see next.

Finding Elements

The now-familiar elegant map() methods to traverse and transform collections won't directly help pick elements from a collection. The filter() method is designed for that purpose.

From a list of names, let's pick the ones that start with the letter *N*. Since there may be zero matching names in the list, the result may be an empty list. Let's first code it using the old approach.

collections/fpij/PickElements.java
```java
final List<String> startsWithN = new ArrayList<>();
for(String name : friends) {
  if(name.startsWith("N")) {
    startsWithN.add(name);
  }
}
```

That's a chatty piece of code for a simple task. We created a variable and initialized it to an empty collection. Then we looped through the collection, looking for a name that starts with the desired letter. If found, we added the element to the collection.

Let's refactor this code to use the filter() method, and see how it changes things.

collections/fpij/PickElements.java
```
final List<String> startsWithN =
  friends.stream()
        .filter(name -> name.startsWith("N"))
        .collect(Collectors.toList());
```

The filter() method expects a lambda expression that returns a boolean result. If the lambda expression returns a true for an element, that element is added to a result collection; it's skipped otherwise. Finally, the method returns a Stream with only elements for which the lambda expression yielded a true. In the end, we transformed the result into a List using the collect() method—we'll discuss this method further in Using the collect Method and the Collectors Class, on page 56.

Let's print the number of elements in the result collection.

collections/fpij/PickElements.java
```
System.out.println(String.format("Found %d names", startsWithN.size()));
```

From the output, it's clear that the method picked up the proper number of elements from the input collection.

```
Found 2 names
```

The filter() method returns a Stream, which is an internal iterator, just like the map() method does, but the similarity ends there. Whereas the map() method returns a collection of the same size as the input collection, the filter() method may not. It may yield a result collection with a number of elements ranging from zero to the maximum number of elements in the input collection. But unlike the map() method, the elements in the result collection that the filter() method returns are a subset of the elements in the input collection.

In the previous example, the list created by the Collectors.toList() may be mutated later on. If you want the iteration to create an immutable list, then instead, use Collectors.toUnmodifiableList() (added in the JDK 10) or the toList() method (added in the JDK 16) instead of collect(Collectors.toList()).

The filter() function is useful to cherry-pick elements in a collection based on the criteria provided in the predicate passed to the function. If we would rather skip processing some elements, we could use the skip() or dropWhile() functions, as we'll see next.

Skipping Values

Given a collection of values, if we want to skip processing a certain number of values or until a certain condition is met, we may use the continue statement along with the if statement in the traditional for loop. In the functional style, we don't use if or continue. Instead, we can control the iteration using the skip() or dropWhile() functions.

If you like to skip the first four values in the collection and only process the rest, pass the number of values you want to skip to the skip() function, like so:

collections/fpij/SkipElements.java
```
friends.stream()
       .skip(4)
       .map(String::toUpperCase)
       .forEach(System.out::println);
```

The call to skip() in the previous example ignores the first four values in the collection from further processing. Thus the output is the transformation of all values except the first four:

```
SARA
SCOTT
```

If, instead of skipping a certain number of values, you want to skip values until an element that meets a certain condition is encountered, use dropWhile(), which was introduced in the JDK 9. In the next example, we skip until we encounter a name whose length isn't greater than 4.

collections/fpij/SkipElements.java
```
friends.stream()
       .dropWhile(name -> name.length() > 4)
       .map(String::toUpperCase)
       .forEach(System.out::println);
```

Whereas filter() works like a garage gate that opens or shuts for each approaching car, skip() and dropWhile() work more like a door that is closed initially, swings open, and then stays open.

In the previous code, since the first element of the collection, Brian, has a length greater than four, it is skipped or dropped from further processing. The next element, Nate, is of length 4, and thus processing starts from that element. Even though the element Scott is greater than four letters in length, it is processed since the door, so to say, has already swung open, as we see in this output:

```
NATE
NEAL
RAJU
SARA
SCOTT
```

We discussed the equivalent of the imperative style continue in the functional style, but what about the popular break statement?

Terminating Iterations

About an hour after I started teaching a class on functional programming for a team of developers, a programmer asked if we had any planned breaks. I quipped "In functional programming we don't have breaks." While that comment was met with chuckles, terminating an iteration is serious business. Java provides at least two ways to exit an iteration before reaching the end of a collection—limit() and takeWhile(), where the latter was added in the JDK 9.

To only process the first three values in a collection, use the limit() function, like so:

collections/fpij/TakeElements.java
```
friends.stream()
       .limit(3)
       .map(String::toUpperCase)
       .forEach(System.out::println);
```

The output shows that only the first three values in the collection were processed and then the iteration was terminated:

```
BRIAN
NATE
NEAL
```

If, instead of a specific number of elements, we want to terminate the iteration upon encountering an element that meets a certain criteria, we can use take-While(), as in the following code:

collections/fpij/TakeElements.java
```
friends.stream()
       .takeWhile(name -> name.length() > 4)
       .map(String::toUpperCase)
       .forEach(System.out::println);
```

In this example, the processing continues as long as the length of the elements encountered is greater than four. The first element, Brian, meets that expectation but the second element, Nate, doesn't and thus the iteration is terminated right away as we see from the output:

```
BRIAN
```

Much like the skip() and dropWhile() functions, the limit() and takeWhile() methods also behave like a door. But instead of initially being shut, these methods behave like a door that is open and then shut forever when the given criteria isn't met.

The conciseness we've achieved by using lambda expressions so far is nice, but code duplication may sneak in quickly if we're not careful. Let's address that concern next.

Reusing Lambda Expressions

Lambda expressions are deceivingly concise and it's easy to carelessly duplicate them in code. Duplicate code leads to poor-quality code that's hard to maintain; if we needed to make a change, we'd have to find and touch the relevant code in several places.

Avoiding duplication can also help improve performance. By keeping the code related to a piece of knowledge concentrated in one place, we can easily study its performance profile and make changes in one place to get better performance.

Now let's see how easy it is to fall into the duplication trap when using lambda expressions, and also consider ways to avoid it.

Suppose we have a few collections of names: friends, editors, comrades, and so on.

```
final List<String> friends =
  Arrays.asList("Brian", "Nate", "Neal", "Raju", "Sara", "Scott");

final List<String> editors =
  Arrays.asList("Brian", "Jackie", "John", "Mike");

final List<String> comrades =
  Arrays.asList("Kate", "Ken", "Nick", "Paula", "Zach");
```

We want to filter out names that start with a certain letter. Let's first take a naive approach to this using the filter() method.

```
collections/fpij/PickElementsMultipleCollection.java
final long countFriendsStartN =
  friends.stream()
         .filter(name -> name.startsWith("N"))
         .count();
```

```
final long countEditorsStartN =
  editors.stream()
        .filter(name -> name.startsWith("N"))
        .count();

final long countComradesStartN =
  comrades.stream()
        .filter(name -> name.startsWith("N"))
        .count();
```

The lambda expressions made the code concise, but quietly led to duplicate code. In the previous example, one change to the lambda expression needs to change in more than one place—that's a *no-no*. Fortunately, we can assign lambda expressions to variables and reuse them, just like with objects.

The filter() method, the receiver of the lambda expression in the previous example, takes a reference to a java.util.function.Predicate functional interface. Here, the Java compiler works its magic to synthesize an implementation of the Predicate's test() method from the given lambda expression. Rather than asking Java to synthesize the method at the argument-definition location, we can be more explicit. In this example, it's possible to store the lambda expression in an explicit reference of type Predicate and then pass it to the function; this is an easy way to remove the duplication.

Let's refactor the previous code to make it DRY.[1] (See the Don't Repeat Yourself— DRY—principle in *The Pragmatic Programmer: From Journeyman to Master [HT00]*, by Andy Hunt and Dave Thomas.)

collections/fpij/PickElementsMultipleCollection.java
```
final Predicate<String> startsWithN = name -> name.startsWith("N");

final long countFriendsStartN =
  friends.stream()
        .filter(startsWithN)
        .count();
final long countEditorsStartN =
  editors.stream()
        .filter(startsWithN)
        .count();
final long countComradesStartN =
  comrades.stream()
        .filter(startsWithN)
        .count();
```

Rather than duplicate the lambda expression several times, we created it once and stored it in a reference named startsWithN of type Predicate. In the three calls

---

1. http://c2.com/cgi/wiki?DontRepeatYourself

to the filter() method, the Java compiler happily took the lambda expression stored in the variable under the guise of the Predicate instance.

The new variable gently removed the duplication that sneaked in. Unfortunately, it's about to sneak back in with a vengeance, as we'll see next, and we need something a bit more powerful to thwart it.

Using Lexical Scoping and Closures

There's a misconception among some developers that using lambda expressions may introduce duplication and lower code quality. Contrary to that belief, even when the code gets more complicated, we still don't need to compromise code quality to enjoy the conciseness that lambda expressions give, as we'll see in this section.

We managed to reuse the lambda expression in the previous example, but duplication will sneak in quickly when we bring in another letter to match. Let's explore the problem further and then solve it using lexical scoping and closures.

Duplication in Lambda Expressions

Let's pick the names that start with *N* or *B* from the friends collection of names. Continuing with the previous example, we may be tempted to write something like the following:

```
collections/fpij/PickDifferentNames.java
final Predicate<String> startsWithN = name -> name.startsWith("N");
final Predicate<String> startsWithB = name -> name.startsWith("B");

final long countFriendsStartN =
  friends.stream()
         .filter(startsWithN)
         .count();
final long countFriendsStartB =
  friends.stream()
         .filter(startsWithB)
         .count();
```

The first predicate tests if the name starts with an *N* and the second tests for a *B*. We pass these two instances to the two calls to the filter() method, respectively. That seems reasonable, but the two predicates are mere duplicates, with only the letter they use being different. Let's figure out a way to eliminate this duplication.

Removing Duplication with Lexical Scoping

As a first option, we could extract the letter as a parameter to a function and pass the function as an argument to the filter() method. That's a reasonable idea, but the filter() method won't accept some arbitrary function. It insists on receiving a function that accepts one parameter representing the context element in the collection and on returning a boolean result. It's expecting a Predicate.

For comparison purposes, we need a variable that will cache the letter for later use and hold onto it until the parameter, name in this example, is received. Let's create a function for that.

collections/fpij/PickDifferentNames.java
```
public static Predicate<String> checkIfStartsWith(final String letter) {
  return name -> name.startsWith(letter);
}
```

We defined checkIfStartsWith() as a static function that takes a letter of type String as a parameter. It then returns a Predicate that can be passed to the filter() method for later evaluation. Unlike the higher-order functions we've seen so far, which accepted functions as parameters, the checkIfStartsWith() returns a function as a result. This is also a higher-order function, as we discussed in Evolution, Not Revolution, on page 12.

The Predicate that checkIfStartsWith() returned is different from the lambda expressions we've seen so far. In return name -> name.startsWith(letter), it's clear what name is: it's the parameter passed to this lambda expression. But what's the variable letter bound to? Since that's not in the scope of this anonymous function, Java reaches over to the scope of the definition of this lambda expression and finds the variable letter in that scope. This is called *lexical scoping*. Lexical scoping is a powerful technique that lets us cache values provided in one context for use later in another context. Since this lambda expression *closes over* the scope of its definition, it's also referred to as a *closure*. For lexical scope access restriction, see Are There Restrictions to Lexical Scoping?, on page 34.

We can use the lambda expression returned by checkIfStartsWith() in the call to the filter() method, like so:

collections/fpij/PickDifferentNames.java
```
final long countFriendsStartN =
  friends.stream()
         .filter(checkIfStartsWith("N"))
         .count();
final long countFriendsStartB =
  friends.stream()
         .filter(checkIfStartsWith("B"))
         .count();
```

Joe asks:
Are There Restrictions to Lexical Scoping?

From within a lambda expression, we can only access local variables that are final or *effectively* final in the enclosing scope.

A lambda expression may be invoked right away, or it may be invoked lazily or from multiple threads. To avoid race conditions, the local variables we access in the enclosing scope aren't allowed to change once initialized. Any attempt to change them will result in a compilation error.

Variables marked final directly fit this bill, but Java doesn't insist that we mark them as such. Instead, Java looks for two things. First, the accessed variables have to be initialized within the enclosing methods before the lambda expression is defined. Second, the values of these variables don't change anywhere else—that is, they're effectively final although they aren't marked as such.

When using lambda expressions that capture local state, we should be aware that stateless lambda expressions are runtime constants, but those that capture local state have an additional evaluation cost.

In the calls to the filter() method, we first invoke the checkIfStartsWith() method, passing in a desired letter. This call immediately returns a lambda expression that is then passed on to the filter() method.

By creating a higher-order function, checkIfStartsWith() in this example, and using lexical scoping, we managed to remove the duplication in code. We didn't have to repeat the comparison to check if the name starts with different letters.

Refactoring to Narrow the Scope

In the preceding (smelly) example, we used a static method, but we don't want to pollute the class with static methods to cache each variable in the future. It would be nice to narrow the function's scope to where it's needed. We can do that using a Function interface.

collections/fpij/PickDifferentNames.java
```
final Function<String, Predicate<String>> startsWithLetter =
  (String letter) -> {
    Predicate<String> checkStarts = (String name) -> name.startsWith(letter);
    return checkStarts;
};
```

This lambda expression replaces the static method checkIfStartsWith() and can appear within a function, just before it's needed. The startsWithLetter variable refers to a Function that takes in a String and returns a Predicate.

This version is verbose compared to the static method we saw earlier, but we'll refactor that soon to make it concise. For all practical purposes, this function is equivalent to the static method; it takes a String and returns a Predicate. Instead of explicitly creating the instance of the Predicate and returning it, we can replace it with a lambda expression.

collections/fpij/PickDifferentNames.java
```
final Function<String, Predicate<String>> startsWithLetter =
  (String letter) -> (String name) -> name.startsWith(letter);
```

We reduced clutter, but we can take the conciseness up another notch by removing the types and letting the Java compiler infer the types based on the context. Let's look at the concise version.

collections/fpij/PickDifferentNames.java
```
final Function<String, Predicate<String>> startsWithLetter =
  letter -> name -> name.startsWith(letter);
```

It takes a bit of effort to get used to this concise syntax. Feel free to look away for a moment if this makes you cross-eyed. Now that we've refactored that version, we can use it in place of the checkIfStartsWith() method, like so:

collections/fpij/PickDifferentNames.java
```
final long countFriendsStartN =
  friends.stream()
         .filter(startsWithLetter.apply("N"))
         .count();
final long countFriendsStartB =
  friends.stream()
         .filter(startsWithLetter.apply("B"))
         .count();
```

We've come full circle with higher-order functions in this section. Our examples illustrate how to pass functions to functions, create functions within functions, and return functions from within functions. They also demonstrate the conciseness and reusability that lambda expressions facilitate.

We made good use of both Function and Predicate in this section, but let's discuss how they're different. A Predicate<T> takes in one parameter of type T and returns a boolean result to indicate a decision for whatever check it represents. We can use it anytime we want to make a go or no-go decision for a candidate we pass to the predicate. Methods like filter() that evaluate candidate elements take in a Predicate as a parameter. On the other hand, a Function<T, R> represents a function that takes a parameter of type T and returns a result of type R. This is more general than a Predicate that always returns a boolean. We can use a Function anywhere we want to transform an input to another value, so it's logical that the map() method uses Function as its parameter.

Selecting elements from a collection was easy. Next, we'll cover how to pick just one element out of a collection.

Picking an Element

It's reasonable to expect that picking one element from a collection would be simpler than picking multiple elements. But there are a few complications. Let's look at the complexity introduced by the habitual approach and then bring in lambda expressions to solve it.

Let's create a method that will look for an element that starts with a given letter, and print it.

collections/fpij/PickAnElement.java

```
public static void pickName(
  final List<String> names, final String startingLetter) {
  String foundName = null;
  for(String name : names) {
    if(name.startsWith(startingLetter)) {
      foundName = name;
      break;
    }
  }
  System.out.print(String.format("A name starting with %s: ", startingLetter));

  if(foundName != null) {
    System.out.println(foundName);
  } else {
    System.out.println("No name found");
  }
}
```

This method's odor can easily compete with passing garbage trucks. We first created a foundName variable and initialized it to null—that's the source of our first bad smell. This will force a null check, and if we forget to deal with it, the result could be a NullPointerException or an unpleasant response. We then used an external iterator to loop through the elements, but had to break out of the loop if we found an element—here are other sources of rancid smells: primitive obsession, imperative style, and mutability. Once out of the loop, we had to check the response and print the appropriate result. That's quite a bit of code for a simple task.

Let's rethink the problem. We simply want to pick the first matching element and safely deal with the absence of such an element. Let's rewrite the pickName() method, this time using lambda expressions.

```
collections/fpij/PickAnElementElegant.java
public static void pickName(
  final List<String> names, final String startingLetter) {

  final Optional<String> foundName =
    names.stream()
         .filter(name ->name.startsWith(startingLetter))
         .findFirst();

  System.out.println(String.format("A name starting with %s: %s",
    startingLetter, foundName.orElse("No name found")));
}
```

Some powerful features in the JDK library came together to help achieve this conciseness. First, we used the filter() method to grab all the elements matching the desired pattern. Then the findFirst() method of the Stream class helped pick the first value from that collection. This method returns a special Optional object, which is the state-appointed null deodorizer in Java.

The Optional class is useful whenever the result may be absent. It protects us from getting a NullPointerException by accident and makes it quite explicit to the reader that "no result found" is a possible outcome. We can inquire if an object is present by using the isPresent() method, and we can obtain the current value using its get() method or the preferred alternative orElseThrow() method that was added in the JDK 10. Alternatively, we could suggest a substitute value for the missing instance, using the method (with the most threatening name) orElse(), like in the previous code.

Let's exercise the pickName() function with the sample friends collection we've used in the examples so far.

```
collections/fpij/PickAnElementElegant.java
pickName(friends, "N");
pickName(friends, "Z");
```

The code picks out the first matching element, if found, and prints an appropriate message otherwise.

```
A name starting with N: Nate
A name starting with Z: No name found
```

The combination of the findFirst() method and the Optional class reduced our code and its smell quite a bit. We're not limited to the preceding options when working with Optional, though. For example, rather than providing an alternate value for the absent instance, we can ask Optional to run a block of code or a lambda expression only if a value is present, like so:

```
collections/fpij/PickAnElementElegant.java
foundName.ifPresent(name -> System.out.println("Hello " + name));
```

When compared to using the imperative version to pick the first matching name, the nice, flowing functional style looks better. But are we doing more work in the fluent version than we did in the imperative version? The answer is no—these methods have the smarts to perform only as much work as is necessary (we'll talk about this more in Leveraging the Laziness of Streams, on page 129).

The search for the first matching element demonstrated a few more neat capabilities in the JDK. Next, we'll look at how lambda expressions help compute a single result from a collection.

Reducing a Collection to a Single Value

We've gone over a few techniques to manipulate collections so far: picking matching elements, selecting a particular element, and transforming a collection. All these operations have one thing in common: they all worked independently on individual elements in the collection. None required comparing elements against each other or carrying over computations from one element to the next. In this section we look at how to compare elements and carry over a computational state across a collection.

Let's start with some basic operations and build up to something a bit more sophisticated. As the first example, let's read over the values in the friends collection of names and determine the total number of characters.

```
collections/fpij/PickALongest.java
System.out.println("Total number of characters in all names: " +
  friends.stream()
        .mapToInt(name -> name.length())
        .sum());
```

To find the total number of characters, we need the length of each name. We can easily compute that using the mapToInt() method. Once we transform the data from the names to their lengths, the final step is to total them. This step we perform using the built-in sum() method. Here is the output for this operation:

```
Total number of characters in all names: 26
```

We leveraged the mapToInt() method, which is a variation of the *map* operation (variations like mapToInt(), mapToDouble(), and so on create type-specialized streams such as IntStream and DoubleStream), and then we *reduced* the resulting length to the sum value.

Instead of using the sum() method, we could use a variety of methods like max() to find the longest length, min() to find the shortest length, sorted() to sort the lengths, average() to find the average of the length, and so on.

The hidden charm in the preceding example is the increasingly popular *MapReduce* pattern,[2] with the map() method being the spread operation and the sum() method being the special case of the more general reduce operation. In fact, the implementation of the sum() method in the JDK uses a reduce() method. Let's look at the more general form of reduce.

As an example, let's read over the given collection of names and display the longest one. If there's more than one name with the same longest length, we'll display the first one we find. One way we could do that is to figure out the longest length and then pick the first element of that length. But that'd require going over the list twice—not efficient. This is where a reduce() method comes into play.

We can use the reduce() method to compare two elements against each other and pass along the result for further comparison with the remaining elements in the collection. Much like the other higher-order functions on collections we've seen so far, the reduce() method iterates over the collection. In addition, it carries forward the result of the computation that the lambda expression returned. An example will help clarify this, so let's get down to the code.

```
collections/fpij/PickALongest.java
final Optional<String> aLongName =
  friends.stream()
         .reduce((name1, name2) ->
            name1.length() >= name2.length() ? name1 : name2);
aLongName.ifPresent(name ->
  System.out.println(String.format("A longest name: %s", name)));
```

The lambda expression we are passing to the reduce() method takes two parameters, name1 and name2, and returns one of them based on the length. The reduce() method has no clue about our specific intent. That concern is separated from this method into the lambda expression that we pass to it— this is a lightweight application of the *strategy pattern*—see *Design Patterns: Elements of Reusable Object-Oriented Software [GHJV95]*, by Gamma et al.

This lambda expression conforms to the interface of an apply() method of a JDK functional interface named BinaryOperator. This is the type of the parameter the reduce() method receives. Let's run the reduce() method and see if it picks the first of the two longest names from our friends list.

```
A longest name: Brian
```

---

2.   http://research.google.com/archive/mapreduce.html

As the reduce() method iterated through the collection, it called the lambda expression first, with the first two elements in the list. The result from the lambda expression is used for the subsequent call. In the second call, name1 is bound to the result from the previous call to the lambda expression, and name2 is bound to the third element in the collection. The calls to the lambda expression continue for the rest of the elements in the collection. The result from the final call is returned as the result of the reduce() method call.

The result of the reduce() method is an Optional because the list on which reduce() is called may be empty. In that case, there would be no longest name. If the list had only one element, then reduce() would return that element and the lambda expression we pass wouldn't be invoked.

Instead of using the reduce() method to compute the maximum, we may also use the specialized max() method. In this case, we have to pass a Comparator as an argument, as in the following:

collections/fpij/PickALongest.java
```
friends.stream()
        .max(java.util.Comparator.comparing(String::length));
```

That's certainly concise compared to passing lambda expressions to the reduce() method—we'll dig further into the use of Comparator in Chapter 3, Strings, Comparators, and Filters, on page 45.

From the example, we can infer that the reduce() method's or the max() method's result is at most one element from the collection. If we want to set a default or a base value, we can pass that value as an extra parameter to an overloaded variation of the reduce() method. For example, if the shortest name we want to pick is Steve, we can pass that to the reduce() method, like so:

collections/fpij/PickALongest.java
```
final String steveOrLonger =
  friends.stream()
        .reduce("Steve", (name1, name2) ->
            name1.length() >= name2.length() ? name1 : name2);
```

If any name was longer than the given base, it would get picked up; otherwise, the function would return the base value, Steve in this example. This version of reduce() doesn't return an Optional since if the collection is empty, the default will be returned; there's no concern of an absent or nonexistent value.

Before we wrap up this chapter, let's visit a fundamental yet seemingly difficult operation on collections: joining elements.

Joining Elements

We've explored how to select elements, iterate, and transform collections. Yet in a trivial operation—concatenating a collection—we could lose all the gains we made with concise and elegant code if not for a newly added join() function. This simple method is so useful that it's poised to become one of the most used functions in the JDK. Let's see how to use it to print the values in a list, comma separated.

Let's work with our friends list. What does it take to print the list of names, separated by commas, using only the old JDK libraries?

We have to iterate through the list and print each element. Since the Java 5 for construct is better than the archaic for loop, let's start with that.

```
collections/fpij/PrintList.java
for(String name : friends) {
  System.out.print(name + ", ");
}
System.out.println();
```

That was simple code, but let's look at what it yielded.

```
Brian, Nate, Neal, Raju, Sara, Scott,
```

Darn it; there's a stinking comma at the end (shall we blame it on Scott?). How do we tell Java not to place a comma there? Unfortunately, the loop will run its course and there's no easy way to tell the last element apart from the rest. To fix this, we can fall back on the habitual loop.

```
collections/fpij/PrintList.java
for(int i = 0; i < friends.size() - 1; i++) {
  System.out.print(friends.get(i) + ", ");
}

if(friends.size() > 0)
  System.out.println(friends.get(friends.size() - 1));
```

Let's see if the output of this version was decent.

```
Brian, Nate, Neal, Raju, Sara, Scott
```

The result looks good, but the code to produce the output doesn't. Beam us up, modern Java.

We don't have to endure that pain. A StringJoiner class cleans up all that mess and the String class has an added convenience method join() to turn that smelly code into a simple one-liner.

collections/fpij/PrintList.java
```
System.out.println(String.join(", ", friends));
```

Let's quickly verify the output is as charming as the code that produced it.

```
Brian, Nate, Neal, Raju, Sara, Scott
```

Under the hood, the String's join() method calls upon the StringJoiner class to concatenate the values in the second argument, a varargs, into a larger string separated by the first argument. We're not limited to concatenating only with a comma using this feature. We could, for example, take a bunch of paths and concatenate them to form a classpath easily thanks to the new methods and classes.

We saw how to join a list of elements; we can also transform the elements before joining them. We already know how to transform elements using the map() method. We can also be selective about which element we want to keep by using methods like filter(). The final step of joining the elements, separated by commas or something else, is simply a reduce operation.

We could use the reduce() method to concatenate elements into a string, but that would require some effort on our part. The JDK has a convenience method named collect(), which is another form of reduce that can help us collect values into a target destination.

The collect() method does the reduction but delegates the actual implementation or target to a collector. We could drop the transformed elements into an ArrayList, for instance. Or, to continue with the current example, we could collect the transformed elements into a string concatenated with commas.

collections/fpij/PrintList.java
```
System.out.println(
  friends.stream()
        .map(String::toUpperCase)
        .collect(joining(", ")));
```

We invoked the collect() on the transformed list and provided it a collector returned by the joining() method, which is a static method on a Collectors utility class. A collector acts as a sink object to receive elements passed by the collect() method and stores it in a desired format: ArrayList, String, and so on. We'll explore the collect() method further in Using the collect Method and the Collectors Class, on page 56.

Here are the names, now in uppercase and comma separated.

```
BRIAN, NATE, NEAL, RAJU, SARA, SCOTT
```

The StringJoiner gives a lot more control over the format of concatenation; we can specify a prefix, a suffix, and infix character sequences if we desire.

We saw how lambda expressions and the newly added classes and methods make programming in Java so much easier, and more fun too. Let's go over what we covered in this chapter.

Wrapping Up

Collections are commonplace in programming and, thanks to lambda expressions and the Stream API, using them is now much easier and simpler in Java. We can trade the long-winded old methods for elegant, concise code to perform the common operations on collections. Internal iterators make it convenient to traverse collections, transform collections without enduring mutability, and select elements from collections without much effort. Using these functions means less code to write. That can lead to more maintainable code, more code that does useful domain- or application-related logic, and less code to handle the basics of coding.

In the next chapter, we'll cover how lambda expressions simplify another fundamental programming task: working with strings and comparing objects.

CHAPTER 3

Strings, Comparators, and Filters

The JDK includes a number of convenience methods that promote the functional style. When using familiar classes and interfaces from the library—String, for example—we need to look for opportunities to use the functional style in place of the imperative style. Also, anywhere we used an anonymous inner class with just one method, we can use lambda expressions to reduce clutter and ceremony.

In this chapter we'll use lambda expressions and method references to iterate over a String, to implement Comparators, to list files in a directory, and to observe file and directory changes. Many of the methods introduced in the previous chapter will appear here again to help with the tasks at hand. The techniques you pick up along the way will help turn long, mundane tasks into concise code snippets you can quickly write and easily maintain.

Iterating a String

The chars() method in the String class from the CharSequence interface returns an IntStream, which is useful for fluently iterating over the String's characters. We can use this convenient internal iterator to apply an operation on the individual characters that make up the string. Let's use it in an example to process a string. Along the way, we'll discuss a few more handy ways to use method references.

```
compare/fpij/IterateString.java
final String str = "w00t";

str.chars()
   .forEach(ch -> System.out.println(ch));
```

The chars() method returns a Stream over which we can iterate, using the forEach() internal iterator. We get direct read access to the characters in the String within the iterator. Here's the result when we iterate and print each character.

```
119
48
48
116
```

The result isn't what we'd expect. Instead of seeing letters, we're seeing numbers. That's because the chars() method returns a stream of Integers representing the letters instead of a stream of Characters. Let's explore the API a bit further before we fix the output.

In the previous code, we created a lambda expression in the argument list for the forEach() method. The implementation was a simple call where we routed the parameter directly as an argument to the println() method. Since this is a trivial operation, we can eliminate this mundane code with the help of the Java compiler. We can rely on it to do this parameter routing for us, using a method reference as we did in Using Method References, on page 25.

We already saw how to create a method reference for an instance method. For example, for the call name.toUpperCase() instance method, the method reference is String::toUpperCase. But in this example, we have a call on a static reference System.out. We can use either a class name or an expression to the left of the double colon in method references. Using this flexibility, it's easy to provide a reference to the println() method, as we see next.

```
compare/fpij/IterateString.java
str.chars()
   .forEach(System.out::println);
```

In this example, we see the smarts of the Java compiler for parameter routing. Recall that lambda expressions and method references may stand in where implementations of functional interfaces are expected, and the Java compiler synthesizes the appropriate method in place (see A Little Sugar to Sweeten, on page 15). In the earlier method reference we used, String::toUpperCase, the parameter to the synthesized method turned into the target of the method call, like so: parameter.toUpperCase();. That's because the method reference is based on a class name (String). In this example, the method reference, again to an instance method, is based on an expression—an instance of PrintStream accessed through the static reference System.out. Since we already provided a target for the method, the Java compiler decided to use the parameter of the synthesized method as an argument to the referenced method, like so: System.out.println(parameter);. Sweet.

The code with the method reference is concise, but we have to dig into it a bit more to understand what's going on. Once we get used to method references, our brains will know to autoparse these.

In this example, although the code is concise, the output isn't satisfactory. We want to see letters and not numbers in their place. To fix that, let's write a convenience method that prints an int as a letter.

compare/fpij/IterateString.java
```
private static void printChar(int aChar) {
  System.out.println((char)(aChar));
}
```

We can use a reference to this convenience method to fix the output.

compare/fpij/IterateString.java
```
str.chars()
    .forEach(IterateString::printChar);
```

We can continue to use the result of chars() as an int, and when it's time to print, we can convert the result to a character. The output of this version will display letters.

```
w
0
0
t
```

If we want to process characters and not int from the start, we can convert the ints to characters right after the call to the chars() method, like so:

compare/fpij/IterateString.java
```
str.chars()
    .mapToObj(ch -> Character.valueOf((char)ch))
    .forEach(System.out::println);
```

The chars() method returns an instance of IntStream. If we call map() on it, then the result will also be an IntStream. But we want a stream of characters (a Stream<Characters>), and to achieve that, we use mapToObj() instead of map().

We used the internal iterator on the Stream that the chars() method returned, but we're not limited to that method. Once we get a Stream, we can use any methods available on it, like map(), filter(), reduce(), and so on, to process the characters in the string. For example, we can filter out only digits from the string, like so:

compare/fpij/IterateString.java
```
str.chars()
    .filter(ch -> Character.isDigit(ch))
    .forEach(ch -> printChar(ch));
```

We can see the filtered digits in the next output.

```
0
0
```

Once again, instead of the lambda expressions we passed to the filter() method and the forEach() method, we can use references to the respective methods.

compare/fpij/IterateString.java
```
str.chars()
   .filter(Character::isDigit)
   .forEach(IterateString::printChar);
```

The method references here helped remove the mundane parameter routing. In addition, in this example we see yet another variation of method references compared to the previous two instances where we used them. When we first saw method references, we created one for an instance method. Later we created one for a call on a static reference. Now we're creating a method reference for a static method—method references seem to keep on giving.

The one for an instance method and the one for a static method look the same structurally: for example, String::toUpperCase and Character::isDigit. To decide how to route the parameter, the Java compiler will check whether the method is an instance method or a static method. If it's an instance method, then the synthesized method's parameter becomes the call's target, as in parameter.toUpperCase(); (the exception to this rule is if the target is already specified as in System.out::println). On the other hand, if the method is static, then the parameter to the synthesized method is routed as an argument to this method, as in Character.isDigit(parameter);. See Appendix 2, Syntax Overview, on page 227, for a listing of method-reference variations and their syntax.

While this parameter routing is convenient, there is one caveat—the ambiguity that results from method collisions. If there's both a matching instance method and a static method, we'll get a compilation error due to the reference's ambiguity. For example, if we write Double::toString to convert an instance of Double to a String, the compiler would get confused whether to use the public String toString() instance method or the static method public static String toString(double value), both from the Double class. If we run into this, no sweat; we simply switch back to using the appropriate lambda-expression version to move on.

Once we get used to the functional style, we can switch between the lambda expressions and the more concise method references, based on our comfort level.

We used the chars() method to easily iterate over characters. Next, we'll explore the enhancements to the Comparator interface.

Implementing the Comparator Interface

The Comparator interface is used in hundreds of places in the JDK library, from searching operations to sorting, reversing, and so on. This good old interface has turned into a functional interface; the benefit is that we can use charmingly fluent syntax to implement comparators.

Let's create a few different implementations of the Comparator to understand the influence of the functional style. Our fingers will thank us for all the keystrokes saved by not having to create anonymous inner classes.

Sorting with a Comparator

We'll build an example to sort a list of people using a few different points of comparison. Let's first create the Person JavaBean.

```
compare/fpij/Person.java
public class Person {
  private final String name;
  private final int age;

  public Person(final String theName, final int theAge) {
    name = theName;
    age = theAge;
  }

  public String getName() { return name; }
  public int getAge() { return age; }

  public int ageDifference(final Person other) {
    return age - other.age;
  }

  public String toString() {
    return String.format("%s - %d", name, age);
  }
}
```

We could implement the Comparable interface on the Person class, but that would limit us to one particular comparison. We'd want to compare on different things—on name, age, or a combination of fields, for example. To get this flexibility, we'll create the code for different comparisons just when we need them, with the help of the Comparator interface.

Let's create a list of people to work with, folks with different names and ages.

```
compare/fpij/Compare.java
final List<Person> people = Arrays.asList(
  new Person("John", 20),
  new Person("Sara", 21),
  new Person("Jane", 21),
  new Person("Greg", 35));
```

We could sort the people by their names or ages and in ascending or descending order. To achieve this in the habitual way, we'd implement the

Comparator interface using anonymous inner classes. But the essence here is the code for the comparison logic, and anything else we write would be pure ceremony. We can boil this down to its essence using lambda expressions.

Let's first sort the people in the list in ascending order by age.

Since we have a List, the obvious choice is the sort() method on the List. But this method has some downsides. It's a void method, which means the list will be mutated when we call it. To preserve the original list, we'd have to make a copy of it and then invoke the sort() method on the copy; that's quite labor-intensive. Instead, we'll seek the help of the Stream.

We can get a Stream from the List and conveniently call the sorted() method on it. Rather than messing with the given collection, it'll return a sorted collection. We can nicely configure the Comparator parameter when calling this method.

```
compare/fpij/Compare.java
List<Person> ascendingAge =
  people.stream()
        .sorted((person1, person2) -> person1.ageDifference(person2))
        .collect(toList());
printPeople("Sorted in ascending order by age: ", ascendingAge);
```

We first transformed the given List of people to a Stream using the stream() method. We then invoked the sorted() method on it. This method takes a Comparator as its parameter. Since Comparator is a functional interface, we conveniently passed in a lambda expression. Finally, we invoked the collect() method and asked it to put the result into a List. Recall that the collect() method is a reducer that will help to target the members of the transformed iteration into a desirable type or format. The toList() is a static method on the Collectors convenience class.

The Comparator's compareTo() abstract method takes two parameters, the objects to be compared, and returns an int result. To comply with this, our lambda expression takes two parameters, two instances of Person, with their types inferred by the Java compiler. We return an int indicating whether the objects are equal.

Since we want to sort by the age property, we compare the two given people's ages and return the difference. If they're the same age, our lambda expression will return a 0 to indicate they're equal. Otherwise, it will indicate the first person is younger by returning a negative number or older by returning a positive number for the age difference.

The sorted() method will iterate over each element in the target collection (people in this example) and apply the given Comparator (a lambda expression in this case) to decide the logical ordering of the elements. The execution mechanism of sorted() is much like the reduce() method we saw earlier. The reduce() method trickles the list down to one value. The sorted() method, on the other hand, uses the result of the comparison to perform the ordering.

Once we sort the instances, we want to print the values, so we invoke a convenience method printPeople(); let's write that method next.

```
compare/fpij/Compare.java
public static void printPeople(
  final String message, final List<Person> people) {

  System.out.println(message);
  people.forEach(System.out::println);
}
```

In this method we print a message and iterate over the given collection, printing each of the instances.

Let's call the sorted() method, and the people in the list will be printed in ascending order by age.

```
Sorted in ascending order by age:
John - 20
Sara - 21
Jane - 21
Greg - 35
```

Let's revisit the call to the sorted() method and make one more improvement to it.

```
.sorted((person1, person2) -> person1.ageDifference(person2))
```

In the lambda expression we're passing to the sorted() method, we're simply routing the two parameters—the first parameter as the target to the ageDifference() method and the second as its argument. Rather than writing this code, we can use the office-space pattern (that is, ask the Java compiler to do the routing again, using a method reference).

The parameter routing we want here is a bit different from the ones we saw earlier. So far, we've seen a parameter being used as a target in one case and as an argument in another case. In the current situation, however, we have two parameters that we want to be split: the first to be used as a target to the method and the second as an argument. No worries. The Java compiler gives us a friendly nod: "I can take care of that for you."

Let's replace the lambda expression in the previous call to the sorted() method with a short and sweet reference to the ageDifference() method.

```
people.stream()
      .sorted(Person::ageDifference)
```

The code is fantastically concise thanks to the method-reference convenience the Java compiler offers. The compiler took the parameters, the two-person instances being compared, and made the first the ageDifference() method's target and the second the parameter. Rather than explicitly connecting these, we let the compiler work a little extra for us. When using this conciseness, we must be careful to ensure that the first parameter is the intended target of the method referenced and the remaining parameters are its arguments.

Reusing a Comparator

We easily sorted the people in ascending order by age, and we can as easily sort them in descending order. Let's give that a shot.

```
compare/fpij/Compare.java
printPeople("Sorted in descending order by age: ",
    people.stream()
        .sorted((person1, person2) -> person2.ageDifference(person1))
        .collect(toList()));
```

We called the sorted() method and passed a lambda expression that conforms to the Comparator interface, much like the previous time. The only difference is the implementation of the lambda expression—we switched the people in the age comparison. The result should be a sort by descending order of their ages. Let's look at the output.

```
Sorted in descending order by age:
Greg - 35
Sara - 21
Jane - 21
John - 20
```

Changing the logic for our comparison was effortless. But we can't refactor this version to use the method reference because the parameter order here doesn't follow the parameter-routing conventions for method reference; the first parameter isn't used as a target to the method, but rather as its argument. There's a way to fix that and, in the process, remove the duplication of effort that crept in. Let's see how.

Earlier we created two lambda expressions: one to order the ages of two people in ascending order and the other to do it in descending order. In so doing, we duplicated the logic and the effort, and we violated the DRY principle.[1] If all we want is a reverse of the comparison, the JDK has us covered with a reversed() method on the Comparator, marked with a special method modifier called default.

---

1. http://c2.com/cgi/wiki?DontRepeatYourself

We'll discuss default methods in A Peek into the default Methods, on page 100, but here we'll use the reversed() method to remove the duplication.

compare/fpij/Compare.java

```
Comparator<Person> compareAscending =
  (person1, person2) -> person1.ageDifference(person2);
Comparator<Person> compareDescending = compareAscending.reversed();
```

We first created a Comparator, compareAscending, to compare the age of the people in ascending order using the lambda expression syntax. To reverse the order of comparison, instead of duplicating the effort, we can simply call reversed() on the first Comparator to get another Comparator with the comparison order in reverse. Under the hood, the reversed() method creates a comparator that swaps its parameters' order of comparison. This makes the reversed() method a higher-order method—this function creates and returns another functional expression with no side effect. Let's use these two comparators in the code.

compare/fpij/Compare.java

```
printPeople("Sorted in ascending order by age: ",
  people.stream()
        .sorted(compareAscending)
        .collect(toList())
);
printPeople("Sorted in descending order by age: ",
  people.stream()
        .sorted(compareDescending)
        .collect(toList())
);
```

It's becoming clear how the modern features in Java can greatly reduce code complexity and duplication of effort, but to get all the benefits, we have to explore the seemingly endless possibilities the JDK offers.

We've been sorting by age, but we could easily sort by name too. Let's sort in ascending alphabetical order by name; again, only the logic within the lambda expression needs to change.

compare/fpij/Compare.java

```
printPeople("Sorted in ascending order by name: ",
  people.stream()
        .sorted((person1, person2) ->
            person1.getName().compareTo(person2.getName()))
        .collect(toList()));
```

In the output we should now see the people with names listed in ascending alphabetical order.

```
Sorted in ascending order by name:
Greg - 35
Jane - 21
John - 20
Sara - 21
```

So far, our comparisons have worked on either the age or the name property. We can make the logic in the lambda expression more intelligent. For example, we could sort based on both name and age.

Let's pick the youngest person in the list. We could find the first person after we've sorted by age in ascending order. But we don't need to go that far; the Stream has us covered with a min() method. This method also accepts a Comparator but returns the smallest object in the collection based on the given comparator.

Let's use that method.

compare/fpij/Compare.java
```
people.stream()
      .min(Person::ageDifference)
      .ifPresent(youngest -> System.out.println("Youngest: " + youngest));
```

We use the reference for the ageDifference() method in the call to the min() method. The min() method returns an Optional because the list may be empty and so there may not be a youngest person. We then print the details of the youngest person that we get access to from the Optional using its ifPresent() method.

Let's look at the output.

```
Youngest: John - 20
```

We can as easily find the oldest person in the list. Simply pass that method reference to a max() method.

compare/fpij/Compare.java
```
people.stream()
      .max(Person::ageDifference)
      .ifPresent(eldest -> System.out.println("Eldest: " + eldest));
```

Let's look at the output for the name and age of the oldest in the list.

```
Eldest: Greg - 35
```

We saw how lambda expressions and method references make implementing comparators concise and easy. For its part, the JDK has evolved with a few convenience methods added to the Comparator interface to make comparisons more fluent, as we'll see next.

Multiple and Fluent Comparisons

Let's look at the convenience methods of the Comparator interface and use them to easily make comparisons based on multiple properties.

We'll continue with the example from the previous section. To sort people by their name we used this:

```
people.stream()
    .sorted((person1, person2) ->
        person1.getName().compareTo(person2.getName()));
```

The syntax is concise compared to the inner-classes syntax from yesteryear. But we can do better thanks to convenience functions in the Comparator interface. We can more fluently express our objectives by using them. For example, to sort people by comparing their names, we can write this:

compare/fpij/Compare.java
```
final Function<Person, String> byName = person -> person.getName();
people.stream()
    .sorted(comparing(byName));
```

In this code we statically imported the comparing() method in the Comparator interface. The comparing() method uses the logic embedded in the provided lambda expression to create a Comparator. In other words, it's a higher-order function that takes in one function (Function) and returns another (Comparator). In addition to making the syntax more concise, the code now reads fluently to express the problem being solved.

We can take this fluency further to make multiple comparisons. For example, here's some cogent syntax to sort people in ascending order by both age and name:

compare/fpij/Compare.java
```
final Function<Person, Integer> byAge = person -> person.getAge();
final Function<Person, String> byTheirName = person -> person.getName();

printPeople("Sorted in ascending order by age and name: ",
  people.stream()
      .sorted(comparing(byAge).thenComparing(byTheirName))
      .collect(toList()));
```

We first created two lambda expressions: one to return the age of a given person and the other to return that person's name. We then combined these two lambda expressions in the call to the sorted() method to compare on both properties. The comparing() method created and returned a Comparator to compare based on age. On the returned Comparator we invoked the thenComparing() method to create a composite comparator that compares based on both age and name. The output from this code shows the net result of sorting by age first and then by name.

```
Sorted in ascending order by age and name:
John - 20
Jane - 21
Sara - 21
Greg - 35
```

As we can see, it's easy to combine the Comparator implementations using the convenience of lambda expressions and the utility classes in the JDK. Next, we'll examine Collectors.

Using the collect Method and the Collectors Class

We've used the collect() method a few times in the examples to gather Stream elements into an ArrayList. This method is a *reduce* operation that's useful for transforming the collection into another form, often a mutable collection. The collect() function, when combined with the utility methods of the Collectors class, provides a wealth of conveniences, as we'll see in this section.

Let's examine the power of collect() using the Person list as an example. Suppose we want to collect only people older than 20 years from the original list. Here's a version that uses mutability and forEach().

```
compare/fpij/OlderThan20.java
List<Person> olderThan20 = new ArrayList<>();
  people.stream()
        .filter(person -> person.getAge() > 20)
        .forEach(person -> olderThan20.add(person)); //BAD IDEA
System.out.println("People older than 20: " + olderThan20);
```

From the Person list we filtered only people who are older than 20 years using the filter() method. Then, within the forEach() method, we added the elements into an ArrayList we initialized before starting the iteration. Let's look at the output from this code before we refactor it.

```
People older than 20: [Sara - 21, Jane - 21, Greg - 35]
```

The code produced the desired result, but there are a few issues. First, the operation of adding an element into the target collection is pretty low-level—imperative rather than declarative. If we decide to make the iteration concurrent, we immediately have to deal with thread-safety concerns—the mutability makes it hard to parallelize. Fortunately, we can easily alleviate these concerns using the collect() method. Let's see how.

The collect() method takes a stream of elements and *collects* or gathers them into a result container. To do that, the method needs to know three things:

- How to make a result container (for example, using the ArrayList::new method)

- How to add a single element to a result container (for example, using the ArrayList::add method)

- How to merge one result container into another (for example, using the ArrayList::addAll method)

The last item may not be necessary for purely sequential operations; the code is designed to work for both sequential and parallel execution.

Let's provide these operations to the collect() method to gather the results of a stream after a filter operation.

```
compare/fpij/OlderThan20.java
List<Person> olderThan20 =
  people.stream()
        .filter(person -> person.getAge() > 20)
        .collect(ArrayList::new, ArrayList::add, ArrayList::addAll); //VERBOSE
System.out.println("People older than 20: " + olderThan20);
```

This version of code produces the same result as the previous version, but this version has many benefits.

First, we're programming with intention and more expressively, clearly indicating our goal of collecting the result into an ArrayList. The collect() method took a factory or supplier as the first parameter, followed by operations that help accumulate elements into the collection.

Second, since we're not performing any explicit mutation in code, it's easy to parallelize the execution of the iteration. Since we let the library control the mutation, it can handle coordination and thread safety for us. This is in spite of the fact that ArrayList isn't itself thread-safe—nifty.

The collect() method can perform parallel additions, as appropriate, into different sublists, and then merge them in a thread-safe manner into a larger list (hence the last parameter to help merge lists).

We saw the benefits of the collect() method over manually adding elements into an ArrayList. Next, let's look at another overloaded version of this method that's simpler and more convenient—it uses a Collector as the parameter. The Collector rolls into an interface the operations of supplier, accumulator, and combiner—the operations we specified as three separate parameters in the previous example—for ease and reuse. The Collectors utility class provides a toList()

convenience method that creates an implementation of the Collector interface to accumulate elements into an ArrayList. Let's modify the previous version to use this version of collect.

```
compare/fpij/OlderThan20.java
List<Person> olderThan20 =
  people.stream()
        .filter(person -> person.getAge() > 20)
        .collect(Collectors.toList());
System.out.println("People older than 20: " + olderThan20);
```

The convenience of this concise version of collect() along with the Collectors utility doesn't stop here. There are several methods on the Collectors to perform various collect or accumulate operations. For example, in addition to toList(), there is toSet() to accumulate into a set, toMap() to gather into a key-value collection, and joining() to concatenate the elements into a string. We can also join multiple combine operations using methods like mapping(), collectingAndThen(), minBy(), maxBy(), and groupingBy().

Let's use groupingBy() to group people by their age.

```
compare/fpij/OlderThan20.java
Map<Integer, List<Person>> peopleByAge =
  people.stream()
        .collect(Collectors.groupingBy(Person::getAge));
System.out.println("Grouped by age: " + peopleByAge);
```

With a simple call to the collect() method we're able to perform the grouping. The groupingBy() method takes a lambda expression or a method reference—called the *classifier function*—that returns the value of the property on which we want to do the grouping. Based on what we return from this function, it puts the element in context into that bucket or group. We can see the grouping in this output:

```
Grouped by age: {35=[Greg - 35], 20=[John - 20], 21=[Sara - 21, Jane - 21]}
```

The instances of Person are grouped based on their age.

In the previous example, we grouped and collected people by age. A variation of the groupingBy() method can combine multiple criteria. The simple groupingBy collector uses the classifier to organize the stream of elements into buckets. The general groupingBy collector, on the other hand, can apply yet another collector to each bucket. In other words, the values collected into buckets can go through more classification and collection downstream, as we'll see next.

Continuing with the previous example, instead of creating a map of all Person objects by age, let's get only people's names, grouped by age.

```
compare/fpij/OlderThan20.java
Map<Integer, List<String>> nameOfPeopleByAge =
  people.stream()
        .collect(
          groupingBy(Person::getAge, mapping(Person::getName, toList())));
System.out.println("People grouped by age: " + nameOfPeopleByAge);
```

In this version, groupingBy() takes two parameters: the first is the age, which is the criteria to group by, and the second is a Collector, which is the result of a call to the mapping() function. These methods are from the Collectors utility class, statically imported for use in this code. The mapping() method takes two details, the property on which to map (name in this case) and the type of the object to collect into, such as a list or set. Let's look at the output from this code:

```
People grouped by age: {35=[Greg], 20=[John], 21=[Sara, Jane]}
```

We see that the list of names is grouped by age.

Let's look at one more combination. Let's group the names by their first character and then get the oldest person in each group.

```
compare/fpij/OlderThan20.java
Comparator<Person> byAge = Comparator.comparing(Person::getAge);
Map<Character, Optional<Person>> oldestPersonOfEachLetter =
  people.stream()
        .collect(groupingBy(person -> person.getName().charAt(0),
          reducing(BinaryOperator.maxBy(byAge))));
System.out.println("Oldest person of each letter:");
System.out.println(oldestPersonOfEachLetter);
```

We first group the names based on their first letter. For this, we pass a lambda expression as the first parameter to the groupingBy() method. From within this lambda expression, we return the first character of the name for grouping purposes. The second parameter in this example, instead of mapping, performs a reduce operation. In each group, it reduces the elements to the oldest person, as decided by the maxBy() method. The syntax is a bit dense due to the combination of operations, but it reads like this: *group by the first character of the name and reduce to the person with the maximum age.* Let's look at the output, which lists the oldest person in each grouping of names that start with a given letter.

```
Oldest person of each letter:
{S=Optional[Sara - 21], G=Optional[Greg - 35], J=Optional[Jane - 21]}
```

We've seen the power of the collect() method and the Collectors. Take a few minutes to examine the Collectors utility class in your integrated development environment or the documentation and get familiar with the facilities it offers. Next, we'll use lambda expressions to stand in for some filters.

Listing All Files in a Directory

It's pretty simple to use the File class's list() method to list all filenames in a directory. To get all the files instead of just their names, we can use the listFiles() method. That's easy, but the challenge is how to proceed once we get the list. Rather than the long-winded traditional external iterator, we can use the elegant functional-style facility to iterate through the list. To achieve this, we have to reach out to the JDK's CloseableStream interface, along with some related higher-order convenience functions.

Here's the code to list the names of all the files in the current directory.

```
compare/fpij/ListFiles.java
Files.list(Paths.get("."))
    .forEach(System.out::println);
```

To list files in a different directory, we can replace "." with the full path of the directory we desire.

We first created a Path instance from the string using the get() method of the Paths convenience class. Then, using the list() method of the Files utility class (in the java.nio.file package), we got a CloseableStream to iterate over the files in the given path. We then used the internal iterator, forEach(), on it to print the filenames.

Let's look at part of the output from this code: listing the files and subdirectories of the current directory.

```
./aSampleFiles.txt
./bin
./fpij
...
```

If we want only the subdirectories in the current directory instead of a listing of all the files, we can use the filter() method:

```
compare/fpij/ListDirs.java
Files.list(Paths.get("."))
    .filter(Files::isDirectory)
    .forEach(System.out::println);
```

The filter() method extracted only the directories from the stream of files. Instead of passing in a lambda expression, we provided a method reference to the Files class's isDirectory() method. Recall that the filter() method expects a Predicate, which returns a boolean result, so this method fits the bill. Finally, we used the internal iterator to print the names of the directories. The output from this code will show the subdirectories of the current directory.

```
./bin
./fpij
./output
...
```

That was simple and took fewer lines than it would have with old-style Java code. Next, let's look at listing only select files that match a pattern.

Listing Select Files in a Directory

Java has long provided a variation of the list() method to cherry-pick filenames. This version of list() takes a FilenameFilter as its parameter. This interface has one method, accept(), that takes two parameters: File dir (representing the directory) and String name (representing a filename). We'd return a true from the accept() method to include the given filename in the list, and a false otherwise. Let's explore the options to implement this method.

It's a habitual practice in Java to pass to the list() method an instance of an anonymous inner class that implements the FilenameFilter interface. For example, let's look at how we'd select only the java files in a fpij directory using that approach.

```
compare/fpij/ListSelectFiles.java
final String[] files =
  new File("fpij").list(new java.io.FilenameFilter() {
    public boolean accept(final File dir, final String name) {
      return name.endsWith(".java");
    }
  });
if(files != null) {
  for(String file: files) {
    System.out.println(file);
  }
}
```

That took some effort and a few lines of code. There's a lot of noise in that code: an object creation, a function call, an anonymous inner class definition, the embedded method within that class, and so on. We don't have to endure that pain anymore; we can simply pass a lambda expression that takes two parameters and returns a boolean result. The Java compiler can take care of the rest for us.

While we could simply replace the anonymous inner class with a lambda expression in the previous example, we can do better than that. The Directory-Stream facility can help traverse large directory structures more efficiently, so let's explore that route. There's a variation of the newDirectoryStream() method, which takes an additional filter parameter.

Let's use lambda expressions to get a list of all java files in the fpij directory.

compare/fpij/ListSelectFiles.java
```
Files.newDirectoryStream(
        Paths.get("fpij"), path -> path.toString().endsWith(".java"))
    .forEach(System.out::println);
```

We got rid of the anonymous inner class and turned the verbose code into short and sweet code. The net effect of the two versions is the same. Let's print the selected files.

The code will display only the .java files in the mentioned directory, as in this partial output:

```
fpij/Compare.java
fpij/IterateString.java
fpij/ListDirs.java
...
```

We picked files based on filenames, but we can easily pick files based on file properties, such as whether a file is executable, readable, or writable. For this, we need a variation of the listFiles() method that takes FileFilter as its parameter. Once again, we can use lambda expressions instead of creating an anonymous inner class. Let's look at an example of listing all hidden files in the current directory.

compare/fpij/ListHiddenFiles.java
```
final File[] files = new File(".").listFiles(file -> file.isHidden());
```

If we're working with a large directory, then we can use the DirectoryStream instead of directly using the methods on File.

The signature of the lambda expression we passed to the listFiles() method conforms to the signature of the FileFilter interface's accept() method. In the lambda expression, we receive a File instance as the parameter, named file in this example. We return a boolean true if the file has the hidden property, or a false otherwise.

We can further reduce the code here; rather than passing a lambda expression, we can use a method reference to make the code more concise:

compare/fpij/ListHiddenFiles.java
```
new File(".").listFiles(File::isHidden);
```

We created the lambda-expressions version and then refactored it to the more concise method-references version. When working on new code, it's perfectly OK to take that route. If we can see the concise code from miles away, then of course we can readily key that in. In the spirit of "make it work, then make it better," it's good to get something simple working first, and once we understand the code, we can take the next step to refactor for conciseness, performance, and so on.

We worked through an example to filter out select files from a directory. Next, we'll look at how to explore subdirectories of a given directory.

Listing Immediate Subdirectories Using flatMap

We saw how to list the members of a given directory. Let's look at the effort to explore the immediate (one-level deep) subdirectories in a given directory, first using a rudimentary operation and then, more conveniently, using the flatMap() method.

Let's use the traditional for loop first to iterate over the files in a given directory. If a subdirectory contains any files, we'll add them to our list; otherwise, we'll add the subdirectory itself to the list. Finally, we'll print the total number of files found. Here's the code—for the hard way.

compare/fpij/ListSubDirs.java
```java
public static void listTheHardWay() {
  List<File> files = new ArrayList<>();

  File[] filesInCurrentDir = new File(".").listFiles();
  for(File file : filesInCurrentDir) {
    File[] filesInSubDir = file.listFiles();
    if(filesInSubDir != null) {
      files.addAll(Arrays.asList(filesInSubDir));
    } else {
      files.add(file);
    }
  }

  System.out.println("Count: " + files.size());
}
```

We fetch the list of files in the current directory and loop through each of the files. For each file, we query for its children and add them, if present, to the list of files. That works, but it comes with the usual culprits: mutability, primitive obsession, imperative, noise.... We can get rid of these using a nice little method called flatMap().

As the name indicates, this method will flatten after mapping. It maps the elements in a collection, much like the map() method does. But unlike the map() method, where we generally return an element from the lambda expression, we return a Stream instead. The method then flattens the multiple streams, obtained by mapping each element, into one flat stream.

We can use flatMap() for various operations, but the problem on hand nicely demonstrates the usefulness of this method. Each subdirectory has a list or stream of files, and we're trying to get a combined (or flattened) list of files in all the subdirectories of the current directory.

Some directories (or files) may be empty and may not have children. In that case, we simply wrap a stream around the no-child directory or file element. In case we choose to ignore a file, the flatMap() method in the JDK can deal with *empty* quite well; it will merge a null reference to a Stream as an empty collection. Let's see the flatMap() method in action.

compare/fpij/ListSubDirs.java
```
public static void betterWay() {
  List<File> files =
    Stream.of(new File(".").listFiles())
        .flatMap(file -> file.listFiles() == null ?
          Stream.of(file) : Stream.of(file.listFiles()))
        .collect(toList());
  System.out.println("Count: " + files.size());
}
```

We obtained a stream of files in the current directory and invoked the flatMap() method on it. To this method we passed a lambda expression that returns a Stream of children for the given file. The flatMap() returns a flattened map of a collection of all the children of the current directory's subdirectories. We collect those back into a List using the toList() methods of collect() and Collectors.

The lambda expression we passed as a parameter to the flatMap() method returned, for a given file, a Stream of its children (if any). Otherwise, it returned a stream with just the file. The flatMap() method gracefully handled that and mapped these streams into a resulting collection of streams and finally flattened it into one final Stream of Files.

flatMap() eliminates so much effort—it nicely combines a sequence of two operations, often called a *monadic composition*—into one single elegant step.

We saw how the flatMap() method simplifies the task of listing the immediate (one-level deep) contents of a subdirectory. Next, we'll create an observer for file changes.

Watching a File Change

We know how to look for files and directories, but if we want to sit back and get alerts when a file is created, modified, or deleted, that's easy as well. Such a facility is useful for monitoring changes to special files like configuration files and system resources. Here we'll explore the facility that's been available since Java 7, the WatchService, to watch for file changes. Most of the features we'll see here are from JDK 7 and the main improvement will be in the convenience of the internal iterator.

Let's create an example to watch for file changes in the current directory. The Path class in the JDK can lead to an instance of the file system, which acts as a factory for the watch service. We can register with this service for any notification, like so:

```
compare/fpij/WatchFileChange.java
final Path path = Paths.get(".");
final WatchService watchService =
  path.getFileSystem()
    .newWatchService();

path.register(watchService, StandardWatchEventKinds.ENTRY_MODIFY);

System.out.println("Report any file changed within next 1 minute...");
```

We've registered a WatchService to observe any change to the current directory. We can *poll* the watch service for any change to files in this directory, and it will notify us through a WatchKey. Once we gain access to the key, we can iterate through all the events to get the details of the file update. Since multiple files may change at once, a poll may return a collection of events rather than a single event. Let's look at the code for polling and iterating.

```
compare/fpij/WatchFileChange.java
final WatchKey watchKey = watchService.poll(1, TimeUnit.MINUTES);

if(watchKey != null) {
  watchKey.pollEvents()
        .stream()
        .forEach(event ->
          System.out.println(event.context()));
}
```

We see an interplay of features from older versions of Java and more recent versions here. We transformed the collection returned by pollEvents() into a Stream and then used an internal iterator on it to display the details of the updated file(s).

Let's run the code, change the sample.txt file in the current directory, and see if the program tattles about the change.

```
Report any file changed within next 1 minute...
sample.txt
```

When we modified the file, the program promptly reported that the file was changed. We can use this facility to watch for changes to various files and perform appropriate tasks in our applications. Or we could register for only file creation or deletion, as we desire.

Wrapping Up

The regular tasks of working with strings and files and creating custom comparators got a lot easier and more concise with lambda expressions and method references. Anonymous inner classes morphed into an elegant style and, along the way, mutability disappeared like the fog in the morning sun. As a bonus for favoring this style, we can benefit from the powerful JDK facilities to iterate efficiently over large directories.

Now you know how to create lambda expressions to pass as parameters to methods. In the next chapter we'll take some of the ideas we saw in this chapter further to almost effortlessly transform data.

CHAPTER 4

Transforming Data

If you're creating business applications, you deal with data all day, from breakfast to dinner and then some. You have to find the average, min, and max; query for the presence of some information; transform one collection into another; slice a collection; group values; and the list goes on.

If you get paid for the number of lines of code you write, then the imperative style is quite suitable. We can write more code and then spend more time trying to figure out why it doesn't work. Some call that job security, but it's that something we'll soon dread.

You're here because you care about results and not the amount of effort. You want to write less code to get the work done and then easily make changes to it when the business needs change. The functional programming API in Java along with the amazing functions provided in the JDK have you covered—they remove the drudgery from the tasks of data transformation.

In this chapter we'll start with computing some statistics over a collection of data and then apply transformations that result in multiple data for each value in a collection. Next, we'll see how to partition the data based on some criteria and also how to group data for different traits or characteristics. We'll conclude this chapter by looking at how to perform not just one, but two different transformations in one shot. Through all of these, we'll see how little code we actually have to write thanks to the powerful utility functions in the Collectors class. Less code to write, less code to change, and more time to get actual work done. Let's start transforming some data.

Computing Statistics

Given a collection of data—a list of stock prices, a set of savings accounts, an array of daily temperature values for a city, for example—we often need to compute different values across the collection, like the average, min, max, and so on. Traditionally, using the imperative style approach, we'd first create a destination variable for the result and initialize it to some value. Then, as we iterate over the elements in the collection, we'd access the appropriate value for each element and update the destination variable accordingly, based on the computation we desire. The result is verbose code that's often hard to understand and maintain and also difficult to parallelize if faster execution is necessary for a large collection of data.

Thanks to the functional capabilities of Java, these concerns disappear like fog that evaporates in the morning sun. In particular, for transforming data, the utility functions that are part of the java.util.stream.Collectors class are great companions for quickly implementing these operations.

We'll explore the benefits that many of the functions in the Collectors class offer using a series of examples. We need a collection of data to work with. For that, we'll first create a Person record which holds a first name, last name, and list of email addresses as Strings.

transforming/fpij/Person.java
```
package fpij;

import java.util.List;

public record Person(
  String firstName, String lastName, List<String> emailAddresses) {

  public String fullName() { return firstName + " " + lastName; }

  public static final List<Person> SAMPLE_DATA = List.of(
    new Person("John", "Doe", List.of()),
    new Person("Sara", "Walker", List.of("sara@example.com")),
    new Person("Mike", "Baker",
      List.of("mike@example.com", "baker@example.com")),
    new Person("Dev", "Shah",
        List.of("dev@example.com", "shah@example.com")),
    new Person("Sara", "Lee",
          List.of("slee@example.org", "lee@example.com")),
    new Person("Nancy", "Xie",
      List.of("nancy@example.com", "xie@example.com", "nx@example.com")),
    new Person("Jill", "Smith", List.of("jill@example.com")));
}
```

If you're using an older version of Java that doesn't support the Records feature, then implement Person as a regular class and provide methods named firstName(), lastName(), and emailAddresses() to access the fields of the class.

We need a list of sample Person instances to work with. Instead of writing a method to create and return a list of Person instances, we store a list in the

SAMPLE_DATA public final field. Records are immutable and so are the lists created by the List.of() method. Thus, record and final, combined with the of() method, give us the power to create immutable data that can be freely accessed without the worry of any inappropriate modifications by the callers. The sample data contains Person instances where different instances have a different number of email addresses associated with the fictitious persons.

Suppose our business requirements ask us to find the average number of email addresses for the people in a list. We want to compute a single value from a collection of values—you'll likely recognize that as a reduce operation; see Chapter 2, Using Collections, on page 19. In addition to the reduce() method, we've seen some specialized reduce operations such as count(), sum(), and collect(). Let's explore a few different options to compute the average number of email addresses for the people in the SAMPLE_DATA.

Let's take the most direct evolutionary approach, applying what we know already:

transforming/fpij/AverageNumberOfEmailAddresses.java
```java
package fpij;

import static java.util.stream.Collectors.*;
import java.util.List;
import static fpij.Person.SAMPLE_DATA;

public class AverageNumberOfEmailAddresses {
  public static void main(String[] args) {
    System.out.println("Average number of email addresses: " +
      SAMPLE_DATA.stream()
        .map(Person::emailAddresses)
        .mapToDouble(List::size)
        .sum()/SAMPLE_DATA.size() * 1.0);
  }
}
```

We got a stream from the SAMPLE_DATA, transformed it to a stream of email addresses using the map() function, then transformed it to a stream of the number of email addresses, determined the sum, and finally computed the average.

Let's execute the code to see what it reports for the given collection:

```
Average number of email addresses: 1.5714285714285714
```

That satisfies the business requirements, but in spite of being in the functional style, that code looks clumsy, especially the last line. As programmers, we often look for ways to improve the levels of abstraction. As it turns out, the DoubleStream interface has an average() method that fits right into what we're looking for. Let's modify the previous code to use that method:

```
System.out.println("Average number of email addresses: " +
  SAMPLE_DATA.stream()
    .map(Person::emailAddresses)
    .mapToDouble(List::size)
    .average()
    .orElse(0));
```

That's better and less noisy than the previous version. The average() method returns an Optional<Double>, and we return the value if present or 0 otherwise. This is reasonable code, and it's good enough for the given problem. This version is easy to arrive at, understand, and maintain.

You may be tempted to combine some of the steps—feel free to do so as a matter of preference, to make the code concise. But keep in mind that the benefit may be mostly aesthetic, and there may not be any gains from the performance or maintainability point of view.

Given that, let's go ahead and combine the steps. We can merge the two map() operations into one, like so:

```
System.out.println("Average number of email addresses: " +
  SAMPLE_DATA.stream()
    .mapToDouble(person -> person.emailAddresses().size())
    .average()
    .orElse(0));
```

It's logical to ask whether the operations of map() and average() may be combined. That question may lead us to explore further into the JDK library. The collect() method accepts as a parameter a Collector that performs the action of collecting the data into a desired form: a list, a set, or a count, for example. You can make your own implementation of the Collector interface, but the creators of the JDK took the time and effort to provide several convenience functions to create Collector implementations for performing different common operations. Using these functions you can readily implement your desired tasks. Let's see how we can do just that for computing the average number of email addresses of the people in the given list.

```
System.out.println("Average number of email addresses: " +
  SAMPLE_DATA.stream()
    .collect(averagingDouble(person -> person.emailAddresses().size())));
```

We iterate over the SAMPLE_DATA collection using the stream() internal iterator and perform the reduce operation using the collect() method. The collect() method accepts as an argument a Collector that can perform various operations on the collection of data. In this example, we use a Collector returned by the averaging-Double() method. We direct the averagingDouble() method to create a Collector that computes the average number of email addresses for the people in the SAMPLE_DATA list.

The output of all four versions of code to compute the average number of email addresses for the people is the same. Pick the version that you feel most comfortable with. It's a good practice to evolve the code into functional style, one step at a time, and refactor as you discover newer functions or more direct functions to get you to the solution.

We computed the average as the double type. The Collectors class also has specialized methods averagingInt() and averagingLong() to compute the average in the integer and long types, respectively.

In addition to computing averages, you may use other specialized functions to compute min and max. If you want to compute the average, min, and max all at the same time, you might wonder if you have to use each one of the individual specialized methods separately. That's one option, but that will make the code verbose, and you'll also end up iterating over the same collection three times instead of just once. Collectors provides specialized methods to get multiple statistical results from a collection in one shot; use summarizing-Double(), summarizingInt(), or summarizingLong() depending on the type of result you would like.

```java
transforming/fpij/Statistics.java
package fpij;

import static java.util.stream.Collectors.*;
import static fpij.Person.SAMPLE_DATA;

public class Statistics {
  public static void main(String[] args) {
    var statistics = SAMPLE_DATA.stream()
      .collect(
        summarizingDouble(person -> person.emailAddresses().size()));

    System.out.println("Number of people: " + statistics.getCount());
    System.out.println(
      "Number of email addresses: " + statistics.getSum());
    System.out.println(
      "Average number of email addresses: " + statistics.getAverage());
    System.out.println(
      "Max number of email addresses: " + statistics.getMax());
    System.out.println(
      "Min number of email addresses: " + statistics.getMin());
  }
}
```

The summarizingDouble() method takes a lambda expression that tells what we want to compute the statistics over. It returns an instance of the Collector that will accumulate the results into an instance of a DoubleSummaryStatistics. Once the computations are completed in one shot, we can get the desired summarizing data from the instance of DoubleSummaryStatistics. This instance provides the min, max, average, count, and sum for the values highlighted by the lambda expressions passed to the summarizingDouble() method.

Let's take a look at the output of the previous code:

```
Number of people: 7
Number of email addresses: 11.0
Average number of email addresses: 1.5714285714285714
Max number of email addresses: 3.0
Min number of email addresses: 0.0
```

We saw how to transform a collection into an average or a summary of statistics. Next, we'll look at another common transformation and get a good grasp of when to use map() and when to go for flatMap().

When to Use map vs. flatMap

As programmers get introduced to the functional style of programming, they quickly learn about and get comfortable using the filter() and map() methods of the Stream API. Whenever we want to transform a collection of data into another collection, we quickly reach for the map() method. That's good, but we have to truly understand when this function is the right choice and when we may have to go beyond.

Let's take a look at the code to get a list of first names from a list of persons.

```
List<String> firstNames = SAMPLE_DATA.stream()
  .map(Person::firstName)
  .toList();

System.out.println(firstNames);
```

That's simple code and it produces the desired result:

```
[John, Sara, Mike, Dev, Sara, Nancy, Jill]
```

We got the first names of each person in the given list of people. Let's take a closer look at the function we passed to the map() function as a method reference. The firstName() method of the Person record is a *one-to-one* function. Given a single instance of Person, this method returns a single String with the value of the first name for that Person instance.

The map() method is ideal for transforming one collection into another collection using a *one-to-one* function as a parameter. But it may not be the right choice if we need to use a *one-to-many* function. Let's dig into this further.

Suppose we're asked to get a list of all email addresses of everyone in a list. We'll have to use the emailAddresses() method for this operation. Given a single instance of Person, the emailAddresses() method returns a collection of email addresses with zero or more elements. Whereas the firstName() is a *one-to-one* function, the emailAddresses() is a *one-to-many* function. Using map() for this problem won't yield the best results. Let's see why and look at how flatMap() will nicely solve the problem.

Let's examine the consequences of passing a *one-to-many* function, the emailAddresses() method, to the map() function:

```
List<List<String>> listOfListOfEmailAdddresses = SAMPLE_DATA.stream()
  .map(Person::emailAddresses)
  .toList();

System.out.println(listOfListOfEmailAdddresses);
```

As we iterated over the SAMPLE_DATA collection, we took each element and applied the emailAddresses() method and collected the result into a list using the toList() method. The output of this code is:

```
[[], [sara@example.com], [mike@example.com, baker@example.com],
  [dev@example.com, shah@example.com], [slee@example.org, lee@example.com],
  [nancy@example.com, xie@example.com, nx@example.com], [jill@example.com]]
```

In the output, we have a list of strings embedded within an outer list. In the code, we stored the result of the iteration into the variable listOfListOfEmailAdddresses of type List<List<String>>. If we want a list of email addresses nested within an outer list, then this code worked spectacularly. But chances are we may actually want a plain and simple one-level list of email addresses and not a multilevel list—that, of course, depends on what the business wants.

Thus, if we have a *one-to-many* function and use the map() method, we'll end up with a nested collection. If we want a collection instead, we have to take an extra step after mapping—we'll have to flatten the generated List<List<String>> to a one-level List<String>.

Unlike languages like Ruby and Kotlin, Java doesn't have a *flatten* function, but, for a moment, let's assume it does so we could write code like this:

```
SAMPLE_DATA.stream().map(Person::emailAddresses).flatten() //hypothetical
```

We'd first map and then flatten to get a one-level list. That's good, but it would still involve making two separate calls. It would be great to merge the two steps into one step. Looking closely, it's quite logical that the single combined step should be called mapFlatten and could be used like so:

```
SAMPLE_DATA.stream().mapFlatten(Person::emailAddresses) //hypothetical
```

But there is no mapFlatten(), fortunately. That's because, about the third time you say the method's name, you'll feel a sharp pain in the muscles on your cheek around the jaw joints. This is due to the awkward movements your lower jaw (mandible) had to endure to say "map flatten." Having a method named *mapFlatten* would have led to repetitive stress injury and turned into an occupational hazard—oh, dear. To avoid that, the method could be named flatMap() instead of mapFlatten().

The method name flatMap() is easier to say, it rolls off the tongue, but remember it does the operation in reverse—it maps first and then flattens.

As it turns out, even though Java doesn't have a flatten method, it does have a flatMap(). The lambda expressions that you pass to the flatMap() method are required to return a Stream. Let's use flatMap() to transform a list of people into a list of their email addresses—one flat list:

```
List<String> emailAddresses = SAMPLE_DATA.stream()
  .flatMap(person -> person.emailAddresses().stream())
  .toList();

System.out.println(emailAddresses);
```

We changed from the call to map() to a call to flatMap() and made sure the lambda expression passed to flatMap() returns a Stream instead of a List. Let's take a look at the output after this change:

```
[sara@example.com, mike@example.com, baker@example.com, dev@example.com,
  shah@example.com, slee@example.org, lee@example.com, nancy@example.com,
  xie@example.com, nx@example.com, jill@example.com]
```

Ah, that's better. We have a simple one-level list of email addresses instead of an outer list containing a list of email addresses.

From this example we get a pretty good idea of when to use the map() vs. flatMap(). Let's summarize the observations:

- Use map() to transform one collection into another collection using a *one-to-one* function

- Use flatMap() to transform one collection into another collection using a *one-to-many* function

Of course, if you want to use a *one-to-many* function to map a collection to a collection nesting another collection—rare but probable—by all means, use the map() method.

Both map() and flatMap() preserve the order when mapping over an ordered collection. Whereas the map() preserves the cardinality (that is, transforming n elements results in an output with n elements), flatMap() doesn't make any such guarantees. For example, if a transformation for an element doesn't yield any values, then the output is compressed for that element.

Checking for Criteria

Transformation of data doesn't always have to result in a particular value like an average or a list. Sometimes a "transformation" may actually be an act of verifying if all the elements in a collection satisfy some characteristics, and the result may be a mere boolean value. This may be perceived as a combination of the filter() operation on a collection followed by reduce(). The Stream API simplifies and provides nice methods for transformations like this, with good efficiency. Let's take a look.

Let's say we're asked to find in a given collection if any person has at least one email address and separately if anyone has at least ten email addresses. We can use the anyMatch() function to check if any element in a collection satisfies a criteria.

```
System.out.println("Anyone has email address: " +
  SAMPLE_DATA.stream()
    .anyMatch(person -> person.emailAddresses().size() > 0));

System.out.println("Anyone has more than 10 email address: " +
  SAMPLE_DATA.stream()
    .anyMatch(person -> person.emailAddresses().size() >= 10));
```

The anyMatch() method takes a predicate that checks on the desired criteria for a given person. The predicate isn't evaluated for every single element in the collection. Instead, efficiently, the anyMatch() method invokes the predicate on elements, but only until it sees a true response. The instant it knows there's one match, it quits evaluating further because such a computation would be redundant.

Here's the output of the previous code:

```
Anyone has email address: true
Anyone has more than 10 email address: false
```

If, instead of checking that any element matches the given criteria, you want to check whether each and every element matches, use the allMatch(). Anytime a call to the predicate returns false for an element, further processing of the collection is terminated by allMatch()—short-circuiting for efficiency. In addition to getting an efficient implementation, a bigger benefit of using these methods is that we can focus on expressing our intent clearly and concisely and leave it to the runtime to figure out the details for efficient execution. Let's put this function to use in an example:

```
System.out.println("Everyone has at least one email address: " +
  SAMPLE_DATA.stream()
    .allMatch(person -> person.emailAddresses().size() > 0));

System.out.println("Everyone has zero or more email address: " +
  SAMPLE_DATA.stream()
    .allMatch(person -> person.emailAddresses().size() >= 0));
```

The output of this evaluation is shown here:

```
Everyone has at least one email address: false
Everyone has zero or more email address: true
```

We're not restricted to only checking for any or all matches. We can also check if none of the elements satisfy a criteria using the noneMatch() method.

In the examples we've seen so far, we got a single value or list as the output. But the Collectors class takes care of us even if we need to transform a collection into multiple collections.

Partitioning a Collection

Sometimes in the middle of processing a pile of data, we may run into a business requirement that needs us to split a collection of data into two groups: elements that satisfy a criteria and those that don't. For example, full-time employees vs. part-time, minors vs. adults, electric- vs. gas-operated machines, honest vs. dishonest politicians, and so on. Well, on second thought, the last one may not need any computational effort. Nevertheless, in general, splitting a collection is a task we want to carry out efficiently.

As we've seen before, the filter() function can be used to pick elements that satisfy a condition and discard the rest from a collection. But if we use this method we'll have to iterate over the collection twice: once for picking the elements that satisfy the condition and another time for picking elements that don't satisfy the condition. That's code duplication and twice the effort—not efficient. This is where the partitioningBy() method of the Collectors class steps in.

Instead of iterating twice using filter(), we can iterate just once using partitioningBy(). In this case, we can pass the same predicate to partitioningBy() that we'd have passed to one of the filter() method calls. The result of the call to collect() that receives the Collector from partitioningBy() will be a Map. The Map will have two keys: true, which contains values corresponding to the list of elements that satisfy the predicate given to partitioningBy(), and false, which contains the values that don't satisfy it.

Let's see this in action with an example where we split the collection of persons into two groups: those with multiple email addresses and those with zero or one email address:

```
Map<Boolean, List<Person>> thoseWithAndWithoutMultipleEmails =
  SAMPLE_DATA.stream()
    .collect(partitioningBy(person -> person.emailAddresses().size() > 1));

System.out.println("Number of people with at most one email address: " +
  thoseWithAndWithoutMultipleEmails.get(false).size());

System.out.println("Number of people with multiple email addresses: " +
  thoseWithAndWithoutMultipleEmails.get(true).size());
```

The partitioningBy() method was used to iterate over the collection just once, but the result is two separate lists stored into the Map. We can fetch the two parts, one after the other, by using the get() method of the Map, and passing a boolean value. The output from the code is shown here:

```
Number of people with at most one email address: 3
Number of people with multiple email addresses: 4
```

The partitioningBy() function splits a collection into two, but we've already seen that the groupingBy() function can split a collection into multiple parts. Let's dig a bit deeper into that function next.

Counting Occurrences

In Using the collect Method and the Collectors Class, on page 56, you saw the amazing capabilities of the groupingBy() function and the mapping() function to split a collection into different groups. We got a taste of the recursive nature of the Collector there. The collect() method takes a Collector as a parameter. We can pass the response from calling groupingBy(), for example. But we saw a variation where we passed the result of a call to the mapping() method as the second argument to groupingBy(). Then again, the mapping() function itself expects a Collector as its second argument. This recursive structure is mind-blowing:

```
//pseudocode
...stream()
.collect(groupingBy(...)) //collect takes a Collector

or

...stream()
.collect(groupingBy(..., mapping(...))) //groupingBy may take a Collector

or
```

```
...stream()
.collect(groupingBy(..., mapping(..., toList())))
//groupingBy may take a Collector and mapping takes a Collector

...
```

In this section we'll revisit the groupingBy() function to explore this recursive nature of Collector related functions.

In the collection of persons, we have people with different names, but some may coincidentally have the same first names and/or last names. Suppose we want to count the number of people in the collection with the same first name. We can use the groupingBy() to group the values in the collection based on the first name. But instead of storing the values for each group or mapping to get a specific detail of a person, we can use the counting() Collectors function, like so:

```
Map<String, Long> namesCount =
  SAMPLE_DATA.stream()
    .collect(groupingBy(Person::firstName, counting()));

System.out.println(namesCount);
```

The groupingBy() function groups the persons in the collection based on their first name, as specified by the first argument to groupingBy(). Instead of storing the result into a list, the values in the group are then processed by the Collector created using the counting() method. The result is a count of the number of people within each group created based on the first names, as we see in this output:

```
{Mike=1, Dev=1, John=1, Nancy=1, Sara=2, Jill=1}
```

The Collector created by the counting() function expects the count to be of type Long. This is inconvenient if our code expects the count to be an int rather than a long. During the reduce operation, we can collect data using the counting()'s Collector and then go on to transform the Long value into an Integer. We can accomplish this by using the collectingAndThen() method to collect data and perform an operation on it.

Let's first change the type of the result, the namesCount variable, from Map<String, Long> to Map<String, Integer>. Then we'll wrap the call to counting() with a call to collectingAndThen(), like so:

```
Map<String, Integer> namesCount =
  SAMPLE_DATA.stream()
    .collect(groupingBy(
      Person::firstName, collectingAndThen(counting(), Long::intValue)));

System.out.println(namesCount);
```

We don't see any difference in the output shown next, but the type of the counts is Integer instead of Long now:

```
{Mike=1, Dev=1, John=1, Nancy=1, Sara=2, Jill=1}
```

The recursive nature of Collector you saw in this section shows the power of composability. You can repeatedly slice and dice the stream in many ways, until you get the desired results. To start, we saw that the groupingBy() method lets us pick a classifier function and use it to map the collection to lists of values based on the classifier. We then saw, using more complicated examples, how to treat the list of values generated, on the fly, as a stream that can be collected further. There's no limit to how deep you can go with this, thanks to the composable nature of Collector. It takes some time for the sheer power of this utility class to sink in. If you play with more examples on your own, you'll soon have a stronger grasp of it and be well on your way to more fully exploiting it.

Counting examines the number of elements, but the operation of summing is a bit more involved. Let's see how that's handled by the Collectors.

Summing Values

By now I'm sure you've recognized that Collectors, with so many functions, may be one of the most comprehensive utility classes in the JDK. If you're looking for an intellectual company to hang out with on a Friday evening, I suggest you invite the Collectors—you won't be disappointed. In addition to all the methods we've seen, the Collectors utility class also has a function to sum values. Let's use that to total the number of email addresses a person has, while grouping the persons in a collection based on their last name.

```
var namesAndEmailAddressesCount =
  SAMPLE_DATA.stream()
    .collect(groupingBy(
      Person::lastName,
      summingInt(person -> person.emailAddresses().size())));

System.out.println(namesAndEmailAddressesCount);
```

As we've seen before, the first argument to the groupingBy() decides the label for the group. The second argument decides what gets stored for each group. In this case, it is the sum of all the numbers of email addresses that it sees for each group. Let's confirm that by viewing the output:

```
{Xie=3, Baker=2, Smith=1, Walker=1, Shah=2, Doe=0, Lee=2}
```

If it gets overwhelming, you're not alone, the Collectors utility class relentlessly keeps on giving. Take a break and then continue with the next couple of examples in this chapter.

Using flatMapping and filtering

You've used the filter() and flatMap() methods on the Stream before. The *ing* ending method names are used within the collect() call instead of directly on the Stream.

When we're in the middle of the reduce operation, collecting data, if we have to deal with a *one-to-many* function, we can use flatMapping() instead of mapping() the same way we can choose flatMap() instead of map() at the stream processing level—see When to Use map vs. flatMap, on page 72.

Also, if we're right in the middle of performing a reduce operation, and we decide to discard some values that are either not visible at the stream level or rather inconvenient to deal with there, we can use the filtering() operation to tailor the collect() operation.

You can use the two methods, filtering() and flatMapping(), independently or together depending on the problem you're trying to solve.

Suppose we're asked to group the persons in a collection based on their last names and store their email addresses that are ending with .com as values. The first thought that comes to mind is filter()—but the data we want to filter is not at the Person level but embedded into one of the properties, emailAddresses. It is rather hard to remove non-".com" addresses at the level of stream processing.

Instead, we'll delay dealing with the email addresses until the collect. We can group based on the last name. Then, we can flatMap, not map, since we have a *one-to-many* relationship. Since this is in the collect phase, we'll use flatMapping() instead of flatMap() to store the email addresses into each group. But we want only email addresses that end with ".com", so we need to use the filtering() method. While the filter operation at the level of a stream is called filter(), when done during collect, it's called filtering(). Let's take a look at the code:

```
var lastNamesAndEmailAddressesFiltered =
  SAMPLE_DATA.stream()
    .collect(
      groupingBy(Person::lastName,
        flatMapping(person -> person.emailAddresses().stream(),
          filtering(address -> address.endsWith(".com"), toList())))));

System.out.println(lastNamesAndEmailAddressesFiltered);
```

Much like flatMap(), the flatMapping() method expects the lambda expression passed to it to return a Stream. In this example, we pass the result of that to the filtering() operation, which lets only those email addresses ending with ".com" go through. We finally pack the resulting email addresses into a list. Let's take a glance at the output to confirm the code worked as expected:

```
{
  Xie=[nancy@example.com, xie@example.com, nx@example.com],
  Baker=[mike@example.com, baker@example.com],
  Smith=[jill@example.com],
  Walker=[sara@example.com],
  Shah=[dev@example.com, shah@example.com],
  Doe=[],
  Lee=[lee@example.com]
}
```

We don't have any non-".com" email addresses in the output; the one address ending with ".org" was discarded during the processing.

The previous code looked for all email addresses ending with .com, but we shouldn't assume that the email addresses will all be lowercase. Unless we have a guarantee that the addresses will all be in lowercase, we can easily take care of any case differences in the email addresses using one more transformation in the middle of the collect operation. We can change the following code snippet:

```
flatMapping(person -> person.emailAddresses().stream()
```

We can replace it with this code snippet to deal with case differences:

```
flatMapping(
  person -> person.emailAddresses().stream().map(String::toLowerCase)
```

This change also shows the power of composability—the ability to transform the lists that are being generated as part of the collect operation.

The filtering() and flatMapping() are relatively new functions that were added to the Collectors class. There's another newer function in that class, and we'll see the awesomeness packed into that next.

Teeing Operations

In almost all the examples we've seen in this chapter, we converted a collection into either a single value or another collection. The only exception to this so far was the partitioningBy() function that produced two separate collections. That's powerful but limited to giving us a collection that satisfies a given criteria and another that doesn't. What if we want to take this idea of producing two different results from one iteration, but the results aren't directly related to each other or mutually exclusive.

The teeing() function creates a Collector that will apply two different transformations on the data that flows through and finally merges the two results into one cumulative result.

Suppose we want to get the full name of a person who has the least number of email addresses and we also want the full name of a person who has the most number of email addresses. We could easily perform the min operation by iterating once and the max operation by iterating again. But as you would agree, that's not desirable. It's verbose, duplicated code with multiple iterations, which won't make us proud when a colleague issues a pull request. We should do better and we can with teeing().

We can invoke the teeing() function in the argument list for the collect() method. The teeing() function takes three parameters. The first is a Collector that works on the data that flows through the functional pipeline, to perform the first operation or transformation we desire. The second parameter is also a Collector that works on the data, just like the first one, but performs a different operation or transformation. Finally, the third parameter, a BiFunction, is used to combine the results of the two operations to produce a combined cumulative result. Let's use teeing() to find the min and max as desired:

```
record MinMax(String least, String most) {}

var leastAndMostEmailAddressPerson =
  SAMPLE_DATA.stream()
    .collect(
      teeing(
        minBy(comparing(person -> person.emailAddresses().size())),
        maxBy(comparing(person -> person.emailAddresses().size())),
        (min, max) ->
          new MinMax(min.map(Person::fullName).orElse(""),
            max.map(Person::fullName).orElse("")))));

System.out.println(leastAndMostEmailAddressPerson);
```

We created a local record MinMax within the method where it's needed. The record makes the intent clear and the code expressive as well. Records are a great way to create tuples in modern Java and are useful for conveniently handling a small arbitrary collection of data. The first argument passed to the teeing() function picks a person with the minimum number of email addresses, using the minBy() function of Collectors. The second argument picks the person with the maximum number of email addresses, using the maxBy() method. If the data that flows is empty, then there may not be a min or max. Thus the results of minBy() and maxBy() are Optional<T>. In the function to combine the two values into a cumulative result, we create an instance of the local record MinMax with the two components or properties. The first, least, will hold the full name of the person picked by the minBy() of Collector; if there is no value, then we return an empty string. Likewise, we create the value for the most. Let's execute the code and check the output:

```
MinMax[least=John Doe, most=Nancy Xie]
```

The code identified a person with the least number of email addresses and the person with the most.

We've seen a number of functions of the Collectors utility class. These functions may be used individually with the collect() method. In addition, we can also combine the methods to solve more complex problems. Because of the recursive nature of the Collectors functions, most of the methods can take additional arguments which are themselves Collectors, as we saw in Counting Occurrences, on page 77.

Wrapping Up

Transforming data is a common operation in programming, and the updates in Java make it possible to meet those challenges with elegance and ease. The power to perform transformations is packed both in the Streams API and particularly in the Collectors utility class. In this chapter we saw quite a few transformations that can be done using different methods in Collectors. We started with some simple transformations, moved on to more complex ones, and finally concluded with the facilities available to perform multiple transformations in one shot, with a single iteration. Take time to get comfortable with the functions in Collectors as it is one of the most comprehensive classes in the JDK.

In the next chapter we'll look at ways to design programs with functional interfaces and lambda expressions.

CHAPTER 5

Designing with Lambda Expressions

OOP has become the de facto standard, but with lambda expressions in Java, we can pull a few more techniques out of our bag of design tricks. In Java, OOP and functional style can complement each other and can nicely interplay. We can use these to create lightweight designs that are flexible to change and easier to extend.

We can replace interfaces, class hierarchies, and anonymous inner classes with concise code. We need fewer lines of code to get the same job done, and we can quickly try out new ideas.

In this chapter lambda expressions bring to life some neat design ideas; where we often use objects, we'll instead use lightweight functions. We'll use lambda expressions to easily separate logic from functions, making them more extensible. Then, we'll apply them to delegate responsibilities and implement the decorator pattern in just a couple of lines of code. Finally, we'll use them to turn mundane interfaces into fluent, intuitive interfaces.

Separating Concerns Using Lambda Expressions

We often create classes to reuse code; we have good intentions, but it's not always the right choice. By using higher-order functions, we can accomplish the same goals without needing a hierarchy of classes.

Exploring Design Concerns

Let's start with an example to sum asset values as a way to illustrate the design idea of separation of concerns. We'll build it in iterations. The design we first create will mix multiple concerns in one method, but we'll quickly refactor the code to make the method more cohesive. Let's start with an Asset class.

```
designing/fpij/Asset.java
public class Asset {
  public enum AssetType { BOND, STOCK };

  private final AssetType type;
  private final int value;

  public Asset(final AssetType assetType, final int assetValue) {
    type = assetType;
    value = assetValue;
  }

  public AssetType getType() { return type; }

  public int getValue() { return value; }
}
```

Asset is a simple JavaBean with two properties: type and value. Suppose we're asked to total the values of all the assets given—let's write a method for that in an AssetUtil class.

```
designing/fpij/AssetUtil.java
public static int totalAssetValues(final List<Asset> assets) {
  return assets.stream()
               .mapToInt(Asset::getValue)
               .sum();
}
```

We used the convenience of lambda expressions within this function. We transformed the List of Assets into a Stream, then mapped that into a Stream of values using the mapToInt() method. Finally, we reduced or totaled the values in this stream to arrive at a single value using the sum() method.

Let's define some assets to try out the code.

```
designing/fpij/AssetUtil.java
final List<Asset> assets = Arrays.asList(
  new Asset(Asset.AssetType.BOND, 1000),
  new Asset(Asset.AssetType.BOND, 2000),
  new Asset(Asset.AssetType.STOCK, 3000),
  new Asset(Asset.AssetType.STOCK, 4000)
);
```

Here's a call to the totalAssetValues() method using these assets.

```
designing/fpij/AssetUtil.java
System.out.println("Total of all assets: " + totalAssetValues(assets));
```

The code will report the total of all the given assets, as we see in the output.

```
Total of all assets: 10000
```

It's good we employed lambda expressions to write the totalAssetValues() method —we used fluent iterators and favored immutability. But let's shift our attention to the design of the method itself. It's tangled with three concerns: how to iterate, what to total, and how to total. This entangled logic will result in poor reuse. Let's see how.

Getting Entangled with the Concerns

Imagine we're asked to total only the bond assets. After a quick glance at the totalAssetValues() method, we realize it does almost everything we need. Why not copy and paste that code? After all, there's a reason the integrated development environments have gone through the trouble to provide keyboard shortcuts for that, right?

We'll leave totalAssetValues() intact, but we'll duplicate it and modify the new version, like so:

designing/fpij/AssetUtil.java
```
public static int totalBondValues(final List<Asset> assets) {
  return assets.stream()
              .mapToInt(asset ->
                 asset.getType() == AssetType.BOND ? asset.getValue() : 0)
              .sum();
}
```

The only difference, other than their names, between totalBondValues() and totalAssetValues(), is in the lambda expressions we send to the mapToInt() function. In this newer method, we pick the price of the asset if it's a bond; otherwise, we use a 0 for the price. Instead of crowding the logic within that one lambda expression, we could use a filter() method to extract only bonds and leave the lambda expression that was passed to the mapToInt() method untouched from the version copied from the totalAssetValues() method.

Let's call this version of the method and make sure it works.

designing/fpij/AssetUtil.java
```
System.out.println("Total of bonds: " + totalBondValues(assets));
```

The output should report only the total of bond prices.

```
Total of bonds: 3000
```

As fate may have it, now we're asked to total only stocks. We know it's morally wrong to copy and paste code once more, but no one's looking.

designing/fpij/AssetUtil.java
```
public static int totalStockValues(final List<Asset> assets) {
  return assets.stream()
```

```
          .mapToInt(asset ->
            asset.getType() == AssetType.STOCK ? asset.getValue() : 0)
          .sum();
}
```

Let's call this version of the method too:

designing/fpij/AssetUtil.java
```
System.out.println("Total of stocks: " + totalStockValues(assets));
```

The output gives us the desired results: a total of stocks only.

```
Total of stocks: 7000
```

Hey, it works and we even used lambda expressions. Time to call it done and celebrate?

Not quite; if our geeky friends discover the duplicates, they'll no longer hang out with us. We need a better design: one that's DRY,[1] one that'll make mothers proud.

Refactoring to Separate a Key Concern

Let's revisit the three methods. They share two out of the three concerns we mentioned earlier. The iteration and the way to total are the same. The "what to total" concern is different and is a good candidate to separate out of these methods.

This seems like a good place for the *strategy* pattern (see Gamma et al.'s *Design Patterns: Elements of Reusable Object-Oriented Software [GHJV95]*). We often create interfaces and classes to implement that pattern in Java, but here lambda expressions will give us a design edge.

Let's refactor the three methods into one that takes a functional interface as a parameter.

designing/fpij/AssetUtilRefactored.java
```
public static int totalAssetValues(final List<Asset> assets,
  final Predicate<Asset> assetSelector) {
  return assets.stream()
               .filter(assetSelector)
               .mapToInt(Asset::getValue)
               .sum();
}
```

This refactored version of totalAssetValues() takes two parameters: the list of assets and a Predicate to evaluate whether an asset should be considered.

---

1. http://c2.com/cgi/wiki?DontRepeatYourself

At first, this may look like what we would've done all along in Java, but it's different in a few ways. Rather than creating our own interface, we've reused the java.util.function.Predicate interface from the JDK. Also, instead of creating classes or anonymous inner classes, we can pass lambda expressions to the refactored version of the totalAssetValue() method.

Let's dig into this refactored version. We filtered the list of assets using the filter() method, then mapped the assets to their prices using the mapToInt() function, and totaled them. We simply passed the Predicate we received on to the filter() method and used a method reference for the mapToInt()'s argument.

The filter method takes care of picking only the assets we're interested in. Under the hood, it calls the given Predicate's test() method to make that decision. If the selector accepts the asset, we use its value to total further down in the chain.

With this refactoring, we turned the three normal methods into one higher-order function that depends on a lightweight strategy to handle a configurable concern, as the following figure illustrates.

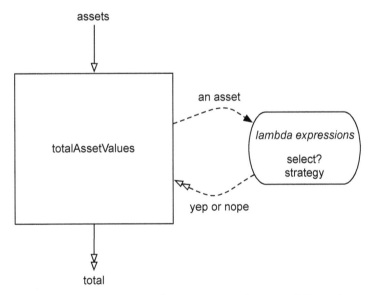

Let's use this refactored version of totalAssetValues() to total the values of all the assets.

designing/fpij/AssetUtilRefactored.java

```
System.out.println("Total of all assets: " +
  totalAssetValues(assets, asset -> true));
```

We invoke the totalAssetValues() function, passing it the list of assets as the first argument and a succinct lambda expression as the second argument. As the function iterates over the assets, it invokes the lambda expression for each asset, asking if the asset's value should be included in the total. Since we want to total all the assets, we return a boolean true here.

We've used the *open/closed principle* in this refactored design.[2] We can easily change the selection criteria without changing the method, as we'll see next.

Let's reuse the function to compute the total of only bonds and then the total of only stocks. We'll pass different lambda expressions as the second argument to the totalAssetValues() function.

designing/fpij/AssetUtilRefactored.java
```
System.out.println("Total of bonds: " +
  totalAssetValues(assets, asset -> asset.getType() == AssetType.BOND));

System.out.println("Total of stocks: " +
  totalAssetValues(assets, asset -> asset.getType() == AssetType.STOCK));
```

Let's quickly run these last three calls to the refactored totalAssetValues() function to ensure the output is the same as that of the previous version.

```
Total of all assets: 10000
Total of bonds: 3000
Total of stocks: 7000
```

We've used lambda expressions to separate the concern from the method. This is a simple use of the strategy pattern, but without the burden of creating extra classes. This pattern does require a bit more from the higher-order function's users—they have to choose the selection logic. But they can save these lambda expressions into variables and reuse them if they desire.

We focused on concerns at a method level in this section; let's apply that technique at the class level next.

Delegating Using Lambda Expressions

> We used lambda expressions and the strategy pattern to separate a concern from a method. We can also use them to separate a concern from a class. From a reuse point of view, delegation is a better design tool than inheritance. With delegation it's easier to vary the implementation we rely on, and we can plug in a different behavior more dynamically. This can help vary the behavior of classes independent of the behavior of the parts they depend on, and make the design more flexible without forcing a deep class hierarchy.

---

2.   http://en.wikipedia.org/wiki/Open/closed_principle

Creating a Delegate

Rather than delegating part of the responsibility to another class, we can delegate it to lambda expressions and method references. This will further reduce class proliferation. Let's explore that idea with an example; we'll start with a class, CalculateNAV, that performs financial calculations with data from a web service.

```
designing/fpij/CalculateNAV.java
public class CalculateNAV {
  public BigDecimal computeStockWorth(
    final String ticker, final int shares) {
    return priceFinder.apply(ticker).multiply(BigDecimal.valueOf(shares));
  }
  //... other methods that use the priceFinder ...
}
```

In the computeStockWorth() method we request the price of a ticker from a (yet to be defined) priceFinder and determine the net worth based on the number of shares. The CalculateNAV may have other methods to perform other calculations, such as yield, with the price returned by the priceFinder. That's a reason for the priceFinder to be a field in the class rather than a parameter to one particular method of CalculateNAV.

Now we need the priceFinder; we have to decide what kind of object it will be. We want to send in a ticker symbol and receive a price, hopefully obtained from a web service. The java.util.function.Function<T, R> functional interface seems like a good lightweight fit for our needs. Its abstract method can take in a value and return another value of possibly a different type. Let's use that to define the field.

```
designing/fpij/CalculateNAV.java
private Function<String, BigDecimal> priceFinder;
```

In the computeStockWorth() method we're already using the Function interface's apply() method. Let's initialize the field through a constructor injection rather than coupling to an implementation directly within the class. In effect, we're using dependency injection and the *dependency inversion principle.*[3] Instead of embedding an implementation, we'll separate the concern and rely on an abstraction. This will make the code more extensible and help shorten the coding and testing time. Here's the constructor for the CalculateNAV class.

```
designing/fpij/CalculateNAV.java
public CalculateNAV(final Function<String, BigDecimal> aPriceFinder) {
  priceFinder = aPriceFinder;
}
```

---

3. http://c2.com/cgi/wiki?DependencyInversionPrinciple

We're all set to use CalculateNAV, but we need to implement a call to the web service. Let's look into that next.

Stubbing the Web Service

We're focused on the design of CalculateNAV; we want to quickly run it and get feedback. When test-driving the design of this class using unit tests, we don't want to depend on external services—that would make the tests brittle. We want to stub the web service.

In general, though, creating a stub (or mock) in Java can be arduous and we often rely on libraries. Thanks to the lambda expressions and their fluency, this just got easier. Let's create a unit test to try out our computeStockWorth() method, stubbing away the implementation of the apply() method.

```
designing/fpij/CalculateNAVTest.java
public class CalculateNAVTest {
  @Test
  public void computeStockWorth() {
    final CalculateNAV calculateNAV =
      new CalculateNAV(ticker -> new BigDecimal("6.01"));
    BigDecimal expected = new BigDecimal("6010.00");
    BigDecimal actual = calculateNAV.computeStockWorth("GOOG", 1000);
    BigDecimal delta = actual.subtract(expected);

    assertEquals(0, delta.doubleValue(), 0.001);
  }

  //...
}
```

Creating the test was effortless. We passed a lambda expression to the CalculateNAV constructor—this is lightweight stubbing of the web service. From within the lambda expression, we returned a contrived value for the price in response to the call. Then, in the test, we asserted that the computeStockWorth() returned the expected result, within a tolerance of 0.001, for a given ticker and the number of shares.

We can also assert that the ticker passed to the lambda expression is the right one. We can take this further quite easily to add other tests—for example, an exception test to ensure code properly handles web-service failures. We can do all this without spending the time to create the code to talk to the web service, but instead merely stubbing away the implementation.

Let's run the test and ensure JUnit reports that it passed.

```
...
Test run finished after 53 ms
[         3 containers found      ]
[         0 containers skipped    ]
[         3 containers started    ]
[         0 containers aborted    ]
[         3 containers successful ]
[         0 containers failed     ]
[         1 tests found           ]
[         0 tests skipped         ]
[         1 tests started         ]
[         0 tests aborted         ]
[         1 tests successful      ]
[         0 tests failed          ]
```

Testing the code was quick; we easily stubbed away the dependency to the web service, which helped to rapidly develop and test the code. But we can't call it done until we run it with a real web service. That's our next task.

Integrating with a Web Service

Let's first invoke the computeStockWorth() on an instance of our CalculateNAV:

designing/fpij/CalculateNAV.java
```
final CalculateNAV calculateNav = new CalculateNAV(FinanceData::getPrice);

System.out.println(String.format("100 shares of Apple worth: $%.2f",
  calculateNav.computeStockWorth("AAPL", 100)));
```

Rather than stubbing away the implementation here, we pass a method reference to a FinanceData's getPrice() method. We need to implement that method to complete this task.

Talking to a real web service is easy if we can find a service that will provide current stock prices. For this example, we'll use the trial URL from Unicorn Data Services[4] to get the stock price for one ticker symbol. The value for the api_token that's hardcoded in the next code works only for select ticker symbols. If you would like to try the example for different stock ticker symbols, register with the site to get your own value for the api_token or use an alternate service you like.

designing/fpij/FinanceData.java
```
public class FinanceData {
  public static BigDecimal getPrice(final String ticker) {
    try {
      final String URL =
        "https://eodhistoricaldata.com/api/eod/%s.US?%s&%s&%s";
```

---

4.   https://eodhistoricaldata.com

```java
      final URL url = new URI(String.format(URL,
        ticker,
        "fmt=json",
        "filter=last_close",
        "api_token=OeAFFmMliFG5orCUuwAKQ8l4WWFQ67YX")).toURL();

      try(Scanner scanner = new Scanner(url.openStream())) {
        return new BigDecimal(scanner.nextLine());
      }
    } catch(Exception ex) {
      throw new RuntimeException(ex);
    }
  }
}
```

In the getPrice() method we send a request to the web service asking only for the latest closing price. We convert the String data returned by the service into a BigDecimal and return. Let's now exercise the call to the computeStockWorth() method we wrote.

```
100 shares of Apple worth: $14264.00
```

In the output, we see the worth of 100 shares of Apple stock at the time the book was written. If we run the code now, the value may be something insanely higher—let's hope.

We have to figure out a way to deal with exceptions that may arise when calling the web service. Suppressing exceptions with empty catch blocks or printing them in arbitrary places is pure evil. Rather than dealing with exceptions within lambda expressions, we have to find the right place to handle them. That requires us to rethrow the exceptions so they can be handled upstream.

Lambda expressions and method references can throw checked exceptions only if those exceptions are declared using the throws clause in the abstract method of the functional interface they stand in for. Since the Function interface's apply() method doesn't specify any expected exceptions, we can't directly throw the checked exception in this example. As a work-around, we wrapped the exception into the unchecked RuntimeException. The lambda expression now simply passes the exception through, and we'll have to handle it upstream in the code. Any runtime exception that's not handled, of course, will abruptly terminate the application.

We delegated part of the responsibility of our class to lambda expressions and method references in this example, as the figure on page 95 demonstrates.

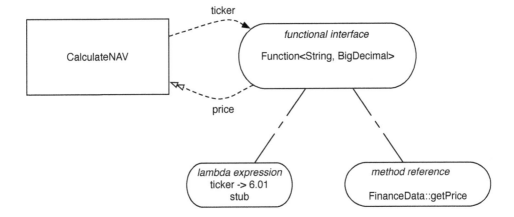

The approach we took helped us to decouple the implementation of the call to the web service from the method that used the data that is fetched from the service. This also helped us to easily stub the service to quickly test our calculate method. Next, we'll use lambda expressions to combine multiple behaviors.

Decorating Using Lambda Expressions

So far we've avoided creating implementation classes to support the delegate interfaces. We needed simple implementations for these interfaces, so that worked out fairly well. Let's increase our demands on these implementations, ask them to interact with multiple delegates, and see how lambda expressions handle that.

Delegation is great, but we can take it further if we can chain delegates to add behavior. We can then create discrete flavors of behavior and sprinkle them onto the classes, like the toppings at the ice cream shop.

The decorator pattern is powerful, but programmers often hesitate to use it due to the burdensome hierarchy of classes and interfaces—like FilterInputStream and FilterOutputStream in the JDK—that are used to implement the pattern (see Gamma et al.'s *Design Patterns: Elements of Reusable Object-Oriented Software [GHJV95]*). We can now realize this pattern with less effort in Java.

In the next example, we'll chain delegates—using lambda expressions, of course—to realize the decorator pattern. This will help us see how we can create a flexible and extensible lightweight design with just a few lines of code.

Designing Filters

Adding filters to a camera is a good example of chaining behavior or responsibilities. We may start with no filters, then add a filter, and then a few more. We want our design to be flexible so that it doesn't care how many filters we have. Let's create an example Camera that'll use filters to process the captured colors.

```java
designing/fpij/Camera.java
@SuppressWarnings("unchecked")
public class Camera {
  private Function<Color, Color> filter;

  public Color capture(final Color inputColor) {
      final Color processedColor = filter.apply(inputColor);
      //... more processing of color...
      return processedColor;
  }

  //... other functions that use the filter ...
}
```

The Camera has a field for the filter, a reference to an instance of Function (much like the delegation example we saw earlier). This filter function can receive a Color and return a processed Color. Looking at what we have so far, the class may appear to use only one filter, but with a design tweak, we'll make it work with multiple filters.

To achieve this flexibility, we'll use a method that belongs to a special type called default methods. In addition to abstract methods, interfaces can have methods with implementation, marked as default. These methods are automatically added to the classes that implement the interfaces. This was done as a trick in Java to enhance existing classes with new methods without having to change each one of them. In addition, interfaces can have static methods.

In addition to the apply() abstract method, the Function interface has a default method, andThen(), to combine or chain multiple Functions. Within the lambda expression that stands in for a Function parameter, we can readily use this method.

The andThen() method can combine or chain two Functions together. Once we combine the functions, a call to apply() will hop through the chained Functions. Let's take a quick look at how that works. Suppose we combine two Functions, target and next, like this:

```java
wrapper = target.andThen(next);
```

Now let's invoke the apply() method on the resulting wrapper.

```
wrapper.apply(input);
```

The result of that call is the same as doing this:

```
temp = target.apply(input);
return next.apply(temp);
```

Without the temporary variable, it would be like this:

```
return next.apply(target.apply(input));
```

Let's write a setFilters() method that takes a *varargs* of Function; we can send zero or more filters to this function. In addition, let's create the constructor for the Camera.

```
designing/fpij/Camera.java
public void setFilters(final Function<Color, Color>... filters) {
  filter =
    Stream.of(filters)
          .reduce((filter, next) -> filter.andThen(next))
          .orElse(color -> color);
}
public Camera() { setFilters(); }
```

In the setFilters() method, we iterate through the filters and combine them into a chain using the andThen() method. If no filter is given, then the reduce() method (we saw this method in Reducing a Collection to a Single Value, on page 38) will return an Optional empty. In that case, we provide a dummy filter as an argument to the orElse() method, and it simply returns the color that the filter would receive for processing. If we provide filters to the setFilters() method, the filter field will refer to the first filter—an instance of Function<Color, Color>—that's at the head of a chain of filters.

We provided a lambda expression as a parameter to the orElse() method of the Optional that the reduce() method returned. The Function interface has an identity() static method that does the same operation as the lambda expression we wrote. Instead of creating our own lambda expression, we can use a reference to that method instead. To do so, we need to change

```
.orElse(color -> color);
```

to

```
.orElseGet(Function::identity);
```

In addition to the setFilters() method, we have a constructor that simply sets the filter to the dummy filter I mentioned previously.

Our design of the camera with filters is complete, so let's try it out. We'll use it with no filters first, but we need a Camera instance to start. Let's create one and assign it to a local variable camera.

designing/fpij/Camera.java
```
final Camera camera = new Camera();
final Consumer<String> printCaptured = (filterInfo) ->
  System.out.println(String.format("with %s: %s", filterInfo,
    camera.capture(new Color(200, 100, 200)))));
```

To see the camera in action, we need a convenience function to print the capture() method's results. Rather than creating a standalone static method, we created a lambda expression to stand in for an instance of the Consumer functional interface, right here within the main() method. We chose a Consumer because printing consumes the value and doesn't yield any results. This function will invoke capture() with the colors 200, 100, and 200 for the *red*, *green*, and *blue* parts of color, respectively, and print the resulting filtered/processed output. Let's ask the camera to capture the given colors.

designing/fpij/Camera.java
```
printCaptured.accept("no filter");
```

Since no filters are given, the captured color should be the same as the input; let's verify that in the output.

```
with no filter: java.awt.Color[r=200,g=100,b=200]
```

Adding a Filter

Adding a filter is a breeze; we simply have to pass the filter to the setFilters() method. The filter can be a simple lambda expression or a method reference. We can use brighter() on the java.awt.Color class as a filter, so let's simply pass a reference of this method to the setFilters() method.

designing/fpij/Camera.java
```
camera.setFilters(Color::brighter);
printCaptured.accept("brighter filter");
```

Let's look at the result of the capture() with this filter in place.

```
with brighter filter: java.awt.Color[r=255,g=142,b=255]
```

The input color has been brightened. As we can see, the output RGB values are higher than the corresponding values in the input. Let's quickly change the filter to a darker shade.

designing/fpij/Camera.java
```
camera.setFilters(Color::darker);
printCaptured.accept("darker filter");
```

This should reduce the brightness of the input, as we can see in the output.

```
with darker filter: java.awt.Color[r=140,g=70,b=140]
```

Adding Multiple Filters

The design is good so far; now let's mix two filters—a brighter one and a darker one—to see the effect of chaining.

```
designing/fpij/Camera.java
camera.setFilters(Color::brighter, Color::darker);
printCaptured.accept("brighter & darker filter");
```

We passed two method references to the setFilters() method—just essence, no ceremony. (We could've passed in lambda expressions instead of method references.) The two filters are now chained, and the filter reference in the Camera instance is referring to the head of the chain. A call to the capture() method will now route the color processing through each of these filters, as we see in the following figure:

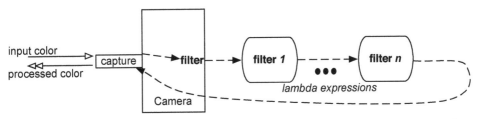

With this filter combination, the input color goes through a series of transformations or filtering. First, it passes through the bright filter, which brightens the shades, and then it goes through the dark filter, which makes the colors darker again, as we can see from the output.

```
with brighter & darker filter: java.awt.Color[r=178,g=99,b=178]
```

Adding more than two filters is no different; we simply pass more comma-separated filters, either as method references or as lambda expressions.

We designed object chaining and implemented the decorator pattern without having to create a hierarchy of classes. The magic happens in just a couple of lines of code within the setFilters() method. We made good use of the JDK Function interface here. We saw lambda expressions and method references really shine in this example.

We ran into another Java feature in this section: the default methods. Let's take a closer look at them next.

A Peek into the default Methods

In the design we explored in the previous section, we used the default methods. default methods aren't intrinsically tied to lambda expressions or the functional style of programming. But many of the convenience methods in collections wouldn't have been possible without them.

Interface evolution is the key motivation behind default methods. The API defined in the early '90s was a good idea back then, but for the platform to stay relevant it needs to evolve. The default methods provide a nondisruptive path for that. Moving forward, when we design with interfaces, we'll likely use default methods. Let's examine their behavior and how they intermix with classes.

The Java compiler follows a few simple rules to resolve default methods:

1. Subtypes automatically carry over the default methods from their super-types.

2. For interfaces that contribute a default method, the implementation in a subtype takes precedence over the one in supertypes.

3. Implementations in classes, including abstract declarations, take precedence over all interface defaults.

4. If there's a conflict between two or more default method implementations, or there's a default-abstract conflict between two interfaces, the inheriting class should disambiguate.

To get a better understanding of these rules, let's create an example with default methods.

```
public interface Fly {
  default void takeOff() { System.out.println("Fly::takeOff"); }
  default void land() { System.out.println("Fly::land"); }
  default void turn() { System.out.println("Fly::turn"); }
  default void cruise() { System.out.println("Fly::cruise"); }
}

public interface FastFly extends Fly {
  default void takeOff() { System.out.println("FastFly::takeOff"); }
}

public interface Sail {
  default void cruise() { System.out.println("Sail::cruise"); }
  default void turn() { System.out.println("Sail::turn"); }
}

public class Vehicle {
  public void turn() { System.out.println("Vehicle::turn"); }
}
```

All the interfaces in this example have default methods. The FastFly interface extends from the Fly interface and overrides the takeOff() method, providing its own default implementation. FastFly also carries forward the other three methods of the Fly interface (*rule 1*). Any class or interface inheriting from FastFly will see the implementation of takeOff() in FastFly, and not the implementation in Fly (*rule 2*).

All three interfaces have implementations for the cruise() and turn() methods. In addition, the Vehicle class implements the turn() method.

Let's create a class that inherits these types.

```java
public class SeaPlane extends Vehicle implements FastFly, Sail {
  private int altitude;
  //...
  public void cruise() {
    System.out.print("SeaPlane::cruise currently cruise like: ");
    if(altitude > 0)
      FastFly.super.cruise();
    else
      Sail.super.cruise();
  }
}
```

SeaPlane extends Vehicle and implements the FastFly and Sail interfaces. Let's take a closer look at the implementation of this class.

There appears to be a conflict for the turn() method, but that's not the case. Even though the turn() method is present in the interfaces, the implementation in the superclass Vehicle takes precedence here (*rule 3*), so there's no conflict to resolve.

But the Java compiler will force us to implement the cruise() method in the SeaPlane class because the default implementations in the FastFly (derived from Fly) and Sail interfaces conflict (*rule 4*).

From within the overridden methods, we can call back into the corresponding default methods. For example, from within the cruise() method, we can see how to call the default methods of both the FastFly and the Sail interfaces.

We can see the logic of why we'd need to specify the interface name, like FastFly or Sail, when invoking the default methods from within the overriding method. At first glance, the use of super may appear superfluous, but it's required. That's how the Java compiler knows if we're referring to a default method (when super is used) or a static method in the interface. In Java, interfaces can optionally have default methods and static methods, possibly with the same name.

To see the behavior of the default methods in action, let's create an instance of SeaPlane and invoke the methods on it.

```
SeaPlane seaPlane = new SeaPlane();
seaPlane.takeOff();
seaPlane.turn();
seaPlane.cruise();
seaPlane.land();
```

Before running the code on the computer, we'll run it mentally; let's go over the code to ensure we've understood the rules.

The call to the takeOff() method should go to the implementation in the FastFly interface (*rules 1 and 2*). The implementation of the turn() method in Vehicle should be picked for the call to the turn() method on the SeaPlane, even though these are available on the interfaces (*rule 3*). Since we were forced to implement the cruise() method on the SeaPlane, that specific implementation of the method should be invoked for the call to cruise() (*rule 4*). Finally, the call to the land() method will land on the implementation in the Fly interface (*rule 1*).

We can now compare the output we got from the mental run of the code with the output from the run on the computer:

```
FastFly::takeOff
Vehicle::turn
SeaPlane::cruise currently cruise like: Sail::cruise
Fly::land
```

We used default methods in interfaces, whereas in the past, interfaces were allowed to have only abstract methods. Seeing this, it may seem that interfaces have evolved into abstract classes, but that's not the case. Abstract classes can have state, but interfaces can't—this eliminates the concerns of the "diamond problem" of collision from multiple inheritance. Also, we can inherit (implement) a class from multiple interfaces, but we only inherit (extend) from at most one abstract class. The good old recommendation to favor interfaces over abstract classes where possible is still a nice rule to follow. And now, thanks to the ability to have default methods, interfaces are even more attractive and powerful than before.

Now that we understand the behavior of default methods, let's shift our attention back to lambda expressions. So far in this chapter, we've seen the different forms the lambda expressions can take and the multiple design goals we were able to achieve using them. Next, we'll cover how they can influence a class's interface.

Creating Fluent Interfaces Using Lambda Expressions

We've been looking at the internals of methods and classes in this chapter. Now let's shift our focus to see how lambda expressions can help shape a class's skin or interface. We can use these techniques to structure the API of our classes to make it more intuitive and fluent for programmers to use.

Starting with a Design

Let's start with a simple Mailer class and evolve the design of its interface.

designing/fpij/Mailer.java
```
public class Mailer {
  public void from(final String address) { /*... */ }
  public void to(final String address)   { /*... */ }
  public void subject(final String line) { /*... */ }
  public void body(final String message) { /*... */ }
  public void send() { System.out.println("sending..."); }

  //...
}
```

The class looks routine—a bunch of void methods. Let's use this class to configure and send out an email.

designing/fpij/Mailer.java
```
Mailer mailer = new Mailer();
mailer.from("build@agiledeveloper.com");
mailer.to("venkats@agiledeveloper.com");
mailer.subject("build notification");
mailer.body("...your code sucks...");
mailer.send();
```

We've all encountered code like this, but it has a couple of smells. First, it's noisy; we had to repeat the mailer so many times. Second, at the end of the call, what do we do with the mailer instance? Can we reuse it for another set of calls, or is it disposable? How do we know?

One answer may be "go read the documentation," but that doesn't help the "put that 'read me' document away and start tinkering with stuff" types among us. Let's design this API so it's more intuitive and fluent.

Using Method Chaining

We discussed two smells: repeated use of mailer reference and unclear object lifetime. Let's address the first smell now.

Rather than repeating the reference, it would be great to continue a conversational state on a context object. We can achieve this using a simple *method chaining* or *cascade method* pattern. In this pattern, rather than having void methods, we make each method return an instance. This returned object is often *this*, the object on which the method is invoked. We use this returned object to build on or chain the subsequent call. Let's evolve the Mailer to use this design; we'll call the new version the MailBuilder. Each method of the class, except the terminal methods like send(), returns a reference instead of being void.

designing/fpij/MailBuilder.java

```
public class MailBuilder {
  public MailBuilder from(final String address) { /*... */; return this; }
  public MailBuilder to(final String address)   { /*... */; return this; }
  public MailBuilder subject(final String line) { /*... */; return this; }
  public MailBuilder body(final String message) { /*... */; return this; }
  public void send() { System.out.println("sending..."); }

  //...
}
```

The new interface will be less noisy to use; we get rid of the repetitive variable name and nicely chain the calls.

designing/fpij/MailBuilder.java

```
new MailBuilder()
  .from("build@agiledeveloper.com")
  .to("venkats@agiledeveloper.com")
  .subject("build notification")
  .body("...it sucks less...")
  .send();
```

We started with a MailBuilder instance and chained the calls to the functions, in sequence, and on the instance that the previous call returned. The method chaining, or a *train wreck* as some like to call it, passed the state from one call to the next as we moved through the chain. The terminal method, send() in this example, wrapped up the sequence.

Even though this design reduced the noise, it has a few disadvantages. The new keyword sticks out, reducing the API's fluency and readability. The design doesn't prevent someone from storing the reference from new and then chaining from that reference. In the latter case, we'd still have the issue with object lifetime, the second smell I mentioned earlier. Also, there are a lot of corner cases—for example, we have to ensure methods like from() are called exactly once.

We need to refine the design further to make it more intuitive and fluent. Let's call our friends, the lambda expressions, for help.

Making the API Intuitive and Fluent

Let's evolve the design further. This time we'll combine the method-chaining approach with lambda expressions. We'll call this version of mailer FluentMailer.

```
designing/fpij/FluentMailer.java
public class FluentMailer {
  private FluentMailer() {}

  public FluentMailer from(final String address) { /*... */; return this; }
  public FluentMailer to(final String address)   { /*... */; return this; }
  public FluentMailer subject(final String line) { /*... */; return this; }
  public FluentMailer body(final String message) { /*... */; return this; }

  public static void send(final Consumer<FluentMailer> block) {
    final FluentMailer mailer = new FluentMailer();
    block.accept(mailer);
    System.out.println("sending...");
  }

  //...
}
```

Just like in the method-chaining version, all the nonterminal methods return the instance. In addition, in this version we made the constructor private. This will disallow direct object creation. We also made the terminal method, send(), a static method and it expects a Consumer as a parameter.

Rather than creating an instance, users will now invoke send() and pass a block of code. The send() method will create an instance, yield it to the block, and, upon return, complete any required validations and perform its final *send* operations.

This may feel a bit roundabout, but we removed the smells we discussed earlier. The object's scope is confined within the block, and once we return from the send() method, the reference is gone. We can also benefit from the fluent method chaining within the block, without the sour new keyword sticking out. Let's use this new API in an example.

```
designing/fpij/FluentMailer.java
FluentMailer.send(mailer ->
  mailer.from("build@agiledeveloper.com")
        .to("venkats@agiledeveloper.com")
        .subject("build notification")
        .body("...much better..."));
```

We invoked the send() method and passed a lambda expression to it. Within the lambda expression, we received an instance of the mailer and invoked the desired chain of methods on it.

The instance's scope is fairly easy to see: we get it, work with it, and return it. For that reason, this is also called the *loan pattern.*

From a mundane repetitive interface, we evolved the design to support a fluent interface. This design is useful in a number of areas in applications. For example, we can use it to configure mailers, to specify database-connection parameters, or anywhere we need to build a series of states on an instance, but in a controlled manner.

Wrapping Up

Lambda expressions aren't just a language feature; they turn into a powerful yet lightweight design tool. Instead of spending the effort to create a hierarchy of interfaces and classes, we can reuse functional interfaces and pass around lambda expressions and method references where possible. This technique can help us easily create delegates to quickly implement the strategy pattern at both the method and the class level. We can also use lambda expressions to implement the decorator pattern. By turning lambda expressions into controlled workhorses, we can create easy-to-read, fluent interfaces as well as configuration details in code.

In the next chapter we'll explore a variation of the loan pattern; we'll use lambda expressions to exert greater control when managing object lifetime.

CHAPTER 6

Working with Resources

We make extensive use of resources when programming—we access files, communicate to remote services, use database connections, and so on. And, that often involves working with issues like the timely release of the resources, locking for synchronization, and handling exceptions that may arise. Dealing with all of these concerns at the same time can get daunting. In this chapter we'll see how we can structure our code, using lambda expressions, to alleviate the pain of managing resource access in general—that is, to deal with the mundane tasks that we'd better not get wrong.

We may have been led to believe that the JVM automates all garbage collection (GC). It's true that we could let the JVM handle it if we're only using internal resources. But GC is our responsibility if we use external resources, such as when we connect to databases, open files and sockets, or use native resources.

Java provides a few options to properly clean up resources, but, as we'll see in this chapter, none are as effective as what we can do with lambda expressions. We'll use lambda expressions to implement the *execute around method (EAM)* pattern, which gives us better control over the sequencing of operations.[1] By using this pattern, as we'll see, we move the burden of managing the resource lifetime from the user of a piece of code to its developer who has better knowledge and control over those details.

We'll then take the ideas of managing resources further to streamline more operations around the use of resources. We'll see how to manage the critical and error-prone task of managing locks in a safe way. Finally, we'll look at how these ideas can also help us with writing exception tests in a concise and elegant way.

---

1. http://c2.com/cgi/wiki?ExecuteAroundMethod

Cleaning Up Resources

GC can be a pain to deal with. A company asked me to help debug a problem —one programmer described the issue as "it works fine...most of the time." The application failed during peak usage. It turned out that the code was relying on the finalize() method to release database connections. The JVM figured it had enough memory and opted not to run GC. Since the finalizer was rarely invoked, it led to external resource clogging and the resulting failure.

We need to manage situations like this in a better way, and lambda expressions can help. Let's start with an example problem that involves GC. We'll build the example using a few different approaches, discussing the merits and deficiencies of each. This will help us see the strengths of the final solution using lambda expressions.

Peeking into the Problem

We're concerned with external resource cleanup, so let's start with a simple example class that uses a FileWriter to write some messages.

resources/fpij/FileWriterExample.java
```
public class FileWriterExample {
  private final FileWriter writer;

  public FileWriterExample(final String fileName) throws IOException {
    writer = new FileWriter(fileName);
  }
  public void writeStuff(final String message) throws IOException {
    writer.write(message);
  }
  public void finalize() throws IOException { //Deprecated in Java 9
    writer.close();
  }
  //...
}
```

In the FileWriterExample class's constructor, we initialize an instance of FileWriter, giving it the name of a file to write to. In the writeStuff() method we write the given message to the file using the instance of the FileWriter we created. Then, in the finalize() method we clean up the resource, calling close() on it with the hope that it will flush the content to the file and close it.

At first glance, the code seems reasonable. After all, classes written in many Java applications use the finalize() method to clean up resources, a standard practice until Java 8, and a lot of legacy code still uses that function. In reality, expecting the resources to be cleaned up automatically is rather wishful thinking.

If the JVM finds that sufficient memory is available, then the GC won't be invoked and thus the finalize() method won't be called for a long time. This will result in the resource not being released in a timely manner and can also lead to resource contention issues. This is one of the reasons why the finalize() method was deprecated in Java 9, to encourage programmers to move away from using that method. We'll look at alternatives to the finalize() method shortly, but first, let's write a main() method to use the FileWriterExample class.

resources/fpij/FileWriterExample.java
```
public static void main(final String[] args) throws IOException {
  final FileWriterExample writerExample =
    new FileWriterExample("peekaboo.txt");

  writerExample.writeStuff("peek-a-boo");
}
```

We created an instance of the FileWriterExample class and invoked the writeStuff() method on it, but if we ran this code, we'd see that the peekaboo.txt file was created but it's empty. The finalizer never ran; the JVM decided it wasn't necessary as there was enough memory. As a result, the file was never closed, and the content we wrote was not flushed from memory.

If we create several instances of the FileWriterExample class in a long-running process, we'll end up with several open files. Many of these files won't be closed in a timely manner since the JVM has a lot of memory and sees no reason to run GC.

Let's fix the problem by adding an explicit call to close(), and let's get rid of the finalize() method.

Say Farewell to finalize()

The finalize() method was deprecated in Java 9. Take a few minutes to examine your own production code to see if the finalize() method is still present in any of the classes. If you find them, note the occurrences down as technical debt and schedule time to clean those up using the techniques you learn in this chapter.

Closing the Resource

Even though the object's memory cleanup is still at the mercy of the JVM's GC, we could convince ourselves that the external resources used by an instance may be quickly cleaned up with an explicit call. That, unfortunately, will result in more issues. To see this, let's write a close() method.

```
resources/fpij/FileWriterExample.java
public void close() throws IOException { //Not a good solution
  writer.close();
}
```

In the close() method, in turn, we call the FileWriter instance's close() method. If we used any other external resources in the FileWriterExample, we can clean them up here, as well. Let's make explicit use of this method in the main() method.

```
resources/fpij/FileWriterExample.java
final FileWriterExample writerExample =
  new FileWriterExample("peekaboo.txt");

writerExample.writeStuff("peek-a-boo");
writerExample.close();
```

If we run the code now and look into the peekaboo.txt file, we'll see the peek-a-boo message. The code works, but it's far from perfect.

The explicit call to close() cleans up any external resources the instance uses as soon as we indicate the instance is no longer needed. But we may not reach the call to the close() method if there was an exception in the code leading up to it. We'll have to do a bit more work to ensure the call to close() happens. Let's take care of that next.

Ensuring Cleanup

We need to ensure the call to close() happens whether or not there's an exception. To achieve this, we can wrap the call in a finally block.

```
resources/fpij/FileWriterExample.java
final FileWriterExample writerExample =
  new FileWriterExample("peekaboo.txt");

try { //Rather verbose
  writerExample.writeStuff("peek-a-boo");
} finally {
  writerExample.close();
}
```

This version will ensure resource cleanup even if an exception occurs in the code, but that's a lot of effort and the code is verbose and smelly. Java 7 introduced a feature to reduce such smells, as we'll see next.

Using ARM

The automatic resource management (ARM) is a feature that has been available since Java 7 and is useful for automatically releasing a resource at the end of its usage. When used properly, ARM can reduce verbosity in code. Rather than using both the try and finally blocks that we used in the previous example, we can use the ARM feature with a special form of the try block with a resource attached to it. When this syntax is used, the Java compiler takes care of automatically inserting, in the bytecode, the finally block and a call to the close() method.

Let's see how the code would look with ARM; we'll use an instance of a new FileWriterARM class.

resources/fpij/FileWriterARM.java
```
try(final FileWriterARM writerARM = new FileWriterARM("peekaboo.txt")) {
  writerARM.writeStuff("peek-a-boo");

  System.out.println("done with the resource...");
}
```

We created the instance of the class FileWriterARM within the safe haven of the *try-with-resources* form and invoked the writeStuff() method within its block. When we leave the scope of the try block, the close() method is automatically called on the instance/resource managed by this try block. For this to work, the compiler requires the managed resource class to implement the AutoCloseable interface, which has just one method, close().

The rules around AutoCloseable have gone through a few changes in Java. First, Stream implements AutoCloseable and, as a result, all input/output (I/O)-backed streams can be used with try-with-resources. The contract of AutoCloseable has been modified from a strict "the resource *must* be closed" to a more relaxed "the resource *can* be closed." If we're certain that our code uses an I/O resource, then we should use try-with-resources.

Here's the FileWriterARM class used in the previous code.

resources/fpij/FileWriterARM.java
```
public class FileWriterARM implements AutoCloseable {
  private final FileWriter writer;

  public FileWriterARM(final String fileName) throws IOException {
    writer = new FileWriter(fileName);
  }

  public void writeStuff(final String message) throws IOException {
    writer.write(message);
  }

  public void close() throws IOException {
    System.out.println("close called automatically...");
    writer.close();
  }

  //...
}
```

Let's run the code and look at the peekaboo.txt file and the console for the code's output.

```
done with the resource...
close called automatically...
```

We can see the close() method was called as soon as we left the try block. The instance we created when entering the try block isn't accessible beyond the point of leaving the block. The memory that instance uses will be garbage-collected eventually based on the GC strategy the JVM employs.

The previous code using ARM is concise and charming, but the programmers have to remember to use it. The code won't complain if we ignore this elegant construct; it will simply create an instance and call methods like writeStuff() outside of any try blocks. If we're looking for a way to ensure timely cleanup and avoid programmer errors, we have to look beyond ARM, as we'll do next.

Using the Execute Around Method Pattern to Clean Up Resources

ARM was a good step in the right direction, but it's not very effective—never trust anything with the word *management* in it, right? Just kidding. Anyone using our class has to figure out that it implements AutoCloseable and remember to use the *try-with-resources* construct. It'd be great if the API we design could guide the programmers and, with the compiler's help, point them in the right direction. We can easily achieve that with lambda expressions and the execute around method (EAM) pattern.

EAM is a powerful pattern that makes use of lambda expressions to wrap a piece of code. As the name alludes to, we can design to perform a pre-op and a post-op around the execution of the code. Thus the user of our design can focus on their business logic and delegate the details of managing the creation and the release of resources to the designers of the code. With the help of this pattern, resource creation can be performed before the execution of the lambda expression, and resource cleanup can be streamlined to run automatically after the execution of the lambda expression. It sounds intriguing and I'm sure you're eager to see this in action. Let's rework the problem at hand to use EAM.

Preparing the Class for Resource Cleanup

We'll design a class, FileWriterEAM, that encapsulates heavy resources that need timely cleanup. In this example we'll use the FileWriter to represent that resource. Let's make both the constructor and the close() methods private—

that'll grab the attention of programmers trying to use the class. They can't create an instance directly, and can't invoke the close() on it either. Before we discuss it further, let's implement the design devised so far.

resources/fpij/FileWriterEAM.java

```java
public class FileWriterEAM  {
  private final FileWriter writer;

  private FileWriterEAM(final String fileName) throws IOException {
    writer = new FileWriter(fileName);
  }

  private void close() throws IOException {
    System.out.println("close called automatically...");
    writer.close();
  }

  public void writeStuff(final String message) throws IOException {
    writer.write(message);
  }
  //...
}
```

The private constructor and the private close methods are in place, along with the public method writeStuff().

Using Higher-Order Functions

Since the programmers can't directly create an instance of FileWriterEAM, we need a factory method for them to use. Unlike the regular factory methods that create an instance and throw it across the fence, our method will yield it to users and wait for them to finish their work with it. We'll use the help of lambda expressions to do this, as we'll see soon. Let's write this method first.

resources/fpij/FileWriterEAM.java

```java
public static void use(final String fileName,
  final UseInstance<FileWriterEAM, IOException> block) throws IOException {

  final FileWriterEAM writerEAM = new FileWriterEAM(fileName);

  try {
    block.accept(writerEAM);
  } finally {
    writerEAM.close();
  }
}
```

In the use() method, we receive two parameters, fileName and a reference to an interface UseInstance (which we haven't defined yet). Within this method we instantiate FileWriterEAM, and within the safe haven of the try and finally block we pass the instance to an accept() method of our soon-to-be-created interface.

When the call returns, we invoke the close() method on the instance in the finally block. Instead of using this construct, we could use ARM within the use() method. In any case, the users of our class don't have to worry about these details.

The use() method represents the structure of the *execute around method* pattern. The main action here is the use of the instance within the accept() method, but the creation and cleanup operations nicely surround this call.

Before we can exercise this code, let's take care of the last missing piece, the UseInstance interface.

resources/fpij/UseInstance.java
```
@FunctionalInterface
public interface UseInstance<T, X extends Throwable> {
  void accept(T instance) throws X;
}
```

UseInstance is a functional interface, an ideal candidate for the Java compiler to automatically synthesize from lambda expressions or method references. We marked the interface with the @FunctionalInterface annotation. This is purely optional, but useful for conveying our intent more explicitly. Whether we use this interface or not, the compiler will automatically recognize functional interfaces structurally, as we discussed in A Little Sugar to Sweeten, on page 15.

We could've used a java.function.Consumer interface instead of defining our own UseInstance; but, since the method may throw an exception, we needed to indicate that in our interface. Lambda expressions can only throw checked exceptions defined as part of the signature of the abstract method being synthesized (see Chapter 10, Error Handling, on page 167). We created the UseInstance interface so that the accept() method can accept an instance of a generic type; in this example, we tied it down to an instance of a concrete FileWriterEAM. We also designed it so this method implementation could potentially throw a generic exception X—again, in this example tied to the concrete class IOException.

Using the Design for Instance Cleanup

As the class's designers, we put in a bit more effort than simply implementing the AutoCloseable interface. This extra investment on our part will quickly pay recurring dividends: each time programmers use our class, they'll get instant resource cleanup, as we can see here:

resources/fpij/FileWriterEAM.java
```
FileWriterEAM.use("eam.txt", writerEAM -> writerEAM.writeStuff("sweet"));
```

First, our class's users can't create an instance directly. This prevents them from creating code that would postpone the resource cleanup beyond its expiration point (unless they go through extreme measures, such as using reflection, to defeat the mechanism). Since the compiler will prevent calls to the constructor or the close() method, the programmers will quickly figure out the benefit of the use() method, which yields an instance for their use. To invoke use(), they can use the short-and-sweet syntax that lambda expressions provide, as we saw in the previous code.

Let's run this version of code and look at the eam.txt file it creates.

```
sweet
```

Let's also glance at the console for the output from the code.

```
close called automatically...
```

We can see that the file has the proper output and that the resource cleanup happened automatically.

In the example, we use the given instance writerEAM for just one call within the lambda expression. If we have to perform more operations with it, we can send it off to other functions as an argument. We can also perform a few operations on it, right within the lambda expression, by using multiline syntax.

```
resources/fpij/FileWriterEAM.java
FileWriterEAM.use("eam2.txt", writerEAM -> {
    writerEAM.writeStuff("how");
    writerEAM.writeStuff("sweet");
 });
```

We can place multiple lines of code within a lambda expression by wrapping them in a {} block. If the lambda expression is expected to return a result, be sure to place a return at the appropriate expression. The Java compiler gives us the flexibility to write just one line or wrap multiple lines, but we should keep lambda expressions short.

Long methods are bad, but long lambda expressions are evil—we'd lose the benefit of code that's concise, easy to understand, and simple to maintain. Instead of writing long lambda expressions, we should move the code into other methods and then use method references for them if possible, or invoke them from within a lambda expression.

In this example, the UseInstance's accept() is a void method. If we were interested in returning some results to the caller of the use() method, we'd have to modify this method's signature to place an appropriate return type, such as a generic parameter R. If we were to make this change, then the UseInstance would be more like the Function<U, R> interface than like the Consumer<T> interface. We'd also have to change the use() method to propagate the return results from the modified apply() method.

We used lambda expressions to implement the *execute around method* pattern. We can benefit from this pattern when designing classes that require a prompt cleanup of resources. Rather than shifting the burden to our class's users, we put in a bit more effort, which made their lives much easier and the behavior of our code a lot more consistent.

This pattern isn't restricted to the cleanup of resources. For me, the pattern came to life on a project where my team had to perform operations within the bounds of transactions. Rather than creating and managing transactions all over the code, we wrapped them into a nice runWithinTransaction() method. The method's callers received a transaction instance, and when they returned, the method took care of checking the status as well as performing actions such as committing or rolling back the transaction and logging.

We used lambda expressions and the *execute around method* pattern to manage resources. Next, we'll use them to manage locks.

Managing Locks

Locks play a critical part in concurrent Java applications since they're essential to ensure the correctness of changes to shared mutable variables from multiple threads. In this section we'll use lambda expressions to gain finer control over locks and open the doors to unit-test the proper locking of critical sections.

synchronized is an age-old keyword used to provide mutual exclusion. A synchronized block of code, such as synchronized { ... }, is a realization of the *execute around method* pattern. This pattern has been around since Java 1.0, but it was restricted and bound to the synchronized keyword in Java. Lambda expressions have now unleashed this pattern's power.

synchronized has some shortcomings—see *Java Concurrency in Practice [Goe06]*, by Brian Goetz, and *Programming Concurrency on the JVM [Sub11]*. First, it's hard to time out a call to synchronized, and this can increase the chance of deadlocks and livelocks. Second, it's hard to mock out synchronized, and that makes it hard to unit-test to see if code adheres to proper thread safety.

To address these concerns, the Lock interface, along with a few implementations such as ReentrantLock, was introduced in Java 5. The Lock interface gives us better control to lock, unlock, check if a lock is available, and easily time out if a lock isn't gained within a certain time span. Because this is an interface, it's easy to mock up its implementation for the sake of unit testing.[2]

There's one caveat to the Lock interface—unlike its counterpart, synchronized, it requires explicit locking and unlocking. This means we not only have to remember to unlock but to do so within the finally block. From our discussions so far in this chapter, we can see lambda expressions and the *execute around method* pattern helping out a lot here.

Let's first look at a piece of code that uses a Lock.

```
resources/fpij/Locking.java
public class Locking {
  Lock lock = new ReentrantLock(); //or mock

  protected void setLock(final Lock mock) {
    lock = mock;
  }

  public void doOp1() {
    lock.lock();
    try {
      //...critical code...
    } finally {
      lock.unlock();
    }
  }
  //...
}
```

We're using a Lock lock field to share the lock between the methods of this class. But the task of locking—for example, within the doOp1() method—leaves a lot to be desired. It's verbose, error-prone, and hard to maintain. Let's turn to lambda expressions for help and create a small class to manage the lock.

```
resources/fpij/Locker.java
public class Locker {
  public static void runLocked(Lock lock, Runnable block) {
    lock.lock();

    try {
      block.run();
    } finally {
      lock.unlock();
    }
  }
}
```

---

2. https://www.agiledeveloper.com/presentations/TestDrivingMultiThreadedCode.zip

This class absorbs the pain of working with the Lock interface so the rest of the code benefits. We can use the runLocked() method in code to wrap critical sections.

resources/fpij/Locking.java

```
public void doOp2() {
  runLocked(lock, () -> {/*...critical code ... */});
}

public void doOp3() {
  runLocked(lock, () -> {/*...critical code ... */});
}

public void doOp4() {
  runLocked(lock, () -> {/*...critical code ... */});
}
```

The methods are concise, and they use the static method runLocked() of the Locker helper class we created (we'd need an import static Locker.runLocked for this code to compile). Lambda expressions come to our assistance once more.

We saw how the *execute around method* pattern helps to make the code concise and less error-prone, but the elegance and conciseness should help remove the ceremony, not hide what's essential. When designing with lambda expressions, we should ensure that the intent of the code and its consequences are clearly visible. Also, when creating lambda expressions that capture local state, we must be aware of the restrictions we discussed in Are There Restrictions to Lexical Scoping?, on page 34.

Let's look at one more benefit the *execute around method* pattern offers in unit testing with JUnit.

Creating Concise Exception Tests

When Java 5 annotations were introduced, JUnit[3] was quick to use them. Overall this was a benefit, but one use in particular, the convenience of exception tests, led to terse rather than concise code. Let's understand the issues and then resolve them using—good guess—lambda expressions. We'll see here that lambda expressions aren't just another language feature; they alter the way we think, design, and even test applications.

Suppose we're driving the design of a class, RodCutter, through unit tests and we expect a maxProfit()method to throw an exception if the argument is zero. Let's look at a few ways we can write the exception tests for it.

---

3. https://junit.org

Attempt 1: Verbose Tests with try and catch

Here's a test for the maxProfit() method with try and catch to check for exceptions.

```
resources/fpij/RodCutterTest.java
@Test public void verboseExceptionTest() {
  rodCutter.setPrices(prices);

  try {
    rodCutter.maxProfit(0);
    fail("Expected exception for zero length");
  } catch(RodCutterException ex) {
    assertTrue(true);
  }
}
```

That's verbose and it may take some effort to understand, but this code is specific about what's expected to fail: the call to the maxProfit() method.

The desire to make the exception tests concise led to the use of annotation for exception tests in JUnit 4. The use of annotation reduces verbosity in tests, but, sadly, makes the test ineffective as we'll see next.

Attempt 2: Rather Terse Tests Using Annotation

Let's quickly take a look at how we wrote exception tests in JUnit 4. It was intended—we could say a failed attempt—to make the tests less verbose using annotation.

```
resources/fpij/RodCutterTest.java
@Test(expected = RodCutterException.class) //JUnit 4 feature
public void TerseExceptionTest() {
  rodCutter.setPrices(prices);
  rodCutter.maxProfit(0);
}
```

The test is short but deceptive—it's rather terse instead of being concise. It tells us that the test should pass if the exception RodCutterException is received, but it fails to ensure that the method that raised that exception is maxProfit(). If the setPrices() method threw that exception, due to some code change, then this test will continue to pass, but for the wrong reason. A good test should pass only for the right reasons—this test deceives us. Thankfully, we don't have to write such tests anymore to enjoy conciseness. Let's see how we can use lambdas in JUnit 5 to write concise tests.

Attempt 3: Concise Test Using Lambda Expressions

The use of annotation in tests is a thing of the past. JUnit 5 has completely reworked how exception tests are written and makes extensive use of lambda expressions. As you may expect, this makes the test concise and at the same time highly effective.

In JUnit 5 you can use a new assertThrows() method to verify if a piece of code throws an expected exception. This method takes two parameters. The first parameter conveys the type of exception that's expected. The second parameter, a lambda expression, is used to exercise the code that's expected to throw that exception. If the code invoked from the lambda expression throws the expected exception, the assert succeeds, otherwise it reports a failure.

Let's use the assertThrows() method to create a concise test.

```
resources/fpij/RodCutterTest.java
@Test
public void ConciseExceptionTest() {
  rodCutter.setPrices(prices);

  Exception ex =
    assertThrows(RodCutterException.class, () -> rodCutter.maxProfit(0));

  assertEquals("length should be greater than zero", ex.getMessage());
}
```

This test is both concise and fine-grained—it'll pass only if the method max-Profit() throws the expected exception. The previous code also shows that, in addition to checking if the expected exception was thrown, we can also optionally check if the exception contains an expected error message.

All the previous tests achieve the same goal, but the last version is better than the others as it's both concise and correct.

We saw how lambda expressions help us write tests that target specific methods for the expected exception, and that helps us create concise, easy-to-read, and less error-prone tests.

Wrapping Up

We managed resources in this chapter. We can't totally rely on automatic garbage collection, especially when our applications use external resources. The *execute around method* pattern can help us gain finer control over the flow of execution, and release external resources. Lambda expressions are a good fit to implement this pattern. In addition to controlling the object lifetime, we can use this pattern to better manage locks and to write concise exception tests. This can lead to more deterministic execution of code, timely cleanup of heavyweight resources, and fewer errors.

In the next chapter we'll use lambda expressions to delay the execution of some parts of code as a way to make the programs more efficient.

CHAPTER 7

Being Lazy

In Java we often execute code eagerly. The arguments are evaluated right at the time of method calls, for example. There's a good reason for that; eager code is easy to write and to think about. But delaying commitments until the last responsible moment is a good agile practice. When executing code, we can gain in performance by being just a little lazy. Eager is simple, but lazy is efficient. But, with lambdas we can easily be lazy and make things simple and efficient at the same time.

Delaying the execution of a function until it's necessary is a good strategy. However, we still need to figure out how to delay the function invocation, and that can take some work. Paradoxically, laziness often requires effort, and this creates an impediment. After all, who wants to work hard to be lazy? In Java we don't have to; we can relax because lambda expressions make running our programs both lazy and fast.

In this chapter we start with a task to postpone the creation of a heavyweight object, and then we turn some eager computations into lazy evaluations. As the last task, we look at creating infinite lazy sequences by exploiting the laziness built into Streams. The tricks from this chapter can help our programs run faster, our code become more concise, and us look smarter.

Delayed Initialization

In object-oriented programming, we ensure that objects are well constructed before any method calls. We encapsulate, ensure proper state transitions, and preserve the object's invariants. This works well most of the time, but when parts of an object's internals are heavyweight resources, we'll benefit if we postpone creating them. This can speed up object creation, and the program doesn't expend any effort creating things that may not be used.

The design decision to postpone creating part of an object shouldn't burden the object's users—it should be seamless. Let's explore some ways to design lazy initialization.

A Familiar Approach

In the following example, we'll craft a way to delay the creation of a heavy-weight instance. Then, we'll improve on the design.

Let's start with a Holder class that needs some heavyweight resources. Creating an instance of this class may take significant time and memory due to the resources it depends on. To address this, we can move the heavyweight resources into another class—say, Heavy. Then an instance of Holder will keep a reference to an instance of Heavy and route calls to it as appropriate.

Let's create the Heavy class.

```
lazy/fpij/Heavy.java
public class Heavy {
  public Heavy() { System.out.println("Heavy created"); }

  public String toString() { return "quite heavy"; }
}
```

This class represents a hypothetical heavyweight resource. In its constructor, we print a message to tell us when it's created. Let's use an instance of this class in the first trial version of the Holder class, named HolderNaive.

```
lazy/fpij/HolderNaive.java
public class HolderNaive {
  private Heavy heavy;

  public HolderNaive() {
    System.out.println("Holder created");
  }

  public Heavy getHeavy() {
    if(heavy == null) {
      heavy = new Heavy();
    }

    return heavy;
  }
}
//...
```

At first glance, this code appears simple. We created a null reference, heavy, and assigned it to a proper instance on the first call to the getHeavy() method. Let's use this class to create an instance of HolderNaive and see if it postpones the creation of the Heavy instance.

lazy/fpij/HolderNaive.java

```
final HolderNaive holder = new HolderNaive();
System.out.println("deferring heavy creation...");
System.out.println(holder.getHeavy());
System.out.println(holder.getHeavy());
```

This is the code's output:

```
Holder created
deferring heavy creation...
Heavy created
quite heavy
quite heavy
```

That appears to work. The solution is familiar, but it's also a rather simplistic solution that fails thread safety. Let's work through it.

Providing Thread Safety

For an instance of HolderNaive, the dependent instance of Heavy is created on the first call to the getHeavy() method. On subsequent calls to this method, the already created instance will be returned. That's exactly what we want, but there's a catch. This code suffers from a race condition.

If two or more threads call the getHeavy() method at the same time, then we could end up with multiple Heavy instances, potentially one per thread. This side effect is undesirable. Let's fix it.

```
public synchronized Heavy getHeavy() {
  if(heavy == null) {
    heavy = new Heavy();
  }

  return heavy;
}
```

We marked getHeavy() with the synchronized keyword to ensure mutual exclusion. If two or more threads call this method concurrently, due to mutual exclusion, only one will be allowed to enter and the others will queue up for their turn. The first one to enter into the method will create the instance. When subsequent threads enter this method, they will see that the instance already exists, and will simply return it.

We averted the race condition, but the solution created another negative impact. Every call to the getHeavy() method now has to endure the synchronization overhead; the calling threads have to cross the memory barrier (see Brian Goetz's *Java Concurrency in Practice [Goe06]*) even if there are no concurrently competing threads.

In fact, the possibility of the race condition is so short-lived it can happen only when the heavy reference is first being assigned, and the synchronization approach is a rather heavy-handed solution. We need thread safety until the reference is first created, and free unhindered access to the reference after that. We'll achieve this by using David Wheeler's advice: "Any problem in computer science can be solved with another level of indirection."[1]

Adding a Level of Indirection

The indirection we'll add in this example comes from a Supplier<T> class. This is a functional interface in the JDK, with one abstract method named get() that returns an instance. In other words, this is a factory that keeps on giving without expecting anything as input, kind of like a mother's love.

In the most rudimentary form, a Supplier will return an instance. For example, we could implement Supplier<Heavy> to return an instance of Heavy, like so:

```
Supplier<Heavy> supplier = () -> new Heavy();
```

Alternatively, we could use a constructor reference instead of the traditional new syntax to instantiate an instance. A constructor reference is much like a method reference, except it's a reference to a constructor instead of a method. We can use a constructor reference anywhere a lambda expression does nothing more than instantiate an instance. Let's look at an example with a constructor reference.

```
Supplier<Heavy> supplier = Heavy::new;
```

We took a look at what a Supplier can do for us, but we need something more than this simple form. We need to postpone and cache the instance. We can do that by moving the instance creation to another function, as we see next, in the final version of the Holder class.

```
lazy/fpij/Holder.java
public class Holder {
  private Supplier<Heavy> heavy = () -> createAndCacheHeavy();

  public Holder() {
    System.out.println("Holder created");
  }

  public Heavy getHeavy() {
    return heavy.get();
  }
  //...
}
```

---

1. http://en.wikipedia.org/wiki/David_Wheeler_(computer_scientist)

The field heavy in this version is an instance of the Supplier<Heavy>. We assign it to a lambda expression, and the Java compiler synthesizes from it an instance with the expected get() method. The implementation simply routes the call to a createAndCacheHeavy() method, which we'll implement soon. The getHeavy() method returns the same thing the Supplier's get method returns.

When an instance of Holder is created, as we can see, an instance of Heavy is not created. This design achieves the goal of lazy initialization. We also need a non-draconian solution to thread safety. This is where the createAndCacheHeavy() method comes in.

Let's first look at the code for this method.

```
lazy/fpij/Holder.java
private synchronized Heavy createAndCacheHeavy() {
  class HeavyFactory implements Supplier<Heavy> {
    private final Heavy heavyInstance = new Heavy();

    public Heavy get() { return heavyInstance; }
  }

  if(!HeavyFactory.class.isInstance(heavy)) {
    heavy = new HeavyFactory();
  }

  return heavy.get();
}
```

We'll mark this method synchronized so threads calling this method concurrently will be mutually exclusive. But within this method, on the first call, we quickly replace the Supplier reference, heavy, with a direct supplier, HeavyFactory, that will return an instance of Heavy. Let's see how this adequately solves thread safety.

Let's consider a scenario in which a new instance of Holder has just been created. Let's assume two threads invoke the getHeavy() method concurrently, followed by a third thread calling this method much later. When the first two threads call the default supplier's get() method in the Holder, the createAndCacheHeavy() method will let one of them through and make the other wait. The first thread to enter will check if heavy is an instance of the HeavyFactory. Since it's not the default Supplier, this thread will replace heavy with an instance of HeavyFactory. Finally, it returns the Heavy instance that this HeavyFactory holds.

The second concurrent thread to enter will again check if heavy is an instance of HeavyFactory, and will bypass the creation. It would simply return the same instance the first thread returned. Here we assume Heavy itself is thread-safe, and we're only focusing on the thread safety of Holder.

We've taken care of the race condition, but since the instance has been created lazily, we no longer need to be so protective. Now that heavy has been replaced with HeavyFactory, subsequent calls to the getHeavy() method will go directly to the HeavyFactory's get() method and will not incur any synchronization overhead.

We designed lazy initialization and, at the same time, avoided null checks. We also ensured the thread safety of the lazy instance creation. This is a simple, lightweight implementation of the *virtual proxy* pattern. Next, we'll use lambda expressions to postpone function evaluations.

Lazy Evaluations

In the previous section, we delayed the creation of heavyweight objects to make code execution faster. We'll explore that further in this section to delay running methods and use that approach to improve our designs. The main objective is to reduce the execution of code to the bare minimum—especially the expensive code—and speed up the execution.

Java already uses lazy execution when evaluating logical operations. For example, in fn1() || fn2(), the call fn2() is never performed if fn1() returns a boolean true. Likewise, if we replace the || with &&, the call to fn2() never happens if fn1() returns a boolean false. Programs benefit from this short-circuiting; we avoid unnecessary evaluation of expressions or functions, and that can help improve performance. Often we rely on such short-circuiting for code correctness, as well.

While Java uses lazy or normal order when evaluating logical operators, it uses eager or applicative order when evaluating method arguments. All the arguments to methods are fully evaluated before a method is invoked. If the method doesn't use all of the passed arguments, the program has wasted time and effort executing them. We can use lambda expressions to postpone the execution of select arguments.

The Java compiler evaluates lambda expressions and method references in the argument list at the called location. The invocation of these is postponed until they're explicitly called from within the methods they're passed to. We can take advantage of this behavior to delay or even avoid method invocation by embedding calls to them within lambda expressions. We can't seamlessly wrap arbitrary arguments into lambda expressions. We have to explicitly design for it, as we'll see here.

Many methods in the JDK—including methods on the Stream class—do lazy evaluation. For instance, the filter() method may not invoke the Predicate, passed as an argument, on all the elements in the target collection.

We can design lazy evaluation of arguments to methods by turning the parameters into functional interfaces. Let's work that approach into an example to get a feel for the design.

Starting with Eager Evaluation

In the example here, methods take significant time to run. We'll call them eagerly and then alter the design to improve speed.

Let's start with a method evaluate() that takes quite a bit of time and resources to run.

```
lazy/fpij/Evaluation.java
public class Evaluation {
  public static boolean evaluate(final int value) {
    System.out.println("evaluating ..." + value);
    simulateTimeConsumingOp(2000);
    return value > 100;
  }
  //...
}
```

A call to evaluate() would take a couple of seconds to run, so we definitely want to postpone any unnecessary calls. Let's create a method, eagerEvaluator(), which is like almost any method we write in Java: all of its arguments will be evaluated before its call.

```
lazy/fpij/Evaluation.java
public static void eagerEvaluator(
  final boolean input1, final boolean input2) {
  System.out.println("eagerEvaluator called...");
  System.out.println("accept?: " + (input1 && input2));
}
```

The method takes two boolean parameters. Within the method, we perform a logical *and* operation on the parameters. Sadly, it's too late to benefit from the lazy evaluation this operation automatically provides since the arguments are evaluated well before we enter this method.

Let's invoke eagerEvaluator() and pass as arguments the results of two evaluate() method calls.

```
lazy/fpij/Evaluation.java
eagerEvaluator(evaluate(1), evaluate(2));
```

If we run this code we'll see both the calls to evaluate() execute well before we enter the eagerEvaluator() method.

```
evaluating ...1
evaluating ...2
eagerEvaluator called...
accept?: false
```

This would take at least four seconds to run because of the cumulative delay from the calls to the evaluate() method. We'll improve on that next.

Designing for Lazy Evaluation

If we know that some arguments may not be used during the execution of a method, we can design the method's interface to facilitate the delayed execution of some or all arguments. The arguments can be evaluated on demand, as in this lazyEvaluator() method:

lazy/fpij/Evaluation.java
```java
public static void lazyEvaluator(
  final Supplier<Boolean> input1, final Supplier<Boolean> input2) {
  System.out.println("lazyEvaluator called...");
  System.out.println("accept?: " + (input1.get() && input2.get()));
}
```

Rather than taking two boolean parameters, the method receives references to the Supplier instances. This JDK functional interface will return an instance, Boolean in this case, in response to a call to its get() method. The logical *and* operation we use within the lazyEvaluator() method will invoke the get() methods only on demand.

If we pass two calls to evaluate() as arguments to the lazyEvaluator() method, the second will be evaluated only if the first call returned a boolean true. Let's run the method to see this.

lazy/fpij/Evaluation.java
```java
lazyEvaluator(() -> evaluate(1), () -> evaluate(2));
```

Each Supplier makes a call to the evaluate() method, but not until the lazyEvaluator() method is invoked. The evaluation is lazy and optional, determined by the flow of execution within the lazyEvaluator() method. We can see this delayed evaluation in the output when we run the code.

```
lazyEvaluator called...
evaluating ...1
accept?: false
```

The arguments aren't evaluated before we enter the lazyEvaluator() method. The second call to evaluate() was skipped in this version. This example call of lazyEvaluator() takes only about two seconds, whereas the previous call to eagerEvaluator() took about four seconds.

We saw the cost savings of the lazy evaluation. This technique is helpful when we have to evaluate a large number of methods or if method evaluations are time/resource consuming.

This technique can significantly boost performance, but its disadvantage is it burdens the caller with packaging the calls in a lambda expression. Sure, lambda expressions are concise, but they're a hindrance compared to the usual way of passing arguments. In some contexts, we may be able to use method references instead of lambda expressions, and this can make the code a bit more concise and ease the burden a little.

The lazy solutions so far have helped us make code more efficient. Next, we'll use it purely for convenience.

Leveraging the Laziness of Streams

In previous chapters we've seen the facilities that the Stream interface offers, but so far we haven't discussed one of their most salient features—they're really lazy, in a good way. The lazy evaluation of Streams is powerful. First, we don't have to do anything special to derive their benefits. In fact, we've used them many times already! Second, they can postpone not just one, but a sequence of evaluations so that only the most essential parts of the logic are evaluated, and only when needed. Let's look at how lazy Streams are and how we benefit from that.

Intermediate and Terminal Operations

Streams have two types of methods: *intermediate* and *terminal*, which work together. The secret behind their laziness is that we chain multiple intermediate operations followed by a terminal operation.

Methods like map() and filter() are intermediate; calls to them return immediately, and the lambda expressions provided to them aren't evaluated right away. The core behavior of these methods is cached for later execution and no real work is done when they're called. The cached behavior is run when one of the terminal operations, like findFirst() and reduce(), is called. But not all the cached code is executed, and the computation will complete as soon as the desired result is found. Let's look at an example to understand this better.

Suppose we're given a collection of names and we're asked to print in all caps the first name that's only three letters long. We can use Stream's functional-style methods to achieve this. But first, let's create a few helper methods.

lazy/fpij/LazyStreams.java
```java
public class LazyStreams {
    private static int length(final String name) {
        System.out.println("getting length for " + name);
        return name.length();
    }
    private static String toUpper(final String name ) {
        System.out.println("converting to uppercase: " + name);
        return name.toUpperCase();
    }
    //...
}
```

The two helper methods simply print the parameters they receive before returning the expected results. We wrote these methods to take a peek at the intermediate operations in the code we'll write next.

lazy/fpij/LazyStreams.java
```java
public static void main(final String[] args) {
    List<String> names = List.of("Brad", "Kate", "Kim", "Jack", "Joe",
        "Mike", "Susan", "George", "Robert", "Julia", "Parker", "Benson");

    final String firstNameWith3Letters =
        names.stream()
            .filter(name -> length(name) == 3)
            .map(name -> toUpper(name))
            .findFirst()
            .orElse("");

    System.out.println(firstNameWith3Letters);
}
```

We started with a list of names, transformed it into a Stream, filtered out only names that are three letters long, converted the selected names to all caps, and picked the first name from that set.

At first glance, it appears the code is doing a lot of work transforming collections, but it's deceptively lazy; it didn't do any more work than was absolutely essential. Let's take a look.

Method Evaluation Order

It would help to read the code from right to left, or bottom up, to see what's going on here. Each step in the call chain will do only enough work to ensure that the terminal operation in the chain completes. This behavior is in direct contrast to the usual eager evaluation, but it is efficient.

If the code were eager, the filter() method would have first gone through all dozen names in the collection to create a list of two names, Kim and Joe, whose length is three (letters). The subsequent call to the map() method would have then evaluated the two names. The findFirst() method finally would have picked the first element of this reduced list. We can visualize this hypothetical eager order of evaluation in the following figure.

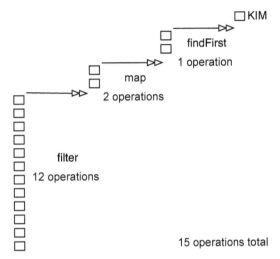

But both the filter() and map() methods are lazy to the bone. As the execution goes through the chain, the filter() and map() methods store the lambda expressions and pass on a façade to the next call in the chain. The evaluations start only when findFirst(), a terminal operation, is called.

The order of evaluation is different as well, as we see in the following figure. The filter() method doesn't plow through all the elements in the collection in one shot. Instead, it runs until it finds the first element that satisfies the condition given in the attached lambda expression. As soon as it finds an element, it passes that to the next method in the chain. This next method, map() in this example, does its part on the given input and passes it down the chain. When the evaluation reaches the end, the terminal operation checks to see if it has received the result it's looking for.

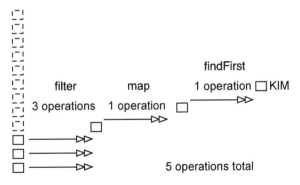

If the terminal operation got what it needed, the computation of the chain terminates. If the terminal operation isn't satisfied, it'll ask for the chain of operations to be carried out for more elements in the collection.

By examining the logic of this sequencing of operations, we can see that the execution will iterate over only essential elements in the collection. We can see evidence of this behavior by running the code.

```
getting length for Brad
getting length for Kate
getting length for Kim
converting to uppercase: Kim
KIM
```

From the output, we can see that most of the elements in the example list were not evaluated once the candidate name we're looking for was found.

The logical sequence of operations we saw in the previous example is achieved under the hood in the JDK using a *fusing* operation—all the functions in the intermediate operations are fused together into one function that's evaluated for each element, as appropriate, until the terminal operation is satisfied. In essence, there's only one pass on the data—filtering, mapping, and selecting the element all happen in one shot.

Peeking into the Laziness

Writing the series of operations as a chain is the preferred and natural way in Java. But to really see that the lazy evaluations didn't start until we reached the terminal operation, let's break the chain from the previous code into steps.

```
lazy/fpij/LazyStreams.java
Stream<String> namesWith3Letters =
  names.stream()
        .filter(name -> length(name) == 3)
        .map(name -> toUpper(name));

System.out.println("Stream created, filtered, mapped...");
System.out.println("ready to call findFirst...");

final String firstNameWith3Letters =
  namesWith3Letters.findFirst()
                   .orElse("");

System.out.println(firstNameWith3Letters);
```

We transformed the collection into a stream, filtered the values, and then mapped the resulting collection. Then, separately, we called the terminal operation. Let's run the code to see the sequence of evaluation.

```
Stream created, filtered, mapped...
ready to call findFirst...
getting length for Brad
getting length for Kate
getting length for Kim
converting to uppercase: Kim
KIM
```

From the output, we can clearly see that the intermediate operations delayed their real work until the last responsible moment when the terminal operation was invoked. And even then, they only did the minimum work necessary to satisfy the terminal operation. Pretty efficient, eh?

This example helped us uncover Stream's true power. Next, we'll use Streams to create infinite collections.

Creating Infinite, Lazy Collections

Using infinite collections can make the code that creates a growing series (such as the Fibonacci numbers) clearer and easier to express. But from our experience in Java, we might think a series can't be infinite due to practical memory limits. The laziness of Streams comes in again here.

In Java, collections are still required to be finite, but streams can be infinite. We will see here how laziness becomes an essential workhorse to make infinite streams possible. We'll use them to create highly expressive, easy-to-understand code to produce an infinitely growing series.

A Desperate Attempt

We'll use a series of prime numbers, 2, 3, 5, 7,... as an example to explore the concepts here. Let's first create a helper function to determine if a number is prime.

```
public static boolean isPrime(final int number) {
  return number > 1 &&
    IntStream.rangeClosed(2, (int) Math.sqrt(number))
            .noneMatch(divisor -> number % divisor == 0);
}
```

A number greater than 1 is prime if it's not divisible by any number between 2 and its square root. Normally, we'd use an external iterator to search for a divisor in that range. Instead, we use more Java goodness here—the range-Closed() static method of the IntStream interface.

The *closed* suffix in the method name emphasizes that the range of values will include the second parameter. For example, rangeClosed(1, 10) will return the range of values 1, 2,..., 10 packed into a Stream. In contrast, the range() method, also a static method in the interface, will return a range of values, up to (but not including) the value in the second parameter.

In the isPrime() method, we use the short and sweet noneMatch() method on the stream returned by the rangeClosed() method. The noneMatch() method takes a Predicate as its parameter and we use this to determine if there's a divisor for the given number. The noneMatch() method will yield a boolean true if the lambda expression returned false for all values in the range—that is, if there are no divisors.

On our first attempt, we'll use the isPrime() method to create a series of prime numbers starting at any given number.

```
//don't try this at the office
public static List<Integer> primes(final int number) {
  if(isPrime(number)) {
    return concat(number, primes(number + 1));
  }

  return primes(number + 1);
}
```

If a given number is prime, we include it in the list of primes that follow the number. Otherwise, we omit it and move on to get that list.

Hold your tweets; no, your humble author hasn't gone mad—that code is enticingly elegant but, sadly, won't work. If we implement the concat() method and run the code, we'll enter into a never-ending recursion and end up with a java.lang.StackOverflowError.

Let's drill into the code just a bit more to see if we can salvage anything from it. The StackOverflowError is from the recursive calls to the primes() method. If we can be lazy about this call, then we won't run into issues.

Reaching for the Stars

Earlier we saw how lazy Streams are. They don't do any real work until we ask them for the results—kind of like my kids. We can rely on that laziness to easily create a lazy, infinite collection.

When we create a Stream, from a collection or through other means, we quickly receive a façade that has the potential to return an infinite list. But it's wickedly clever; it returns to us only as many elements as we ask for, producing the elements just in time. We can use that capability to express an infinite collection and generate as many (finite) elements as we like from that list. Let's see how.

The Stream interface has a static method iterate() that can create an infinite Stream. It takes two parameters, a *seed* value to start the collection, and an instance of a UnaryOperator interface, which is the supplier of data in the collection. The Stream the iterate() method returns will postpone creating the elements until we ask for them using a terminating method. To get the first element, for example, we could call the findFirst() method. To get ten elements we could call the limit() method on the Stream, like so: limit(10).

Let's see how all these ideas shape up in code.

```
lazy/fpij/Primes.java
public class Primes {
  private static int primeAfter(final int number) {
    if(isPrime(number + 1)) {
      return number + 1;
    }

    return primeAfter(number + 1);
  }

  public static List<Integer> primes(final int fromNumber, final int count) {
    return Stream.iterate(primeAfter(fromNumber - 1), Primes::primeAfter)
                 .limit(count)
                 .collect(toList());
  }
  //...
}
```

We first defined a convenience method, primeAfter(), that returns a prime number that's after the given number. If the number next to the given number is prime, it's immediately returned; otherwise, the method recursively asks for the prime number that follows. The code that deals with the infinite series is in the primes() method. It's short for what it does; the real complexity is hidden within the iterate() method and the Stream.

The primes() method will create an infinite series of prime numbers, starting with the first prime greater than or equal to the number given as a parameter. In the call to the iterate() method, the first parameter provides the seed for the infinite series. If the given number is prime, it's used as the seed. Otherwise, the first prime after the number is used. The second parameter, a method reference, stands in for a UnaryOperator that takes in a parameter and returns a value. In this example, since we refer to the primeAfter() method, it takes in a number and returns a prime after the number.

The result of the call to the iterate() method is a Stream that caches the UnaryOperator it's given. When we ask for a particular number of elements, and only then, the Stream will feed the current element (the given seed value is used as the first element) to the cached UnaryOperator to get the next element, and then feed that element back to the UnaryOperator to get the subsequent element. This sequence will repeat as many times as necessary to get the number of elements we asked for, as we see in the following figure.

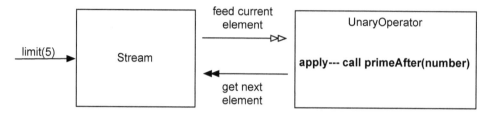

Execute only on demand

Let's call the primes() method first to get ten primes starting at 1, and then five primes starting at 100.

lazy/fpij/Primes.java
```
System.out.println("10 primes from 1: " + primes(1, 10));

System.out.println("5 primes from 100: " + primes(100, 5));
```

The primes() method creates a Stream of an infinite collection of primes, starting at the given input. To get a particular number of elements from the collection, we call the limit() method. Then we convert the returned collection of elements into a list and print it. This call to collect() triggers the evaluation of the sequence. The method limit() is also an intermediate operation that lazily notes the number of elements needed for later evaluation! Let's look at this code's output.

```
10 primes from 1: [2, 3, 5, 7, 11, 13, 17, 19, 23, 29]
5 primes from 100: [101, 103, 107, 109, 113]
```

The code produced two series of primes, one starting at 1 and the other starting at 100. These were extracted from the infinite series we created so succinctly within the primes() method, thanks to the laziness of Streams and the power of lambda expressions/method references.

We saw how lambda expressions and the Stream implementations work in tandem to make the execution efficient. While lambda expressions and method references make code elegant, expressive, and concise, the real performance gains in Java applications will come from Streams. Lambda expressions are the gateway drug to Java, but Streams are the real addiction—be ready to get hooked on them as you develop Java applications.

We got a lot done within just a few lines of code; it's perfectly fine to take a few minutes to admire the power of lambda expressions, functional interfaces, and the efficiency of Streams. In the next chapter, we're ready to take the use of lambda expressions up another notch to make recursions more efficient.

Wrapping Up

Efficiency got a boost in Java with the introduction of lambdas; we can be lazy and postpone the execution of code until we need it. We can delay the initialization of heavyweight resources and easily implement the virtual proxy pattern. Likewise, we can delay the evaluation of method arguments to make the calls more efficient. The real heroes of the improved JDK are the Stream interface and the related classes. We can exploit their lazy behaviors to create infinite collections with just a few lines of code. That means highly expressive, concise code to perform complex operations that we couldn't even imagine in Java before.

In the next chapter we'll look at the roles lambda expressions play in optimizing recursions.

CHAPTER 8

Optimizing Recursions

Recursion is a powerful and charming way to solve problems. It's highly expressive—using recursion we can provide a solution to a problem by applying the same solution to its subproblems, an approach known as *divide and conquer*. Various applications employ recursion, such as for finding the shortest distances on a map, computing minimum cost or maximum profit, or reducing waste.

Most languages in use today support recursion. Unfortunately, problems that truly benefit from recursion tend to be fairly large and a simple implementation will quickly result in a stack overflow. In this chapter we'll look at the tail-call optimization (TCO) technique to make recursions feasible for large inputs. Then, we'll look into problems that can be expressed using highly recursive overlapping solutions and examine how to make them blazingly fast using the memoization technique.

Using Tail-Call Optimization

The biggest hurdle to using recursion is the risk of stack overflow for problems with large inputs. The brilliant TCO technique can remove that concern. A tail call is a recursive call in which the last operation performed is a call to itself. This is different from a regular recursion, where the function, in addition to making a call to itself, often performs further computations on the result of the recursive call(s). TCO lets us convert regular recursive calls into tail calls to make recursions practical for large inputs.

Java doesn't directly support TCO at the compiler level, but we can use lambda expressions to implement it in a few lines of code. With this solution, sometimes called *trampoline calls*, we can enjoy the power of recursion without the concern of blowing up the stack.

We'll implement TCO using a very simple and common example, computing a number's factorial.

Starting with an Unoptimized Recursion

Let's start with a piece of code for computing a factorial using a simple unoptimized recursion.

recur/fpij/Factorial.java

```
Line 1   public class Factorial {
     2     public static int factorialRec(final int number) {
     3       if(number == 1) {
     4         return number;
     5       }
     6
     7       return number * factorialRec(number - 1);
     8     }
     9   }
```

The recursion terminates when we get down to the value of 1. For higher values, we recursively call the number times the *factorial* of number minus 1. Let's try out this method using the number 5.

recur/fpij/Factorial.java

```
System.out.println(factorialRec(5));
```

Here's the output for the factorial value.

```
120
```

That seems to work, but let's try it again, this time with a larger input value.

recur/fpij/Factorial.java

```
try {
  System.out.println(factorialRec(20000));
} catch(StackOverflowError ex) {
  System.out.println(ex);
}
```

We coded that call defensively; let's look at the output to see how it turned out.

```
java.lang.StackOverflowError
```

The recursion didn't handle the large input size. It went down with a bang. This is a showstopper in adopting this powerful and expressive technique.

The problem isn't the recursion itself. It's caused by holding the partial result of computations while waiting for the recursion to complete. Let's take a closer look at line 7 in the factorialRec() method. The last operation we perform on that line is multiplication (*). While we hold on to the given number, we wait for the result of the next call to factorialRec() to return. As a consequence, we climb the call stack for each call, and the execution of code will eventually blow up if the input size keeps growing. We need a way to be recursive without holding on to the stack.

In *Structure and Interpretation of Computer Programs [AS96]*, Abelson and Sussman discuss the TCO technique, where they convert a recursion into a pure iteration under the hood. Ideally, we'd like to rely on the compiler to provide such optimization, but since it doesn't, we can use lambda expressions to do this manually, as we'll see next.

Turning to Tail Recursion

Before we can use the TCO technique, we have to redesign our code so it doesn't build up the stack. Instead of waiting to perform the multiplication on line 7 in the factorialRec() method, we can compute the partial product with what we have so far, and pass that on as an extra parameter to the subsequent call. This will remove the need to perform any arithmetic when we return from the recursive call. That's a good first step, but it's not adequate. In addition, we have to step down from the current level of the stack before we recursively call the method. In other words, we need to turn an eager call to factorialRec() into a *lazy* call. We'll use a TailCall functional interface and a companion TailCalls class for this purpose. We'll soon design these two, but let's pretend for now that they already exist.

First, let's add static imports to the methods of the TailCalls class.

```
recur/fpij/Factorial.java
import static fpij.TailCalls.done;
import static fpij.TailCalls.call;
```

We'll use these two methods in the new recursive version to compute a factorial, the factorialTailRec() method.

```
recur/fpij/Factorial.java
public static TailCall<Integer> factorialTailRec(
  final int factorial, final int number) {
  if (number == 1) {
    return done(factorial);
  }

  return call(() -> factorialTailRec(factorial * number, number - 1));
}
```

This version to compute the factorial is tail recursive; that is, the last operation is a (delayed/lazy) call to itself, and there's no further computation to carry out on the result upon return. And, rather than calling the method factorialTail-Rec() eagerly, we wrapped it into a lambda expression for lazy/later execution.

Creating the TailCall Functional Interface

When we call the factorialTailRec() method, it returns immediately with an instance of TailCall. The key idea here is that if we call the done() method, we signal the recursion's termination. On the other hand, if we were to go through the call() method, we'd be asking for the recursion to continue, but only after we step down from the current stack level. To fully understand how this works, we have to look inside these methods, so let's drill down into the TailCall interface and the TailCalls companion class. We'll start with the interface.

```
recur/fpij/TailCall.java
@FunctionalInterface
public interface TailCall<T> {

  TailCall<T> apply();

  default boolean isComplete() { return false; }

  default T result() { throw new Error("not implemented"); }

  default T invoke() {
    return Stream.iterate(this, TailCall::apply)
               .filter(TailCall::isComplete)
               .findFirst()
               .get()
               .result();
  }
}
```

We have four methods in this interface: one abstract and the remaining default. The isComplete() method simply returns a false value. The default implementation of the result() method blows up if called—we'd never call this method as long as the recursion is in progress; an alternate implementation of the TailCall interface will take care of the situation when the recursion does terminate.

Critical work is done in the short code within the invoke() method. This method collaborates with the apply() method, which will return the next TailCall instance waiting for execution. The invoke() method has two responsibilities. First, it has to repeatedly iterate through the pending TailCall recursions until it reaches the end of the recursion. Second, upon reaching the end, it has to return the final result (available in the result() method of the terminal TailCall instance).

The invoke() method is short, but there's a lot going on here, so let's slow down and dig into it.

We have no clue how many recursions will be evaluated; it's not infinite, but we can treat it as a series of unknown length. Once we get our heads around treating this as a series of TailCall objects, we can easily use lazy iteration over a Stream of pending TailCall instances. The technique we used in Creating Infinite,

Lazy Collections, on page 133, will help us here to lazily produce the next pending TailCall instance. Let's take a closer look at how.

To create a lazy list of pending TailCall instances, we use the Stream interface's iterate() static method. This method takes an initial seed value and a generator. We use the current TailCall instance, this, as the seed. The generator, a UnaryOperator, takes in the current element and produces the next element. For the generator to return the next pending TailCall instance, it can use the apply() method of the current TailCall. We use the method reference TailCall::apply for this purpose to create the generator.

In short, we've designed the invoke() method so that the iteration will start at the seed, the first instance of TailCall, and iterate through subsequent instances of TailCall produced by the generator until it finds an instance of TailCall that signals the termination of recursion.

Creating the TailCalls Convenience Class

The iteration continues until the isComplete() method reports a completion. But the default() implementation of this method in the TailCall interface always returns a false value. This is where the companion TailCalls class comes in. It provides two different implementations of the TailCall functional interface: one in the call() method and the other in the done() method.

```
recur/fpij/TailCalls.java
public class TailCalls {
  public static <T> TailCall<T> call(final TailCall<T> nextCall) {
    return nextCall;
  }
  public static <T> TailCall<T> done(final T value) {
    return new TailCall<T>() {
      @Override public boolean isComplete() { return true; }
      @Override public T result() { return value; }
      @Override public TailCall<T> apply() {
        throw new Error("not implemented");
      }
    };
  }
}
```

In this class we implement two static methods, call() and done(). The call() method simply receives a TailCall instance and passes it along. It's a convenience method so the recursive calls (such as factorialTailRec()) can nicely end with a symmetric call to either done or call.

In the done() method, we return a specialized version of TailCall to indicate the recursion's termination. In this method, we wrap the received value into the specialized instance's *overridden* result() method. The specialized version's isComplete() will report the end of the recursion by returning a true value. Finally, the apply() method throws an exception because this method will never be called on this terminal implementation of TailCall, which signals the end of the recursion.

We can see in this design how the TailCall returned through call() continues recursion, and the one returned from done() terminates it. Also, the recursive calls are all evaluated lazily in a loop in the invoke() default method, thus never increasing the stack level like a simple recursion would.

We designed TailCall and TailCalls for use with factorialTailRec(), but they're reusable for any tail-recursive function.

Using the Tail-Recursive Function

We saw a tail-recursive function factorialTailRec(), a functional interface TailCall, and a convenience class TailCalls. Let's walk through a scenario to understand how all these work together.

Let's start with a call to the factorialTailRec() to compute the factorial of 2, like so:

```
factorialTailRec(1, 2).invoke();
```

The first argument, 1, is the initial value for the factorial; the second argument, 2, is the value for which we'd like to find the factorial. The call to factorialTailRec() will check if the given number is equal to 1 and, since it's not, will use the call() method and pass a lambda expression that synthesizes an instance of TailCall.

This synthesized instance will lazily call the factorialTailRec() with two arguments, 2 and 1, respectively. Back outside the call to the factorialTailRec() method, the call to the invoke() method will create a lazy collection with this first instance of TailCall as the seed and explore the collection until a terminating instance of TailCall is received. When the apply method of the seed TailCall is called, it will result in a call to the factorialTailRec() with the two arguments we mentioned previously. This second call to factorialTailRec() will result in a call to the done() method.

The call to done() will return a terminating specialized instance of TailCall, signaling the recursion's termination. The invoke() method will now return the final result of the computation, 2 in this case.

The TCO of the factorial recursion is complete. Let's take the factorialTailRec() method for a spin. We'll call it with a small value for the input parameter first.

recur/fpij/Factorial.java
```
System.out.println(factorialTailRec(1, 5).invoke());
```

We seed the factorialTailRec() with an initial factorial value, 1 and the number. The result of this call is a TailCall instance and we call the invoke() method on it. That call's result should be the same as the unoptimized recursion version we saw earlier.

```
120
```

Let's run this version with the large input value.

recur/fpij/Factorial.java
```
System.out.println(factorialTailRec(1, 20000).invoke());
```

The previous version ran into a stack overflow. Let's check this version's fate.

```
0
```

Our efforts paid off. We averted blowing up the stack, but the result was 0 due to arithmetic overflow; the factorial result is a very large number. We'll soon fix that—we need to use BigInteger instead of int. Before we address that, let's revisit the solution. We have some cleaning up to do.

Cleaning Up the Recursion

The implementation of the factorialTailRec() is alluringly simple. It has one downside, though: we polluted the method's interface. Rather than passing a nice and simple input number, now we have to pass two arguments. We rely on the callers to supply 1 for the first parameter; an argument like 0 would derail the result. We also have to call invoke() on the result of the call to factorialTailRec()—not pleasant. We can easily fix these issues by introducing one more level of indirection.

We can turn factorialTailRec() into a private method and introduce a public method that calls it.

recur/fpij/Factorial.java
```
public static int factorial(final int number) {
  return factorialTailRec(1, number).invoke();
}
```

This method brings back the simple interface and encapsulates the details of tail recursion. It deals with the extra parameter and takes care of calling the necessary invoke() method in the end. Let's use this modified version.

recur/fpij/Factorial.java
```
System.out.println(factorial(5));
System.out.println(factorial(20000));
```

We ran the latest version with a small value and the preposterously large value; let's check out the output.

```
120
0
```

The result was good for the small value, but the large value requires a fix. Let's attend to that as the last step.

Fixing the Arithmetic Overflow

The factorial code was nice and sweet with the int primitive type. To avert the arithmetic overflow, we have to switch to BigInteger. Sadly, we'll lose the fluency of simple arithmetic operators like * and - and have to use methods on BigInteger to perform these. We'll reduce clutter in the code by creating small functions for these operations in a BigFactorial class.

recur/fpij/BigFactorial.java
```java
public class BigFactorial {
  public static BigInteger decrement(final BigInteger number) {
    return number.subtract(BigInteger.ONE);
  }

  public static BigInteger multiply(
    final BigInteger first, final BigInteger second) {
    return first.multiply(second);
  }

  final static BigInteger ONE = BigInteger.ONE;
  final static BigInteger FIVE = new BigInteger("5");
  final static BigInteger TWENTYK = new BigInteger("20000");

    //...
}
```

We wrote some convenience methods and fields to work with BigInteger. Now let's look at the important parts, the encapsulated tail-recursive function and the fluent wrapper around it.

recur/fpij/BigFactorial.java
```java
private static TailCall<BigInteger> factorialTailRec(
  final BigInteger factorial, final BigInteger number) {
  if(number.equals(BigInteger.ONE)) {
    return done(factorial);
  }

  return call(() ->
    factorialTailRec(multiply(factorial, number), decrement(number)));
}
```

```
public static BigInteger factorial(final BigInteger number) {
  return factorialTailRec(BigInteger.ONE, number).invoke();
}
```

Where we used int in the earlier version, we instead use BigInteger in this version. The rest of the code is pretty much the same, using the TailCall interface, the TailCalls class, and the TCO technique.

Let's call this modified version of factorial().

recur/fpij/BigFactorial.java
```
public static void main(final String[] args) {
  System.out.println(factorial(FIVE));
  System.out.println(String.format("%.10s...", factorial(TWENTYK)));
}
```

Now that we used BigInteger, the operation should go well.

```
120
1819206320...
```

We see the correct value of the factorial for the number 5 and the trimmed output value for the large input.

With only a few lines of code we turned an unoptimized recursion into a tail recursion and averted stack overflow, thanks to lambda expressions, functional interfaces, and infinite Streams.

With this technique on hand, we can boldly implement recursive solutions, with a minor redesign to turn them into tail calls.

The approach we used here made recursions feasible for large input. Next, we'll see how to make them practical from a performance point of view.

Speeding Up with Memoization

Quick, what's 25 * 12?

Unless you have some superpowers, you'll take some effort and time to arrive at the result of 300. Now, if I ask again what's 25 * 12, right away, you'll instantaneously snap back the response of 300. How did you get that good so fast? Well, you remembered the result, temporarily memorized it—or should we say you *memoized* it.

If you evaluated an expression or looked up some information recently, and if you need that again, you most likely use the details from your memory instead of repeating the task. But computers can do that kind of stuff a lot more efficiently than we can. Reusing the result of a computation, instead of repeating its evaluation, is a technique called memoization.

This is especially useful in recursive problems where the solution contains multiple subproblems with identical solutions.

Let's look at how memoization can turn excessively recursive problems into incredibly fast execution. We'll explore a problem, implement it using recursion, and take note of how it gets exponentially slow as the problem size increases. Then we'll use the memoization technique to speed it up and along the way see how lambda expressions help with the solution.

An Optimization Problem

We can see optimization problems in various domains, such as economics, finance, and resource allocation, where an optimal solution is selected from several feasible ones. For example, we may have to find the maximum profit from sales of assets or the shortest route between locations. In an algorithmic technique called *dynamic programming*, we apply recursion extensively to solve a problem. This takes recursion to the next level; the solution to a problem overlaps with solutions to subproblems.

If we naively implement such recursion, we'd end up with computations that take exponentially increasing amounts of time to run for increasing input sizes. This is where *memoization* comes in. In this technique, we look up solutions, if they already exist, and perform and store computations just once. The redundancy that exists in repeatedly asking for the overlapping solutions doesn't translate into recomputations, but instead, it turns into a quick lookup for the results. This technique transforms the exponential time complexity to mere linear time. Let's implement this using an example: the rod-cutting problem.[1]

We'll employ a solution for a company that buys rods at wholesale and sells them at retail. They figured that by cutting the rods into different sizes, they could maximize profits. The price that the company can charge for different lengths of rods changes often, so the company wants us to write a program to reveal what the maximum profit would be for a given size of rod. Let's find a simple solution, and then improve on it.

We'll start with a class that stores the prices for different lengths of rods.

```
recur/fpij/RodCutter.java
public class RodCutter {
  private final List<Integer> prices;
```

---

1. http://en.wikipedia.org/wiki/Cutting_stock_problem

```
public RodCutter(final List<Integer> pricesForLengths) {
  prices = pricesForLengths;
}
//...
```

Let's work with some sample prices for different lengths, starting with 1".

recur/fpij/RodCutter.java
```
final List<Integer> priceValues =
  Arrays.asList(2, 1, 1, 2, 2, 2, 1, 8, 9, 15);

final RodCutter rodCutter = new RodCutter(priceValues);
```

Plain-Vanilla Recursion

We can solve the problem using a simple recursion. If we're given a 5" rod, we can look up the price for that length. In this example, that would get us $2. We can do better than that—after all, a 4" rod also would fetch $2, so we could cut the rod into two pieces—4" and 1"—to increase profit. Continuing with this approach, we find that the maximum profit for an arbitrary length n is the maximum of the profits from each of the possible 2^{n-1} cuts of that length. That is, max(no cut, cut(1, n - 1), cut(2, n - 2), ...), for a given length n. The following figure is an example of profits from all possible cuts for a 5" rod.

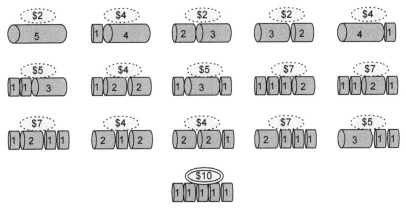

To compute the maximum profit for 5" we need to compute the maximum profit for 4", 3", 2", and 1". Likewise, to compute the maximum profit for 4", we need to compute the maximum profit for the smaller sizes. The solution nicely introduces overlapping recursion; we'll implement this without any optimization first, and then improve on it.

Let's implement the logic for maximum profit.

recur/fpij/RodCutter.java
```
public int maxProfit(final int length) {
  int priceAtLength = length <= prices.size() ? prices.get(length - 1) : 0;
```

```
    return Math.max(priceAtLength,
       IntStream.range(1, length)
                .map(i -> maxProfit(i) + maxProfit(length - i))
                .max()
                .orElse(0));
}
```

In the maxProfit() method we look up the price for a particular length. Then, we recursively find the profit for cuts that add up to the given length and pick the maximum from them. The implementation turns out to be simple. Let's try it for a few lengths.

recur/fpij/RodCutter.java
```
System.out.println(rodCutter.maxProfit(5));
System.out.println(rodCutter.maxProfit(22));
```

Let's look at the output for the different lengths.

```
10
44
```

The output seems reasonable, but the computation for this takes several minutes. If we increase the length slightly from 22, the program will slow a lot, into hours. That's because the time complexity of this computation is exponential—$O(2^{n-1})$—we're performing the computations redundantly for various lengths. We need to memoize the results to speed up execution—a lot.

Memoizing the Results

Memoization is a simple, yet smart, technique to make recursive overlapping computations fast. Using this technique, as the program runs, we make calculations only if they haven't been made already. Each time a new calculation happens, we cache the results and reuse those for subsequent calls for the same input. This technique is useful only if the computations are expected to return the same result each time for a given input. Our rod-cutting problem fits that expectation: the profit is the same for a given length and a given set of prices, no matter how many times we ask. Let's memoize the result of the profit calculation.

When seeking the profit for a sublength, we can skip the computation if the profit for that length has already been computed. This will speed up the program, as the redundant calls to find the profit will turn into a quick lookup of a hashmap. It sounds good, but it would be nice to have reusable code for that. Let's create a reusable class; we'll call it the Memoizer. It doesn't yet exist, but we'll pretend it does and write the code to use it. Let's refactor the maxProfit() method to use a static method, callMemoized(), of the Memoizer class.

```java
public int maxProfit(final int length) {
  return callMemoized(this::computeMaxProfit, length);
}

private int computeMaxProfit(
  Function<Integer, Integer> memoizedFunction, int length) {

  int priceAtLength = length <= prices.size() ? prices.get(length - 1) : 0;

  return Math.max(priceAtLength, IntStream.range(1, length)
    .map(i -> memoizedFunction.apply(i) + memoizedFunction.apply(length - i))
    .max()
    .orElse(0));
}
```

Let's look at the crux of the design before we dig into the code. We create a function, computeMaxProfit(), and memoize it. The memoized version will look up values before making a call to the actual implementation. Let's discuss how we achieve this.

In the maxProfit() method, we call the (yet-to-be-implemented) Memoizer's callMemoized() method. To this function we pass a method reference to the computeMaxProfit() method as the first argument and the rod length that we're computing the max profit for as the second argument.

The computeMaxProfit() method takes two parameters—the first is a reference to the memoized version of the function and the second is the length for which we want to compute the max profit. Within the computeMaxProfit() method, we perform our task, and when it's time for recursion, we route the call to memoizedFunction, the memoized function reference. This will return quickly if the value has been cached or memoized. Otherwise, it will recursively route the call to the computeMaxProfit() method to compute for that length. We'll get a full picture of how this happens when we see the callMemoized() method.

The missing piece of the puzzle is how the memoized function is created from the argument passed to callMemoized() method. Let's look at the Memoizer class's implementation to get a good understanding of that.

```java
recur/fpij/Memoizer.java
public class Memoizer {
  public static <T, R> R callMemoized(
    final BiFunction<Function<T,R>, T, R> functionToMemoize, final T input) {

    Function<T, R> memoizedFunction = new Function<T, R>() {
      private final Map<T, R> store = new HashMap<>();

      public R apply(final T input) {
```

```
      if(!store.containsKey(input)) {
        store.put(input, functionToMemoize.apply(this, input));
      }

      return store.get(input);
    }
  };

  return memoizedFunction.apply(input);
  }
}
```

The Memoizer has just one short function. In callMemoized() we create an implementation of Function in which we check to see if the solution for a given input is already present in the store HashMap. If a value is present for the given input, we return it; otherwise, we compute the value for the given input, store it in the store HashMap, and return the computed value.

This version of the maxProfit() method nicely encapsulates the details of memoization. The call to this method looks the same as the previous version:

```
System.out.println(rodCutter.maxProfit(5));
System.out.println(rodCutter.maxProfit(22));
```

Let's run the memoized version and ensure the maximum profit reported is the same as in the previous version.

```
10
44
```

The profit is consistent between the versions, but the execution speeds are a world apart. The memoized version took less than 0.05 seconds, compared to many minutes for the previous version. With this memoized version, we can easily bump up our rod lengths to large values and still take only a fraction of a second to get the results. For example, a length of 500" makes no dent in the execution time; it's blazingly fast.

In this chapter we used lambda expressions and infinite Streams to implement TCO and memoization. The examples show us how the features in Java can come together to create powerful solutions. You can use similar techniques to create nifty solutions to your own complex problems.

Wrapping Up

Recursions are a valuable tool in programming, but a simple implementation of recursion is often not useful for practical problems. Functional interfaces, lambda expressions, and infinite Streams can help us design tail-call optimization to make recursions feasible in such cases. We can also combine recursions and memoization to make the execution of over-lapping recursions fast.

In the next chapter we'll explore a practical example that employs lambda expressions, and then we'll parallelize it with little effort.

CHAPTER 9

Composing Functions with Lambda Expressions

With Java we have two powerful tools: the object-oriented approach and the functional style. They aren't mutually exclusive; they can work together for the greater good.

In OOP we often mutate state. If we combine OOP with the functional style, we can instead transform objects by passing lightweight objects through a series of cohesive functions. This can help us create code that's easier to extend—to produce a different result we simply alter the way the functions are composed. We can use the functions, in addition to the objects, as components to program with.

In this chapter we look into function composition. Then we use that to create a practical working example of the popular MapReduce pattern, where we scatter independent calculations, and gather the results to create the solution. As a final step, we parallelize those calculations almost effortlessly, thanks to the ubiquitous JDK library.

Using Function Composition

The OOP paradigm helps us realize abstraction, encapsulation, and polymorphism; inheritance is the weakest link in the paradigm. When programming in the functional style, we compose higher-order functions, and as much as possible, promote immutability and functions. We can leverage our experience with OOP, and, at the same time, intermix the elegant functional style in Java.

Let's get a feel for object transformation. Suppose we need change, and we ask a friend to break a $10 bill. We don't expect our buddy to tear up the bill and return the pieces. Instead, we'd like the bill to disappear into our friend's pocket and some smaller bills to appear. Mixing OOP and functional style is like that; we send lightweight objects to functions and expect other objects to emerge.

In this combined approach, to achieve a task, we chain a series of appropriate functions. As objects pass through the functions in the series, they transform into new objects to produce the desired result. We can see the difference between a pure OOP and a mixed OOP-functional style in the following figure. In pure OOP, at least the way it's used in Java, over time an object's state goes through transitions. In the combined approach, we see lightweight objects transform into other objects rather than the state of the objects transitioning.

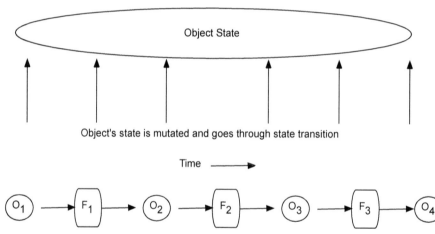

Let's work with an example to get a better feel for this. We'll start with a list of ticker symbols and, from it, create a sorted list, with each item's corresponding stock valued over $100. In the habitual approach, we'd walk through the list using an external iterator and update a mutable collection. Instead, we'll transform objects. We'll filter the tickers list into a list of tickers priced over $100, then sort the list, and finally report.

We need a sample list of ticker symbols, so let's start with that.

```
applying/fpij/Tickers.java
public class Tickers {
  public static final List<String> symbols = Arrays.asList(
    "AMD", "HPQ", "IBM", "TXN", "VMW", "XRX", "AAPL", "ADBE",
    "AMZN", "CRAY", "CSCO", "SNE", "GOOG", "INTC", "INTU",
    "MSFT", "ORCL", "TIBX", "VRSN", "RIVN");
}
```

We have some twenty symbols in this sample list. We need to determine the price for each stock. We saw the code to fetch the latest price from a web service in Integrating with a Web Service, on page 93. That service works only for a few tickers when the hardcoded api_token is used. If you'd like to use that service for fetching prices for any ticker symbol, you'll have to get your own token. Instead of going through that effort, we'll create a function in this chapter to return some fake prices for tickers. Here's the code for that:

```
applying/fpij/FinanceData.java
public class FinanceData {
  public static BigDecimal getPrice(final String ticker) {
    Map<String, String> fakePrices = new HashMap<>() {
      {
        put("AMD", "81"); put("HPQ", "33"); put("IBM", "135");
        put("TXN", "150"); put("VMW", "116"); put("XRX", "15");
        put("AAPL", "131"); put("ADBE", "360"); put("AMZN", "106");
        put("CRAY", "130"); put("CSCO", "43"); put("SNE", "72");
        put("GOOG", "2157"); put("INTC", "36"); put("INTU", "369");
        put("MSFT", "247"); put("ORCL", "67"); put("TIBX", "24");
        put("VRSN", "157"); put("RIVN", "26");
      }
    };

    try { Thread.sleep(200); } catch(Exception ex) {} //simulate a call delay

    return new BigDecimal(fakePrices.get(ticker));
  }
}
```

The getPrice() method returns some fake price for a given ticker symbol. Since we're looking for only stocks valued over $100, we can use Stream's filter() method to trim down the list. Once we get the short list, we can sort it easily using Stream's sorted() method. Finally, we can concatenate the symbols to print. These are all operations we've seen before, coming together here to help with this task. Let's look at the code.

```
applying/fpij/Stocks100.java
final BigDecimal HUNDRED = new BigDecimal("100");

System.out.println("Stocks priced over $100 are:");

System.out.println(
  Tickers.symbols
        .stream()
        .filter(
          symbol -> FinanceData.getPrice(symbol).compareTo(HUNDRED) > 0)
        .sorted()
        .collect(joining(", ")));
```

The series of operations flows nicely in a chain. The operations are associative; the stream of ticker symbols is filtered, sorted, and concatenated. As we move through the composed functions, the original list of symbols is left unmodified, and we first create a filtered stream of symbols from it, and then a stream of sorted symbols. We finally join the symbols in this last stream for printing. If instead of sorting we want to pick a particular symbol, let's say the first, we only have to slightly alter the chain; we can reuse most of the functions. Let's visit our fake stock market to see which stocks in the list are valued at over $100.

```
Stocks priced over $100 are:
AAPL, ADBE, AMZN, CRAY, GOOG, IBM, INTU, MSFT, TXN, VMW, VRSN
```

The ability to compose functions into a chain of operations is powerful and has a few benefits. It makes the code easier to understand. The lack of mutability reduces the chance of errors and makes it easier to parallelize the code. We can alter a few links in the chain and also easily alter the behavior along the way. We'll see these benefits come to life in the next examples.

Using MapReduce

In the *MapReduce* pattern we express two sets of operations: one to perform on each element in a collection and one to combine these results to arrive at a final result. This pattern is gaining attention due to its simplicity and power to exploit multicore processors.

The JVM is all geared up to utilize multicore processors. To fully benefit from the true power of the JVM and multicore processors, we have to change the way we code. In this section we'll explore the MapReduce pattern with an example, and in the next section we'll build on that example to parallelize it.

Let's continue with the example we've been using. Given a list of ticker symbols, let's pick the highest-priced stock whose value is less than $500. Let's work this example first using the imperative style and quickly evolve it to the functional style. This will help us see the difference in style and how to transition from the familiar style to the functional style in a more of a real-world scenario.

Preparing the Computations

To start we need some utility functions to get the prices, compare them, and so forth. Let's cover those first.

To help easily work with the stock names and prices, let's create a class with immutable fields.

```
applying/fpij/StockInfo.java
public class StockInfo {
  public final String ticker;
  public final BigDecimal price;

  public StockInfo(final String symbol, final BigDecimal thePrice) {
    ticker = symbol;
    price = thePrice;
  }

  public String toString() {
    return String.format("ticker: %s price: %g", ticker, price);
  }
}
```

The StockInfo is simply a value object; it holds a ticker symbol and its price. Given a ticker, we need a function to create an instance of StockInfo with the price information filled in. We'll reuse the fake FinanceData's getPrice() method in the implementation of this function.

```
applying/fpij/StockUtil.java
public class StockUtil {
  public static StockInfo getPrice(final String ticker) {
    return new StockInfo(ticker, FinanceData.getPrice(ticker));
  }
  //...
}
```

The getPrice() method is simply a wrapper, a convenience method.

We need a method to tell us if the price is less than the desired amount, so let's create that.

```
applying/fpij/StockUtil.java
public static Predicate<StockInfo> isPriceLessThan(final int price) {
  return
    stockInfo -> stockInfo.price.compareTo(BigDecimal.valueOf(price)) < 0;
}
```

This is a higher-order method. It takes a price value and returns a Predicate that can be evaluated later to check if a given instance of StockInfo is less than the price value cached in the lambda expression.

The last convenience method will help us pick the highest-priced stock from a pair.

```
applying/fpij/StockUtil.java
public static StockInfo pickHigh(
  final StockInfo stock1, final StockInfo stock2) {
  return stock1.price.compareTo(stock2.price) > 0 ? stock1 : stock2;
}
```

pickHigh() simply returns an instance of StockInfo with the highest price from the pair of instances given to it. We've created the functions we need and we're all set to put them to work. Let's create the imperative version of the code to get the highest-priced stock in the range.

Moving from the Imperative Style…

We're accustomed to imperative programming, but as we'll see here, it can be a lot of work.

```
applying/fpij/PickStockImperative.java
final List<StockInfo> stocks = new ArrayList<>();

for(String symbol : Tickers.symbols) {
  stocks.add(StockUtil.getPrice(symbol));
}

final Predicate<StockInfo> isPriceLessThan500 = StockUtil.isPriceLessThan(500);
final List<StockInfo> stocksPricedUnder500 = new ArrayList<>();

for(StockInfo stock : stocks) {
  if(isPriceLessThan500.test(stock))
    stocksPricedUnder500.add(stock);
}

StockInfo highPriced = new StockInfo("", BigDecimal.ZERO);

for(StockInfo stock : stocksPricedUnder500) {
  highPriced = StockUtil.pickHigh(highPriced, stock);
}

System.out.println("High priced under $500 is " + highPriced);
```

We created three loops. In the first one, we made a list of StockInfo filled with the price for each of the symbols. In the second loop, we made a trimmed-down list of stock info, restricting it to stocks under $500. In the final loop, we picked the highest-priced stock from among the candidates. Let's see which stock gets picked.

```
High priced under $500 is ticker: INTU price: 369.000
```

In that code, we see three distinct steps: from symbols to stocks, then to selected stocks, and finally to the highest-priced stocks from among the selected ones. We can combine the operations all into one loop if we like. Here's the clubbed imperative version:

```
applying/fpij/PickStockImperativeClubbed.java
StockInfo highPriced = new StockInfo("", BigDecimal.ZERO);
final Predicate<StockInfo> isPriceLessThan500 = StockUtil.isPriceLessThan(500);

for(String symbol : Tickers.symbols) {
  StockInfo stockInfo = StockUtil.getPrice(symbol);
```

```
  if(isPriceLessThan500.test(stockInfo))
    highPriced = StockUtil.pickHigh(highPriced, stockInfo);
}

System.out.println("High priced under $500 is " + highPriced);
```

With this step, we gained some and lost some. We reduced the code and removed a few loops; less code is better. But we're still being imperative, mutating variables. Furthermore, if we want to change the logic—say we want to pick the highest-priced stock under $1,000—we have to modify this code. No part of it is reusable. Going back to our three-step version of the code, we could modularize each part into a function for reuse. Rather than combining the steps, if we keep them as distinct steps we can convert them easily from the imperative style to the functional style, as we'll see next.

...To the Functional Style

We used three different loops in the imperative version, but the JDK provides specialized functional-style methods for each of those steps. We can easily use those convenience methods and we won't have to manually create any internal iterators to program the logic in the functional style. Let's refactor the code into the functional style; this version is declarative, preserves immutability, is concise, and uses function composition.

```
applying/fpij/PickStockFunctional.java
public static void findHighPriced(final Stream<String> symbols) {
  final StockInfo highPriced =
    symbols.map(StockUtil::getPrice)
           .filter(StockUtil.isPriceLessThan(500))
           .reduce(StockUtil::pickHigh)
           .get();

  System.out.println("High priced under $500 is " + highPriced);
}
```

In the method findHighPriced(), we employ method chaining and transform objects. We start with a Stream of symbols and flow into streams of stocks. We first map the symbols into stocks filled with prices. Following the map operation, we trim down the list and reduce it to a single value. The reduce() function gives us some extra control, but if we simply want to pick the highest value, we could instead use the max() method on the Stream.

This version has about half as many lines as the multistep imperative version. It has about the same number of lines as the clubbed imperative version. In addition to being concise, this code has a few benefits. The biggest gain is that the ability to parallelize this code comes for free, as we'll see in the next section. We derive this benefit by using function composition and higher-order functions, and avoiding mutability. This version of code is easier to understand —the symbols are mapped into StockInfo, then filtered to the desired range, and finally reduced to a single object containing the highest value and the corresponding ticker symbol.

We need to convert from the List of symbols, in Tickers, to a Stream of symbols before we call the findHighPriced() method.

applying/fpij/PickStockFunctional.java
```
findHighPriced(Tickers.symbols.stream());
```

Let's run the code and ensure the result is the same as the imperative version.

```
High priced under $500 is ticker: INTU price: 369.000
```

The code is concise, and this version picked the same stock, at the same price as the previous version.

Let's take a minute to visualize, in the following figure, the operations we performed in this example.

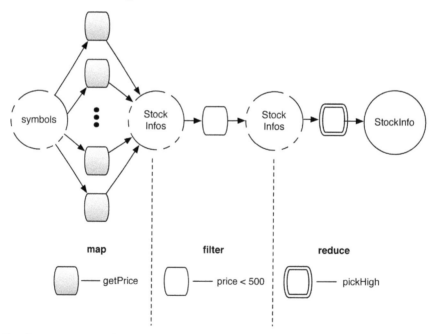

In the figure, we see the *map* operation applies the function to fetch the stock prices on each element in the symbols collection. This gives us the stream of StockInfo instances, which we then *filter* to select stocks, and finally we apply the *reduce* operation to distill this to one StockInfo object. The layout of the operations in the figure shows the potential for parallelization. We'll dig into that next.

Taking a Leap to Parallelize

In the previous example, we fetched the prices for many stock symbols. Whether we use a simulated time delay to generate fake data, as in the example, or make a network call to get real data from a service, fetching data for each symbol will take some non-trivial amount of time. The more symbols we deal with, the longer it will take to run the code sequentially. Even though we executed the function to fetch the price sequentially, in the previous diagram we showed these calls stacked vertically. That helps to visualize that the functions, instead of being run one after the other, may be run in parallel. That is, we don't have to wait for the fetch of the price for one symbol to complete before we start the fetch of the next symbol in the list. Running the functions to fetch the prices in parallel will greatly reduce the execution time. Thanks to the functional programming capabilities of Java and the Stream API, we can ˌeasily parallelize the previous example to speed up the execution.

Let's take a closer look at the code before we make any changes. We send the tickers through the map() method, which sequentially invokes the attached function to get the price from our fake service. Once all the prices arrive, we sequentially trim the list to stocks within the desired price range. In the last step, which is also sequential, we pick the highest-priced stock from among them.

Of these three operations, the first is the slowest. It involves a call to the web service, incurs a network delay, and has to perform the operation 20 times—once for each ticker symbol. The remaining operations involve light arithmetic and hardly take any time. Thankfully, in this problem, the slowest parts are independent of each other and can be performed all at once.

We don't have to wait for the (fake) web service to respond to the price for one ticker symbol before we send out the request for the next. Web services are capable of handling multiple requests concurrently, barring any limits imposed by a particular vendor to set free-of-charge or basic service apart from premium services they may sell.

Let's run the previous version once more to see how long it took to pick the highest-priced stock valued under $500. The following output was produced by running the program with the UNIX-based time utility.

```
High priced under $500 is ticker: INTU price: 369.000

real    0m4.147s
user    0m0.058s
sys     0m0.019s
```

If we were using a real web service to fetch the stock prices, the time it takes to run would vary, depending on the quality of the network connection and the time for the service to respond. Since we're using a fake service in this example, we'll incur only the simulated delays. The program took about 4 seconds for the functional, sequential version to pick the appropriate stock. Let's parallelize the code and see how that fares.

Making code concurrent is a big topic—where do we start and how do we proceed? We have to distribute the tasks onto multiple threads, then collect the results, and then move on to the sequential steps. While we're at it, we must ensure there are no race conditions; we don't want threads to collide with other threads' updates and mess up the data.

There are two concerns here: one is how to do it and the other is how to do it properly. For the first concern, we can seek the help of libraries to manage threads. The responsibility for doing it right falls on us. Race conditions arise largely from shared mutability. If multiple threads try to update an object or a variable at the same time, we have to ensure thread safety. This concern disappears if we follow good functional style and honor immutability.

Surprisingly, with the design we created, the code is only one step away from running parallel rather than sequentially. We need to switch only one call, from this:

```
findHighPriced(Tickers.symbols.stream());
```

to this:

```
findHighPriced(Tickers.symbols.parallelStream());
```

stream() and parallelStream() have the same return type, but the instances they return are different. parallelStream()'s returned instance runs methods like map() and filter() in parallel across multiple threads, managed by a thread pool under the hood. The benefit is that we can easily switch between sequential and concurrent versions, and methods like findHighPriced() can be oblivious to parallelism.

Let's run the parallelized version of the code and look at the time it takes to run. Again, I produced the following output using the time utility.

```
High priced under $500 is ticker: INTU price: 369.000
real    0m0.470s
user    0m0.076s
sys     0m0.023s
```

The first bit of good news is that this version picked the same stock as the sequential version. After all, there's no point running really fast to get some wrong results. The second bit of good news is the speed of execution. The parallelized version took about 0.4 seconds, which is much less than the time taken by the sequential versions.

When deciding whether to call stream() or parallelStream(), we have to consider a few issues. First, do we want to run the lambda expressions concurrently? Second, the code should be able to run independently without causing any side effects or race conditions. Third, the correctness of the solution shouldn't depend on the order of execution of the lambda expressions that are scheduled to run concurrently. For example, it wouldn't make sense to parallelize calls to the forEach() method and print results from within the lambda expression we provide. Since the order of execution isn't predictable, the order of output might be confusing. On the other hand, methods like map() and filter() that can perform computations and forward their results for further processing are good candidates; see the following sidebar.

Joe asks:

Should We Choose Parallel Streams?

The library makes it easy to go parallel, but sometimes that's not the right choice. It depends on your data and your computation. Sometimes a parallel computation may be *slower* than its sequential counterpart.

We often look to concurrency to speed up execution. But there is a cost—execution time—to make things concurrent. We have to evaluate to make sure that the time saving far outweighs the cost of using concurrency.

For small collections, if the tasks per element are fairly short and quick, the sequential execution may beat any concurrent solution. The benefits of concurrency will shine only if the tasks are time-consuming and the collection is fairly large.

Even though parallel streams in Java make it pretty easy to make code concurrent, we still have to evaluate the problem at hand and the data size to determine whether there's an execution-time saving.

The change from sequential to parallel was effortless, but we did a number of things to make this possible. First, we avoided mutability and kept the functions pure, with no side effects. We avoided race conditions and thread-safety issues, which is critical for correctness—there's no point in being fast and incorrect. We should take extreme care to ensure that lambda expressions passed to stream operations are free of side effects.

Second, the way we composed the functions helped. The decision to run sequentially or in parallel was made upstream, when we transformed the List to a Stream. The rest of the code in the findHighPriced() method didn't change; the two versions share it in common. Going from sequential to parallel was as simple as toggling a switch.

Wrapping Up

Lambda expressions help compose functions into a chain of operations, which lets us put problems into an associative series of object transformations. In addition, by preserving immutability and avoiding side effects we can easily parallelize the execution of parts of the chain's operations and gain speed.

So far, we've discussed features that show how amazing the functional programming capabilities of Java are. Next, we'll see an exception to that, the gnarly topic of exception handling.

Error Handling

Murphy's law says that if something can fail it will. Software systems will fail; errors are inevitable. The code we write should anticipate and properly react to errors that may happen at runtime. Error handling should not be an afterthought. The way you handle errors should depend on the application requirements and the code should align with those expectations. Whether we code in the imperative style or the functional style, proper error handling is our responsibility.

Functional style code is amazing, concise, less complex, and easy to work with...until we hit exception handling. Exception handling is fundamentally an imperative style of programming idea. Throwing exceptions is incompatible with functional programming. But we still have to deal with failures in code written using the functional programming paradigm.

When programming with the functional pipeline we don't have the luxury of throwing an exception as we do in the imperative style of programming. This is one area where the imperative style may have an upper hand compared to functional programming.

You're not allowed to throw a checked exception from the functional pipeline. Don't throw a runtime exception either. Sure, the compiler doesn't stop you from doing so, but you'll abruptly end the functional pipeline processing and the previously processed data may be lost. Throwing exceptions in a functional pipeline is simply not an option.

In this chapter we'll take a close look, using concrete examples, at why exception handling isn't always the right choice in functional programming. To illustrate this, we'll first start with the familiar imperative style where throwing exceptions is the norm. We'll then convert the code to the functional style to reap the benefits of this paradigm, but as you'll see, we'll quickly run into issues with exceptions. We'll then, instead of throwing exceptions, treat errors as forms of data and deal with the failure downstream. By the end of this chapter, you'll have a good sense of how to program to deal with failures, and you'll be able to apply those ideas to your own projects that use the functional style.

Taking a Holistic View of Error Handling

Before we dive into code we need to step back and think about handling errors. We'll discuss an example application here and use that to drive the discussions on error handling in the rest of this chapter.

Suppose we're asked to write a program to print the names of the airports given a list of IATA codes. The happy path is simple to visualize—given the list, map it to the names, and print. But there are a few things that could go wrong in the process. We may run into a network error when accessing the details from a remote web service that provides the mapping of IATA codes to airport names. It's also possible that one or more of the given IATA codes are not valid or not recognized by the web service.

As programmers, we may quickly recognize the possible failures, but what we do about them isn't in our hands. The business and the requirements should decide that. Should we gracefully fail the entire program if the request for the name of one of the IATA codes runs into a failure? Should we ignore the failures and report only the names of the IATA to name mappings that mapped successfully? Should we report the names and the failures all in sequences? Should we organize the names into one group and the failures into another group? Those are all good options in different circumstances, but the implementation has to align with what the business wants.

Suppose we approach the business for clarification, and they suggest to print the names when successful and print error details upon failures; we can design for that. But, if they change their mind, we want our design to accommodate that with as little change to the code as possible. For this reason, the place where the error happens is often not the right place to deal with the errors. Most of our code may have to propagate the result and failures to the calling code, and let the code at the edge deal with the display of results or the proper handling of errors, based on the requirements.

Next, we're going to write a small program that uses imperative style code to deal with exceptions.

Exception Handling and Imperative Style

Your users don't care what programming style you use. Whether you implement code using the imperative style or the functional style, the result should be the same. Your programs have to handle failures gracefully, no matter which paradigm you chose. In this section, we'll start with imperative style code that takes us directly into the heart of dealing with failures. Once we see how the code handles exceptions and the output of the program, we'll look at options to turn that code into the functional style and verify that the output matches that of the imperative style code.

We're going to work with the requirements from the previous section: given a list of airport IATA codes, retrieve and print the names of the airports, and print the error details for the names that can't be found. Let's start with the code that retrieves the name of an airport when given its IATA code:

```
exceptionhandling/fpij/AirportInfo.java
package fpij;

import java.util.Scanner;
import java.net.URL;
import java.io.IOException;

public class AirportInfo {
  public static String getNameOfAirport(String iata)
    throws IOException, AirportInfoException {
    var url = "https://soa.smext.faa.gov/asws/api/airport/status/" + iata;

    try(var scanner = new Scanner(new URL(url).openStream())) {
      var response = scanner.nextLine();

      if(!response.contains("Name")) {
        throw new AirportInfoException("Invalid airport code " + iata);
      }

      return response.split("\"")[3]; //a bruteforce way to get the Name
    }
  }
}
```

The getNameOfAirport() method takes an IATA code for an airport, talks to a web service to get information about that airport, and extracts the name of the airport from the response. Due to the nature of the code—there may be failures accessing the remote web service or the service may not recognize the given code—failures are inevitable.

The getNameOfAirport() method isn't the right place to handle any errors. If the call to the service fails, we merely propagate the IOException from the URL to the caller of getNameOfAirport(). If, on the other hand, the service call succeeded but we didn't get the airport details we're looking for, the getNameOfAirport() method throws a domain-specific checked exception AirportInfoException, which is defined as shown next:

exceptionhandling/fpij/AirportInfoException.java

```java
package fpij;

public class AirportInfoException extends Exception {
  public AirportInfoException(String message) {
    super(message);
  }

  public AirportInfoException(Throwable cause) {
    super(cause);
  }

  public AirportInfoException(String message, Throwable cause) {
    super(message, cause);
  }
}
```

Now that we have the code for getting the name of an airport given its IATA code, let's focus on the next higher-level function. We want to get the names of all the airports in a given list of IATA codes. Let's look at how we'd write the code in the imperative style first—after that, we'll see how to do the same thing in the functional style.

The getNamesOfAirports() method takes a list of airports, calls the getNameOfAirport() method of the AirportInfo class, and returns a list of names. That will take care of the happy path, but we also need to consider the possibility of failures. Programmers are often tempted to throw or propagate an exception in the case of a failure. That may work if we have a stop-the-show requirement, but it's not a solution when the users want to see the results, both for successes and failures. We need to capture both successful results and details of failures and pass them to the caller.

Here's the implementation of the getNamesOfAirports() method in a new AirportNames class:

exceptionhandling/fpij/AirportNames.java

```java
public class AirportNames {
  public static List<DataOrException<String>> getNamesOfAirports(
    List<String> iataCodes) {

    List<DataOrException<String>> result = new ArrayList<>();

    for(var iataCode: iataCodes) {
      try {
        result.add(DataOrException.of(
          AirportInfo.getNameOfAirport(iataCode).toUpperCase()));
```

```
    } catch(IOException | AirportInfoException ex) {
        result.add(DataOrException.of(ex));
    }
  }

  return result;
}
```

In the previous code, a DataOrException serves as a wrapper of the result—a String for an airport name or an Exception in case of a failure. The getNamesOfAirports() of AirportNames iterates, imperatively, through a list of IATA codes, and fetches the name of the airport from the service using the getNameOfAirport() method we wrote previously. If the call succeeds, the method converts the obtained name to upper case, wraps it into an instance of DataOrException, and adds that to the result list. If the call fails, the method instead adds the details of the failure, wrapped into an instance of DataOrException, to the result list in the catch block. The imperative style, even though it's verbose, is rather good at handling exceptions, and we took advantage of that here. Let's take a quick look at the DataOrException interface that's used to wrap the data or the Exception:

exceptionhandling/fpij/DataOrException.java
```
package fpij;

public sealed interface DataOrException<T> {
  public default boolean isDataPresent() { return true; }

  public default T getDataOrThrow() {
    throw new RuntimeException("No data");
  }

  public default Exception getExceptionOrThrow() {
    throw new RuntimeException("No Exception");
  }

  public static <T> DataOrException<T> of(T data) {
    return new Data<T>(data);
  }

  public static <T> DataOrException<T> of(Exception exception) {
    return new TheException<T>(exception);
  }
}

record Data<T>(T data) implements DataOrException<T> {
  public T getDataOrThrow() { return data; }
}

record TheException<T>(Exception exception) implements DataOrException<T> {
  public boolean isDataPresent() { return false; }

  public Exception getExceptionOrThrow() { return exception; }
}
```

The first overloaded of() static method of DataOrException returns a wrapper instance that carries the given data. The second overloaded version of the method returns a wrapper instance that carries the exception. Using this we can conveniently transport data or exceptions between functions.

Let's call the getNamesOfAirports() method from a main() method, providing a few IATA codes for airports in my favorite Lone Star state of Texas:

exceptionhandling/fpij/AirportNames.java

```java
  public static void main(String[] args) {
    var iataCodes = List.of("AUS", "DFW", "HOU", "IHA", "SAT");

    for(var result: getNamesOfAirports(iataCodes)) {
      if(result.isDataPresent()) {
        System.out.println(result.getDataOrThrow());
      } else {
        System.out.println("Error: " +
          result.getExceptionOrThrow().getMessage());
      }
    }
  }
}
```

Let's take that code for a short flight and see how it works.

```
AUSTIN-BERGSTROM INTL
DALLAS-FORT WORTH INTL
WILLIAM P HOBBY
Error: Invalid airport code IHA
SAN ANTONIO INTL
```

The output shows the names of the airports for IATA codes that were valid. Instead of IAH, I had typed in IHA, and it turns out there is no airport with that code. No worries, the code handled that gracefully, told us politely what had happened, and moved on to display the name for the next airport in the list.

The main() method, being the edge function, can decide how to deal with the exceptions based on the requirements. It can evolve based on the change to the requirements: to print only the successful names, to print only the errors, to group them separately, and so on. From the design point of view, this solution is easier to extend. For example, in the future, if one caller to getNamesOfAirports() wants all the results and failures but another caller wants to fail fast upon the first exception, we can modify the getNamesOfAirports() so that it can return a full list of successes/failures or only the first failure based on the caller's preference, which could be passed in as a parameter.

The previous code was in the imperative style, but what about the functional style, you may wonder? We know that functional style code is elegant compared to imperative style, but it should also be graceful in handling errors. Let's see how the efforts to refactor the code to the functional style turn out next.

Checked Exceptions and Functional Style with Streams

If we don't consider the exceptions for a moment, refactoring the imperative style code to functional style code is easy. We have a list of IATA codes, we can invoke the stream() method on the list, call map() to get the name for a given IATA code, and then call map() again to convert the name to uppercase, and finally use the toList() method to place the result in a list. Code, like life, is easy when we don't have to deal with errors. But fun without the risk of failure isn't an option.

Using the Stream API with code that throws exceptions poses some serious challenges. Let's use the functional style to rewrite the imperative solution and see what issues pop up:

```
public static List<String> getNamesOfAirports(List<String> iataCodes) {
  return iataCodes.stream()
    .map(iataCode -> AirportInfo.getNameOfAirport(iataCode))
    .map(String::toUpperCase)
    .toList();
  //ERROR: This code will not compile
}
```

As one would expect from the functional style, the code is beautiful, elegant, concise, reads well to convey the intent, and...it doesn't work, sadly. Go ahead and compile, and you'll see the following error:

```
fpij/AirportNames.java:10: error:
  unreported exception IOException; must be caught or declared to be thrown
      .map(iataCode -> AirportInfo.getNameOfAirport(iataCode))
                                   ^
1 error
```

The error is from the lambda expression we're passing to the map() method. The parameter of Stream's map() method takes Function<T, R> as its parameter. The abstract method of that functional interface, R apply(T) doesn't have any throws clause. Thus, the lambda expression or method reference that will be used as an argument to map() isn't allowed to throw any checked exceptions.

That seems like a serious limitation at first glance. Some developers have complained about it. Some have even taken the extreme measure of forking the JDK code and adding the throws clause. But the folks behind the Java language have done what is right—it's not an oversight. Let's see why.

Exception Handling vs. Functional Style

It's worth reiterating:

Exception Handling

 Exception handling is fundamentally an imperative style of programming idea. Exception handling and functional programming are incompatible.

Some programmers think the issue with the Stream API and exception handling is the fact that the functional interfaces used by methods like filter(), map(), and so on don't deal with checked exceptions. This leads them towards a poor solution of throwing an unchecked exception that wraps the underlying checked exceptions. This may provide a temporary relief by quieting the compiler from complaining that the exception should be caught or thrown. But this doesn't address the fundamental issue of how the error is handled by the program.

Let's try out the often-attempted bad solution by refactoring the previous code to eliminate the compiler error. Then we'll discuss why this is a terrible idea.

In the lambda expression passed to the map() method, we wrap the checked exception within a RuntimeException. Here's the code—please don't try this at the office or anywhere in public for that matter.

```
public static List<String> getNamesOfAirports(List<String> iataCodes) {
  return iataCodes.stream()
    .map(iataCode -> { //Bad idea
      try {
        return AirportInfo.getNameOfAirport(iataCode);
      } catch(Exception ex) {
        throw new RuntimeException(ex);
      }})
    .map(String::toUpperCase)
    .toList();
}
```

If Airport's getNameOfAirport() method returns an airport name, we forward that to the next map() method for transformation to uppercase. But if there is a failure, the code blows up with an unchecked exception.

Throwing an exception from the middle of a functional pipeline is a terrible idea for a few reasons. The functional pipelines are executed either lazily or in parallel. The exception in the pipeline might have been thrown from another thread if the stream is executed in parallel. Also, the lambda expression passed to any function in the pipeline, like filter(), map(), and so on may be executed lazily. In either case, the caller may not be in the control flow to properly receive the exception.

What if the entire pipeline along with the terminal operation is fully embedded within a function and the execution of the stream is sequential, you may ask? In the previous code, the exception blows up the call stack. If you carefully examine the code, you'll see we're not catching the exception anywhere. So, it will result in the abrupt termination of the program. You may be tempted to put a try-catch within the getNamesOfAirports() method, moving the current body of the method into the try block. That may help catch the exception, but by then you will be out of the functional pipeline, and you'll have no way to continue processing for any remaining IATA code or gathering the results for the previously successful IATA codes. All is lost, and nothing is gained, as you see in the output:

```
Exception in thread "main" java.lang.RuntimeException:
  fpij.AirportInfoException: Invalid airport code IHA
      ...
```

The output of this code is far different from the output of the imperative style code. Let's think through the fundamental issue that caused this.

In functional programming, and especially in using the Stream API, we're working with a functional pipeline of functions. Blowing up in the middle of the pipeline doesn't make much sense if we want to gracefully handle the failure and continue processing for other elements in the collection.

Don't Blow Up

 Don't raise or propagate exceptions from within a functional pipeline.

Imagine a friend calls you frantically and says they have a flat tire while driving on the middle lane of a major freeway. The worst advice you may give, especially if you don't want to abruptly end that friendship: "Blow up and start driving in reverse." Now, you'd never do that... right? You'd most likely suggest: "Carefully drive forward, exit the freeway or pull over to the shoulder, and deal with it downstream."

That's right, *deal with it downstream.*

Dealing with It Downstream

Ideally, the operations we perform in the functional pipeline are pure operations with no side-effects. The data flows in harmony as it gets transformed from one stage of the functional pipeline to the next. In reality, things go wrong, Murphy's law intervenes, and we have to gracefully deal with the messes we may run into.

A good strategy to deal with errors and exceptions in functional programming is to treat an error as a form of data, move it down the pipeline, and deal with it downstream.

Wrap the Exception Received into an Object

 Treat errors and exceptions as forms of data. Wrap the details in an object and move it downstream.

To treat an error as a form of data, we need to capture and encapsulate the result or the error into an object. In short, we need a Union Type.[1] A Union Type is a data structure that can hold one of many different types of data, but an instance of it can hold data of only one of the expected types at runtime. In our case, we need objects of a Union Type that hold only one of two types: either the result or an error. In functional programming, the Union Type is often referred to as an *Either monad* since it carries either the data or an error through the stages of the functional pipeline.

Incidentally, we already went this route earlier in this chapter when we created the DataOrException wrapper to carry data or an error in the imperative style code. Now, in the context of functional programming, we need more operations on a wrapper as it flows through the functional pipeline, and we carry forward that idea of using a Union Type. In the spirit of such solutions in languages like Scala[2] and libraries like Vavr,[3] we'll call our new implementation Try.

Our Try may exist in one of two forms: a Success, which carries data or a result, or a Failure, which carries an exception in the form of Throwable. We'll build our functional pipeline so that each stage in the pipeline will process the result that's carried in the Try given to it. In response, each stage will create another Try. This Try will contain the result of that stage if successful or an error otherwise. If a stage in the pipeline receives a Failure instead of receiving a Success, the function in that stage will merely pass along that failure downstream without processing.

---

1. https://en.wikipedia.org/wiki/Union_type
2. https://www.scala-lang.org/api/2.13.6/scala/util/Try.html
3. https://www.javadoc.io/doc/io.vavr/vavr/0.9.2/io/vavr/control/Try.html

Instead of data flowing through a Stream API, we'll model it so that either data or an error, captured into a Success or Failure, is passed down the pipeline, as shown in the following figure.

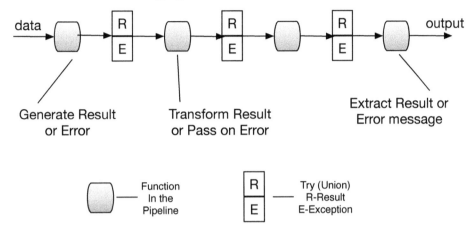

In this design, the pipeline starts with the collection of data given as input. As each element is processed, an instance of Try, in the form of Success or Failure, is passed down the chain. The final stage in the pipeline extracts the result from the success it receives or the details of the error if it receives a Failure.

Let's rewrite the getNamesOfAirports() method to use this approach, using the yet-to-be-written Try interface and Success, and Failure classes.

```
public static List<Try<String>> getNamesOfAirports(List<String> iataCodes) {
  return iataCodes.stream()
    .map(iataCode -> Try.of(() -> AirportInfo.getNameOfAirport(iataCode)))
    .map(name -> name.map(String::toUpperCase))
    .toList();
}
```

Structurally, this version of getNamesOfAirports() is the same as the first functional style version we wrote. Whereas the first version ran into compilation errors, in this version we're better equipped to deal with exceptions.

We take a collection of IATA codes and, using the StreamAPI, process each element through the pipeline. In the first map() method call, in the lambda expression passed as an argument, we invoke the AirportInfo's getNameOfAirport() method, passing the given IATA code. This method, as you know, may return a name of an airport or throw an exception.

We wrap the call to getNameOfAirport() in another lambda expression and pass that to the yet-to-be- written Try's of() method. Since this lambda expression will return a name, it appears that a suitable functional interface to represent this would be a Supplier<T>. But the abstract method get() of that interface doesn't permit any exceptions. Instead, the good old Callable<T> interface in java.util.concurrent will work great here—other than method names, the main difference between Callable and Supplier is that the former will permit exceptions to be thrown from its call() method implementation whereas the latter won't allow any such thing from its get() method implementation.

The result of the first map() call is a Try, but in reality, it may be Success, which carries an airport name, or Failure, which carries the details of what went wrong. Thus, both Success and Failure are classes that implement the Try interface.

The lambda expression passed as an argument to the second map() call, in the functional pipeline, transforms the name to uppercase if the received Try is a Success or passes on Failure as is in case of an error. This is done using the map() method of Try. In the final step of the functional pipeline, we return a list of Try instances to the caller. This way the caller of the getNamesOfAirports() has control over what to do with data and exceptions, based on the overall system requirements.

For the previous code to work, we need to create the Try, Success, and Failure. We have a couple of different options to create these. If the version of Java you're using supports sealed classes, you can follow along with the code given here. If you're using an older version of Java, then leave out the sealed and permits clause from the definition of Try.

Let's implement the Try interface which represents either a success or a failure.

exceptionhandling/fpij/Try.java

```
package fpij;

import java.util.concurrent.Callable;
import java.util.function.Function;

public sealed interface Try<T> permits Success, Failure {
  T getResult();
  Throwable getError();

  static <T> Try<T> of(Callable<T> code) {
    try {
      return new Success<T>(code.call());
    } catch(Throwable throwable) {
      return new Failure<T>(throwable);
    }
  }

  default <R> Try<R> map(Function<T, R> mapper) {
    if(this instanceof Success<T>) {
      return of(() -> mapper.apply(getResult()));
    } else {
```

```
      return new Failure<R>(getError());
    }
  }
}
```

The interface has two abstract methods: one static factory method and one default method. The getResult() is for fetching the result, if present. On the other hand, the getError() is to get the exception if there is a failure.

The of() static method acts as a factory method to return an instance of Success if the given Callable's call method returns a result. Otherwise, it captures the generated exception and passes it on as an instance of Failure. Both Success and Failure conform to the Try interface.

The last method in the Try interface is the map() method which transforms the result, if present, using the Function given as an argument. If the Try holds an error instead of the result, that is, if it's a Failure, then the map() method simply passes on the failure without applying the given function.

All the necessary logic is in the Try interface. The implementing classes of this interface are merely holders of results or errors. Let's write Success as a record:

exceptionhandling/fpij/Success.java
```java
package fpij;

public record Success<T>(T result) implements Try<T> {
  @Override
  public T getResult() { return result; }

  @Override
  public Throwable getError() {
    throw new RuntimeException("Invalid invocation");
  }
}
```

There isn't much to this record—it is merely a carrier of data and conforms to the Try interface.

Similarly, the Failure class is pretty straightforward:

exceptionhandling/fpij/Failure.java
```java
package fpij;

public record Failure<T>(Throwable throwable) implements Try<T> {
  @Override
  public T getResult() { throw new RuntimeException("Invalid invocation"); }

  @Override
  public Throwable getError() { return throwable; }
}
```

Chapter 10. Error Handling • 180

Success is a carrier of results and Failure is a carrier of bad news. Take another look at the getNamesOfAirports() method to see how these classes are used.

As a final step, let's see how the functional style implementation of the get-NamesOfAirports() can be used:

```java
public static void main(String[] args) {
  var iataCodes = List.of("AUS", "DFW", "HOU", "IHA", "SAT");

  getNamesOfAirports(iataCodes).stream()
    .map(name -> switch(name) {
      case Success(String result) -> result;
      case Failure(Throwable throwable) -> "Error: " + throwable.getMessage();
    })
    .forEach(System.out::println);
}
```

We've pushed the error handling all the way to the edge where we can align the code to the business requirements. By preserving all the information in a strongly typed form, we can gracefully evolve the program as the requirements change. The main() method gets a list of Try instances from the getNamesOfAirports() method and iterates over it using the stream() internal iterator. In the map() call, we extract the result from the Try if it is a success; otherwise, we extract the error details.

We're using the amazing feature of the switch expression of Java. If you're using an older version of Java, you may use the traditional if-else instead—the code will be a tad verbose but will get the job done.

Run the code and take a look at the output:

```
AUSTIN-BERGSTROM INTL
DALLAS-FORT WORTH INTL
WILLIAM P HOBBY
Error: Invalid airport code IHA
SAN ANTONIO INTL
```

It worked...and the output is exactly the same as the output of the imperative style version. Phew!

Before we end this chapter, let's bring together everything we've covered on handling errors in functional style code.

Handling Failures in Functional Programming

When programming with the functional style and the Stream API, treat errors as forms of data. If a lower-level function called in one of the stages of the pipeline throws an exception, capture and wrap that into a failure object. Instead of writing your pipeline so that it moves only data, design it to move a union object that may carry either data or an error. This is a good way to deal with errors in a functional pipeline, but there are consequences to this approach.

If none of the stages in a functional pipeline may have errors, then the functions can nicely focus on dealing with data. But, if errors are possible in any stage of the pipeline, then the stages downstream have to be written to work with the union object and take actions to transform data upon success or push the error downstream upon failure. This makes the functions in the pipeline less cohesive. They can't focus only on data transformation, they need to also process the error or at least move that along downstream.

If you have to deal with errors, you have to choose between using the imperative style or functional style. If complex error handling is needed, the imperative style may be a better option. If you want to use the functional style, the code will have to be designed to pass the union objects and not merely the data, and that takes more effort than simply writing a pipeline to deal with data. Evaluate your options, prototype, and get a feel to see if using the imperative style or the functional style is better for your use case.

Wrapping Up

Dealing with failure is hard, both in life and in programming. Exception handling is fundamentally an imperative style of programming idea, and we can't mix exceptions and functional style code. One way to deal with failures is to treat errors as forms of data. In this chapter we took a close look at how to do this with a practical example. The solution is effective in handling errors but makes the code a tad complex and less cohesive. Use caution in how you deal with errors when writing functional style code.

In the next chapter we'll apply our learnings by taking some legacy code written using the imperative style and turning it into functional style.

CHAPTER 11

Refactoring to Functional Style

In the past, Java programmers could only write object-oriented code using the imperative style of programming. Today they can write object-oriented code using either the imperative style or the functional style. It's nice to have such choices when writing code. Functional style code may not be ideal all the time, for example, to deal with side-effects or exceptions as we saw in the previous chapter. But it does win over the imperative style by reducing accidental complexity and making code easier to read and understand.

When we sit down to write new code, we can reach out to our functional programming skills. But many enterprise applications aren't greenfield. We're often thrown into a codebase that has been around for years and written by someone who's not around in the company anymore.

There's a lot of imperative style Java code in the world. There are two main reasons for that. First, the imperative style was the way of life in Java, and most programmers are very familiar with that style since that was the only option for a long time. Second, even though functional programming has been possible in Java since version 8, it's natural for us to fall back on the ways we're comfortable with and highly used to because they're familiar. It's unrealistic to expect that we wake up one morning and write functional style code with as much ease as we did imperative style code the night before. Thus, more new imperative style code has been written in the past years.

The code works, so you may wonder why bother refactoring to functional style. The simplest reasons are to reduce accidental complexity, make the code easier to understand, and above all, for it to be more obviously correct. With the functional style, the accidental complexity is tucked away, out of our sight into the underlying library of code, and our code appears to read more like the problem statement. This reduces the impedance mismatch and the cost of maintaining the code. That sounds great, but does that mean we have to refactor all the existing code? Certainly not.

It's not practical—and I certainly don't suggest—that you change all existing imperative style code to functional style code. Don't go out on a mission to change code for the sake of changing. There are a few opportunities when we can, and should, refactor imperative style code to functional style code. We benefit by being pragmatic instead of being dogmatic.

Modules of code that have no other reasons to change aren't worth spending time refactoring from imperative to functional. However complex that code may be, no one is touching it, so it's wise to spend our time and effort elsewhere.

In applications that have been around for a while, when you touch a piece of code—whether making an enhancement to an existing feature, adding a new feature, or fixing a bug—is a great time to refactor. The code you're changing is likely to continue to change and deserves to be less complex, easier to read, and cost-effective to maintain.

When writing new code, both in greenfield and existing applications, we may be tempted to write code in the imperative style because it's familiar. That's quite fine. We're not in a competition—don't let anyone, especially yourself, ridicule you for writing code in the imperative style. I'm a big fan of the mantra "Make it work, then make it better real soon." If you find it easier to express your ideas in the imperative style, so be it. Once you have the code working, with good tests around it, refactor the new code to the functional style and verify that the tests are passing. You captured the logic and then reduced the complexity, that's noble. As you gain experience with the functional style, you'll find yourself gradually writing code in that style first rather than having to write in the imperative style and then refactor it. Give yourself and your colleagues the time to make that transition.

As you may have realized already, writing code in the functional style isn't about learning a particular set of syntax. It's a paradigm shift that takes changing the way we think and involves exploring, trying out ideas, prototyping, and patience. Refactoring code from the imperative style to the functional style is one of the best ways to get that practice.

In this chapter, we'll refactor code for a number of common programming tasks that we run into every day, from the imperative style to the functional style. Working through the refactoring steps for these tasks will help you to think through the ways to program in the functional style. As you look at each of the problems, try out the code and rework the solution in the functional style. Then resume reading to compare your line of thinking with the details outlined and the resulting code.

Before we dive into the first refactoring task, let's discuss a key step that's essential for refactoring—having a set of automated tests.

Creating a Safety Net for Refactoring

Refactoring should make the internals of code better without affecting its external behavior. We're often eager to reap the benefits of refactoring but have to be mindful of the risks as well. It's reasonable to worry about the code behaving differently after the change. Due to the hidden complexity in the code, it's possible that we haven't fully understood the code we set out to change. Irrespective of how charming the functional style code may look, it's no good if it doesn't produce the same results as the imperative style code it's replacing. Automated tests serve as a safety net for refactoring.

Once we have passing tests, with each change we can quickly verify that the code that worked before continues to work the same way. When writing new code, whether in the imperative or functional style, write tests. Even if we write code in the functional style in the first place, we're sure to find ways to improve the design and quality of code. The tests will give a great deal of confidence that the refactoring didn't break the existing functionality.

Legacy code poses additional challenges as it may not contain automated tests to verify the behavior. If possible, write automated unit tests on the code before refactoring. If that's not possible, identify integration tests that touch the code you plan to refactor. If none of those options exist, rely on manual tests that verify the code's behavior. Once you identify tests that provide the feedback as quickly and reliably as possible, then set out to refactor the code.

For each example in this chapter, we'll start with an imperative style code for a task along with a set of unit tests that verify the code's behavior. As you practice along, key in both the code and the accompanying tests, and verify the tests pass. Then refactor the code to the functional style. Finally, verify that the tests still pass to confirm that the functional style code produces the same result as the imperative style code it replaces.

Let's start with our first refactoring task—we'll begin with a relatively simple problem to warm up.

Refactoring the Traditional for Loop

Existing codebases are littered with for loops. We use them to iterate over collections of data but also over a range of indexes. To illustrate how we can refactor the traditional imperative for loop into functional style code, we'll look at using a for loop to compute the factorial of numbers in a range. But, of course, we'll start with a test to provide the safety net we just discussed.

refactoring/fpij/FactorialTest.java
```java
public class FactorialTest {
  Factorial factorial;

  @BeforeEach
  public void init() {
    factorial = new Factorial();
  }

  @Test
  public void computeFactorial() {
    assertAll(
      () -> assertEquals(BigInteger.ONE, factorial.compute(1)),
      () -> assertEquals(BigInteger.TWO, factorial.compute(2)),
      () -> assertEquals(BigInteger.valueOf(6), factorial.compute(3)),
      () -> assertEquals(BigInteger.valueOf(120), factorial.compute(5))
    );
  }
}
```

The test verifies that the yet-to-be-seen Factorial class's compute() method returns proper factorial values for the given upper limit of values. Let's now take a look at the Factorial class where the compute() method is implemented in the imperative style:

refactoring/fpij/Factorial.java
```java
public class Factorial {
  public BigInteger compute(long upTo) {
    BigInteger result = BigInteger.ONE;

    for(int i = 1; i <= upTo; i++) {
      result = result.multiply(BigInteger.valueOf(i));
    }

    return result;
  }
}
```

Much like the traditional use of for to loop, we're iterating over a range from 1 to the value in the variable upTo. Your mission: pause reading, run the test, and verify it passes. Then refactor the compute() method to the functional style.

Verify the tests pass and then read on. We'll refer to these steps in the sections that follow as:

Pause, refactor, and continue.

Now that you're back, let's compare the steps you took to those I suggest here. It's not always clear where to start and how to proceed when trying to refactor from the imperative to the functional style. One technique that's helpful is to *think declaratively and then program functionally.*

As we discussed before, the imperative style is where we tell the code what to do and also how to do it. In the declarative style we focus on the what and delegate the how to underlying libraries.

Functional style == declarative style + the use of higher-order functions

One of the key strengths of the functional style of programming is its declarative nature. Before jumping into the functional style, take some time to think declaratively—it can help you identify some key elements in how to implement the code differently from the imperative style. Rather than focusing on how each step is carried out, think of the problem as a series of high-level steps that transform the data from the given input to the desired output. Let's dive into the problem at hand to see how this approach can help.

To compute the factorial, we work with a range of values from 1 to the given number as the upper limit. For each number in the range, we need its BigInteger representation. Finally, we accumulate the product of the BigInteger values—that's a reduce operation. The problem at hand appears as the series or pipeline: range => map => reduce. We can refactor the code to bring those ideas to fruition.

As the first step, we need to get a range of long values from 1 to a given number. A quick search through the JDK shows that the LongStream interface has a static method named rangeClosed() that will generate a LongStream to iterate through the values in the specified range. Once we have a LongStream, we want to transform the values in the range to values that are a BigInteger representation of the values. We can't use the map() method because it expects to transform a LongStream to another LongStream, not a Stream<BigInteger>, so we'll use the map-ToObj() method. As the final step, we can use the reduce() operation. Let's put those steps together in code:

```
public BigInteger compute(long upTo) {
  return LongStream.rangeClosed(1, upTo)
    .mapToObj(BigInteger::valueOf)
    .reduce(BigInteger.ONE, BigInteger::multiply);
}
```

In addition to using the Stream API, we also used method references instead of creating lambda expressions, making the code more concise and expressive. No explicit mutability, less clutter, more expressive—these are all benefits that we can expect from the functional style.

Next, let's look at a problem that has a tad more complexity.

Refactoring More Complex Loops

Traditional for loops allow us to increment or decrement the range by different step values. Let's take a look at a countFrom1900() method of a LeapYears class that computes the number of leap years since 1900 to a given year.

Let's start with the test first:

```
refactoring/fpij/LeapYearsTest.java
public class LeapYearsTest {
  LeapYears leapYears;

  @BeforeEach
  public void init() {
    leapYears = new LeapYears();
  }

  @Test
  public void countFrom1900() {
    assertAll(
      () -> assertEquals(25, leapYears.countFrom1900(2000)),
      () -> assertEquals(27, leapYears.countFrom1900(2010)),
      () -> assertEquals(31, leapYears.countFrom1900(2025)),
      () -> assertEquals(49, leapYears.countFrom1900(2100)),
      () -> assertEquals(0, leapYears.countFrom1900(1800))
    );
  }
}
```

The tests verify that the countFrom1900() method is returning the correct result for different years passed as arguments.

Let's now take a look at the imperative style code that we'd like to refactor:

```
refactoring/fpij/LeapYears.java
public class LeapYears {
  public int countFrom1900(int upTo) {
    int numberOfLeapYears = 0;

    for(int i = 1900; i <= upTo; i += 4) {
      if(Year.isLeap(i)) {
        numberOfLeapYears++;
      }
    }
```

```
      return numberOfLeapYears;
   }
}
```

Since leap years occur at most once every four years, the for loop steps over the index in increments of 4. It then uses the isLeap() method from the JDK library to check if a year is a leap year and increments a count accordingly.

Pause, refactor, and continue.

We need to find a functional style equivalent for the for loop that steps over in arbitrary increments. Let's take a closer look at the for statement, but with functional eyes:

```
for(int i = 1900; i <= upTo; i += 4) {
```

reads like

```
for(seedValue, predicate to check upper limit, step function)
```

The for loop starts with an initial value, and it can use a Predicate to check if the loop should continue and a function to increment an index value. Now we need to look for such a function in the JDK. It turns out that the IntStream has exactly what we're looking for—the iterate() function. Let's rethink, once again, how the for loop will look in the functional style, using the iterate() function:

```
iterate(1900, year -> year <= upto, year -> year + 4)
```

The loop can start at the value of 1900. The second argument, a Predicate can check if the year as it progresses through the iteration is within the limits of the value in upTo. The third argument, a Function can increase the value of year by the desired step value of 4. The iterate() function will generate a stream of numbers, starting at the seed value and stepping by the given increments up to the value checked in the Predicate. We can use this stream to refactor the imperative style code:

```
public int countFrom1900(int upTo) {
  return (int) IntStream.iterate(
      1900, year -> year <= upTo, year -> year + 4)
    .filter(Year::isLeap)
    .count();
}
```

Once we arrive at the functional equivalent of the for, the rest of the steps are fairly straightforward. The more complex loop of the imperative style turned into an elegant functional pipeline. Next, we'll refactor an unbounded imperative style loop into another elegant functional style iteration.

Refactoring Unbounded Loops

The traditional for loops, albeit complex, are quite versatile. Specifying no upper bounds is a nice capability that makes it easier to execute a loop until a condition is met. Let's take a look at a variation of the countFrom1900() method that makes use of this capability. Oh, yeah, test first, of course.

```
refactoring/fpij/LeapYearsUnboundedTest.java
public class LeapYearsUnboundedTest {
  LeapYearsUnbounded leapYearsUnbounded;

  @BeforeEach
  public void init() {
    leapYearsUnbounded = new LeapYearsUnbounded();
  }

  @Test
  public void count() {
    assertAll(
      () -> assertEquals(25,
        leapYearsUnbounded.countFrom1900(year -> year <= 2000)),
      () -> assertEquals(27,
        leapYearsUnbounded.countFrom1900(year -> year <= 2010)),
      () -> assertEquals(31,
        leapYearsUnbounded.countFrom1900(year -> year <= 2025)),
      () -> assertEquals(49,
        leapYearsUnbounded.countFrom1900(year -> year <= 2100)),
      () -> assertEquals(0,
        leapYearsUnbounded.countFrom1900(year -> year <= 1800))
    );
  }
}
```

Instead of passing an upper bound for a year to the countFrom1900() method, the tests pass a lambda that checks a given year to determine if the upper limit has been reached. Let's take a look at the imperative style version that is a candidate for refactoring:

```
refactoring/fpij/LeapYearsUnbounded.java
interface Continue {
  boolean check(int year);
}

public class LeapYearsUnbounded {
  public int countFrom1900(Continue shouldContinue) {
    int numberOfLeapYears = 0;

    for(int i = 1900;; i += 4) {
      if(!shouldContinue.check(i)) {
        break;
      }
```

```
    if(Year.isLeap(i)) {
      numberOfLeapYears++;
    }
  }

  return numberOfLeapYears;
  }
}
```

The method uses an interface named Continue with a check() method, and countFrom1900() receives an instance that implements that interface as the parameter. Within the method, the loop is unbounded and uses the passed-in Continue to determine if the loop should continue or break out.

Pause, refactor, and continue.

As the first refactoring opportunity, we can replace the custom Continue interface with the functional interface Predicate of the JDK.

The functional style equivalent of the unbounded for loop won't need a Predicate since it doesn't have to check for an upper bound. The creators of the iterate() method of IntStream anticipated this use and provided an overloaded version of the method that takes two parameters, without the Predicate, instead of three parameters.

The imperative style for loop uses the break statement to exit out of the loop. In functional programming there is no break, but, we have takeWhile()—see Terminating Iterations, on page 29. We can refactor the imperative-style unbounded loop by chaining the call to iterate() with a call to takeWhile(), like so:

```
public int countFrom1900(Predicate<Integer> shouldContinue) {
  return (int) IntStream.iterate(1900, year -> year + 4)
    .takeWhile(shouldContinue::test)
    .filter(Year::isLeap)
    .count();
}
```

We have one less interface, and the method became concise and expressive. Refactoring for the win. In the next task, we'll refactor an imperative style code that uses the *for-each* loop to the functional style.

Refactoring for-each

As Java programmers, we've come to like and extensively use the so-called for-each syntax, which is of the form for(Type variable: iterable). It's a lot simpler than the traditional for loop when we don't need the index and care only about the elements in a collection. But it's not uncommon to use break and continue with both versions of for. The result is verbose code that takes effort to maintain in the long run. Let's take a stab at refactoring code that uses for-each to functional style.

Keeping up with our tradition, let's start with the tests:

refactoring/fpij/AgencyTest.java
```java
public class AgencyTest {
  Agency agency;

  @BeforeEach
  public void init() {
    agency = new Agency();
  }

  @Test
  public void isChaperoneRequired() {
    assertAll(
      () -> assertTrue(agency.isChaperoneRequired(
        Set.of(new Person("Jake", 12)))),
      () -> assertTrue(agency.isChaperoneRequired(
        Set.of(new Person("Jake", 12), new Person("Pam", 14)))),
      () -> assertTrue(agency.isChaperoneRequired(
          Set.of(new Person("Shiv", 8),
              new Person("Sam", 9), new Person("Jill", 11)))),
      () -> assertFalse(agency.isChaperoneRequired(
          Set.of(new Person("Jake", 12), new Person("Pam", 18)))),
      () -> assertFalse(agency.isChaperoneRequired(Set.of()))
    );
  }
}
```

The test makes use of a Person which can be implemented as a record (or a class in older versions of Java).

refactoring/fpij/Person.java
```java
public record Person(String name, int age) {}
```

An agency is responsible for deciding if a chaperone is required for trips taken by a group of people. The logic to make that decision is in the Agency class's isChaperoneRequired() method:

refactoring/fpij/Agency.java
```java
public class Agency {
  public boolean isChaperoneRequired(Set<Person> people) {
    boolean required = true;

    if(people.size() == 0) {
      required = false;
    } else {
      for(var person: people) {
        if(person.age() >= 18) {
```

```
            required = false;
            break;
        }
      }
    }
  }

  return required;
}
}
```

What the method does is rather simple, but it does it with a lot of noise. If anyone in the group is 18 years or older or the group is empty, then no chaperone is needed. This code can use some refactoring to reduce clutter and remove mutability.

Pause, refactor, and continue.

We know that instead of using for-each we can iterate over a collection using the stream() method. Given a collection of people, we want to know if anyone in the list is older than 17, to decide if a chaperone is needed. We can use the noneMatch() of Stream for that, like so:

```
public boolean isChaperoneRequired(Set<Person> people) {
  return people.size() > 0 &&
    people.stream()
      .noneMatch(person -> person.age() >= 18);
}
```

The conciseness of this code is hard to match. In the refactoring examples we've seen so far, we've managed to keep the logic the same while converting from the imperative to the functional style. That may not be possible all the time and, sometimes, we may have to rework the algorithm or the logic, as we'll see next.

Refactoring to Rework the Logic

Sometimes when refactoring to the functional style, we may have to step back and rethink the logic or the algorithm instead of merely trying to map from the imperative to functional style. If we don't take an alternative approach in such cases, either we may have issues creating functional style code or the refactored version may be complex and leave us wanting for a better solution. We'll look at one such problem in this section—this was raised by a developer who was interested in solving this problem and was having a hard time creating a functional equivalent.

Given a string, we want to find the first letter that's repeated anywhere else in the string. For example, in the string hellothere, the first letter that's repeated is h, even though the letters l and e are also repeated. When dealing with such problems, and especially when we desire to refactor the code, tests are one of the best ways to clarify the details and resolve any ambiguity. Here are some tests for this problem:

refactoring/fpij/FirstRepeatedLetterTest.java

```java
public class FirstRepeatedLetterTest {
  FirstRepeatedLetter firstRepeatedLetter;

  @BeforeEach
  public void init() {
    firstRepeatedLetter = new FirstRepeatedLetter();
  }

  @Test
  public void findFirstRepeating() {
    assertAll(
      () -> assertEquals('l', firstRepeatedLetter.findIn("hello")),
      () -> assertEquals('h', firstRepeatedLetter.findIn("hellothere")),
      () -> assertEquals('a', firstRepeatedLetter.findIn("magicalguru")),
      () -> assertEquals('\0', firstRepeatedLetter.findIn("once")),
      () -> assertEquals('\0', firstRepeatedLetter.findIn(""))
    );
  }
}
```

Let's look at the imperative style code that passes the previous tests:

refactoring/fpij/FirstRepeatedLetter.java

```java
public class FirstRepeatedLetter {
  public char findIn(String word) {
    char[] letters = word.toCharArray();

    for(char candidate: letters) {
      int count = 0;

      for(char letter: letters) {
        if(candidate == letter) {
          count++;
        }
      }

      if(count > 1) {
        return candidate;
      }
    }

    return '\0';
  }
}
```

We iterate over the letters in the given word in the outer loop. In the inner loop, we check the number of times a letter picked in the outer loop occurs among the letters of the given word. As soon as we realize that a letter has been repeated, we return it as the result. The code is verbose, noisy, and hard to read, but once we see the logic hidden in it, we can agree that it's fairly straightforward. Of course, we want the code to be easier to read and understand, so we want to refactor it to the functional style. Let's give that a shot.

Pause, refactor, and continue.

If we directly try to translate the two loops into the functional style equivalent, it will be rather messy at the best. Instead, we can step back and rethink the approach to solving this problem. Along the way, we can leverage the lazy evaluation capabilities of the functional pipeline.

A letter is repeated if the position of its last occurrence in the given word is greater than the position of its first occurrence. If it's not repeated, its last occurrence position will be the same as its first occurrence position. From the given word, we can filter out letters that are repeated. At first thought, that appears to be rather inefficient. Why bother getting all of them when we need only the first one? But, thanks to lazy evaluation (see Chapter 7, Being Lazy, on page 121), the computation can stop as soon as the first repeated letter is found, and the letters that follow don't have to be processed. We can achieve this by using the findFirst() method. Let's refactor the code by applying these ideas.

```
public char findIn(String word) {
  return Stream.of(word.split(""))
    .filter(letter -> word.lastIndexOf(letter) > word.indexOf(letter))
    .findFirst()
    .map(letter -> letter.charAt(0))
    .orElse('\0');
}
```

Once again the code is expressive, concise, and easy to read. If you prefer, you can move the lambda expression into a separate function, named isDuplicated(), to make the code a tad more readable.

The Stream API can be readily used to process a collection of data in memory. Next, we'll see how to deal with data that's in a file.

Refactoring File Processing

Reading data from a file is a common operation in programming and I'm sure you've done that countless number of times. But the code to perform that operation was rather verbose and messy in the past. Let's take a look at a function that reads the contents of a file and counts the number of occurrences of a word in it. Then we'll refactor to use the functional style.

Let's start with a small set of tests to verify that a countInFile() function works as expected:

refactoring/fpij/WordCountTest.java
```java
public class WordCountTest {
  WordCount wordCount;

  @BeforeEach
  public void init() {
    wordCount = new WordCount();
  }

  @Test
  public void count() {
    assertAll(
      () -> assertEquals(2,
        wordCount.countInFile("public", "fpij/WordCount.java")),
      () -> assertEquals(1,
        wordCount.countInFile("package", "fpij/WordCount.java"))

    );
  }
}
```

The tests illustrate that the method under test takes a search word and the path to the file to search in. Here's the imperative style code that's crying to be refactored:

refactoring/fpij/WordCount.java
```java
public class WordCount {
  public long countInFile(
    String searchWord, String filePath) throws IOException {

    long count = 0;

    BufferedReader bufferedReader =
      new BufferedReader(new FileReader(filePath));

    String line = null;

    while((line = bufferedReader.readLine()) != null) {
      String[] words = line.split(" ");

      for(String word: words) {
        if(word.equals(searchWord)) {
          count++;
        }
      }
    }

    return count;
  }
}
```

The function checks if there are more lines to read from the file by checking the content read against null—eek, that's rather unsightly. We need easier ways to read and process the contents of files and thankfully the JDK has newer functions that bring forward the charm of functional style for that.

Pause, refactor, and continue.

Given the contents of a file, we want to look for the number of occurrences of a word in it. we can use the filter operation to check if each word is what we're looking for, followed by a reduce operation to count the number of appearances. But, to take those steps, we need a stream of the contents of the file. The Files class in the JDK's java.nio.file package has the right function for it. The lines() method returns a Stream<String>, and we can apply our favorite Stream operations to process the contents of the file. Let's use that function to refactor the countInFile() method:

```
public long countInFile(
  String searchWord, String filePath) throws IOException {

  return Files.lines(Paths.get(filePath))
    .flatMap(line -> Stream.of(line.split(" ")))
    .filter(word -> word.equals(searchWord))
    .count();
```

The lines() method creates an internal iterator to work with one line of file contents at a time. But we need to work with the words in the file and not just the lines. We can call split() to break a line into words so that we can perform further processing on the words. Since splitting a line into words is a one-to-many mapping, we have to use flatMap() instead of map() to transform the data from a stream of lines to a stream of words—see When to Use map vs. flatMap, on page 72. Once we get the stream of words, we can filter and then finally count.

In addition to concise and expressive code, as a bonus, we don't have to mess with null and that's a big win in itself.

Next, we'll work with an example where the data is in a Map.

Refactoring Data Grouping Operations

Grouping data based on some criteria is a common operation in business applications. We may want to group employees based on their work location, projects based on their business units, products based on their latest revenues, and so on. Creating a Map for the group and adding values for its keys can get verbose in the imperative style and may also involve some inefficiencies. You'll see a stark contrast between the imperative style version of code that does such processing and its equivalent functional style code.

To gain insight into refactoring code that does grouping operations, we'll take a collection of hypothetical scores from a game, provided as key-value pairs of player names and scores. Let's start with some tests that verify that a function namesForScores() groups the data based on the scores and creates a list of names associated with for each store.

refactoring/fpij/ScoresTest.java
```
public class ScoresTest {
  Scores scores;

  @BeforeEach
  public void init() {
    scores = new Scores();
  }

  @Test
  public void namesForScores() {
    assertAll(
      () -> assertEquals(Map.of(), scores.namesForScores(Map.of())),
      () -> assertEquals(
        Map.of(1, Set.of("Jill")), scores.namesForScores(Map.of("Jill", 1))),
      () -> assertEquals(
        Map.of(1, Set.of("Jill"), 2, Set.of("Paul")),
          scores.namesForScores(Map.of("Jill", 1, "Paul", 2))),
      () -> assertEquals(
        Map.of(1, Set.of("Jill", "Kate"), 2, Set.of("Paul")),
          scores.namesForScores(Map.of("Jill", 1, "Paul", 2, "Kate", 1)))
    );
  }
}
```

To group the data based on the scores, we'll have to iterate over the given Map's key set. For each player, we check if their score value is already in the destination map. If it is, we add the name to the existing key's value set. If the score isn't already present as a key, then we create a new set with the name of the player and add the set as a value for the new key in the destination map. Here's the code that does those mundane operations:

refactoring/fpij/Scores.java
```
public class Scores {
  public Map<Integer, Set<String>> namesForScores(
    Map<String, Integer> scores) {

    Map<Integer, Set<String>> namesForScores = new HashMap<>();

    for(String name : scores.keySet()) {
      int score = scores.get(name);
```

```
    Set<String> names = new HashSet<>();
    if(namesForScores.containsKey(score)) {
      names = namesForScores.get(score);
    }

    names.add(name);
    namesForScores.put(score, names);
  }

  return namesForScores;
  }
}
```

Lots of garbage variables, explicit mutation, low-level operations, and the list goes on—shudder.

Pause, refactor, and continue.

The entire body of the namesForScores() method can be refactored to literally three lines of code:

```
public Map<Integer, Set<String>> namesForScores(
  Map<String, Integer> scores) {

  return scores.keySet()
    .stream()
    .collect(groupingBy(scores::get, toSet()));
}
```

We iterate over the key set using the stream() method and ask the values to be grouped based on the value of the score for each name. We then ask the names to be placed into a set, by providing the Collector returned by toSet() to the groupingBy() function. The code is shockingly potent.

Through each example, we've worked with increasing complexity, and each example has given a few new ideas to consider when refactoring to functional style. The next example, the last one in this refactoring series of tasks, has a nice added complexity and brings along a powerful set of solutions—let's take a look.

Refactoring Nested Loops

The imperative style code you see in this section was sent to me by a developer who was interested in applying functional programming and was curious to learn how to refactor it into the functional style. The code creates Pythagorean triples[1] of positive numbers (a, b, c) which satisfy the condition $a^2 + b^2 = c^2$.

---

1.   https://en.wikipedia.org/wiki/Pythagorean_triple

Let's start with a few tests to verify the results of the compute() method of a PythagoreanTriples class:

refactoring/fpij/PythagoreanTriplesTest.java
```java
public class PythagoreanTriplesTest {
  PythagoreanTriples pythagoreanTriples;

  @BeforeEach
  public void init() {
    pythagoreanTriples = new PythagoreanTriples();
  }

  @Test
  public void compute() {
    assertAll(
      () -> assertEquals(List.of(), pythagoreanTriples.compute(0)),
      () -> assertEquals(List.of(triple(3, 4, 5)),
        pythagoreanTriples.compute(1)),
      () -> assertEquals(
        List.of(triple(3, 4, 5), triple(8, 6, 10), triple(5, 12, 13)),
        pythagoreanTriples.compute(3)),
      () -> assertEquals(
        List.of(triple(3, 4, 5), triple(8, 6, 10),
                triple(5, 12, 13), triple(15, 8, 17),
                triple(12, 16, 20)),
        pythagoreanTriples.compute(5))
    );
  }
}
```

Next, an implementation of the compute() method using the imperative style:

refactoring/fpij/PythagoreanTriples.java
```java
record Triple(int a, int b, int c) {
  public static Triple triple(int a, int b, int c) {
    return new Triple(a, b, c);
  }

  public String toString() { return String.format("%d %d %d", a, b, c); }
}

public class PythagoreanTriples {
  public Triple getTripleEuclidsWay(int m, int n) {
    int a = m * m - n * n;
    int b = 2 * m * n;
    int c = m * m + n * n;

    return triple(a, b, c);
  }

  public List<Triple> compute(int numberOfValues) {
    if(numberOfValues == 0) {
      return List.of();
    }
```

```
    List<Triple> triples = new ArrayList<>();
    int count = 1;

    for(int m = 2; ; m++) {
      for(int n = 1; n < m; n++) {
        triples.add(getTripleEuclidsWay(m, n));
        count++;

        if(count > numberOfValues)
          break;
      }

      if(count > numberOfValues)
        break;
    }

    return triples;
  }
}
```

We store the Pythagorean triple values into a tuple represented by the Java Record named Triple. A static method triple() of the record is provided to help create an instance using triple(...) instead of new Triple(...), for the sake of a little fluency.

The getTripleEuclidsWay() method uses Euclid's algorithm to create a Pythagorean triple for the given positive values of m and n, where m > n.

The compute() method takes as a parameter the number of triple values we expect to be created. It then iterates over a value of m from 2 onwards. For values of n from 1 to m - 1, it uses the getTripleEuclidsWay() method to compute the desired number of triples.

In addition to the verbosity, the really smelly parts of the code are the two checks to see if the desired number of values has been computed.

Pause, refactor, and continue.

For every value of m we create many values of the triples. You got it; it's a one-to-many problem, and from our discussions in When to Use map vs. flatMap, on page 72, you know it's a problem that will benefit from flatMap(). Let's use that to refactor the code to the functional style:

```
public List<Triple> compute(int numberOfValues) {
  return Stream.iterate(2, e -> e + 1)
    .flatMap(m -> IntStream.range(1, m)
      .mapToObj(n -> getTripleEuclidsWay(m, n)))
    .limit(numberOfValues)
    .toList();
}
```

Sweet.

We create an unbounded/infinite stream of values for m, starting with 2. For each value of m, we then create a series of m - 1 triples. We finally ask the stream to limit the number of values to the desired value in the parameter numberOfValues and package the values into a list.

The biggest challenge in this code is recognizing it as a flatMap problem. Once we've done that, the rest is relatively simple to put in place.

Speaking of recognizing, let's discuss some common patterns we can lean on when refactoring real-world code.

Real-World Refactoring

The examples you've seen in this chapter may give you the confidence to refactor your own code in the applications you're working on. Code that we have to deal with in the real world, unfortunately, rarely appears as an amiable candidate for refactoring. The journey to refactor the code can be daunting and, at times, dissuading. The frustrations may lead us to feel hopeless and tempt us to throw in the towel. But remember that it doesn't have to be an all-or-nothing effort.

Big-bang refactoring may result in a big-bang failure. Instead, refactor incrementally. You can start by converting imperative loops into functional iterations using internal iterators like Stream, IntStream, and so on. The if conditions may be refactored into filter(), and the operations inside the loops may be refactored into map(). Such changes may help us to reduce some complexity in code, make it more readable, and move us further towards more functional style code. That may be still worth it, even if the code might not have transformed into the most elegant and fully functional style code, yet.

When you refactor code to functional style, look for some common patterns for refactoring. When you know the common patterns to map to, you can quickly identify suitable functions to use. See the table on page 203 for some functional style alternatives to common imperative style code constructs.

Use the table as a reference when refactoring code. As you move along, if you find other such patterns emerge from your code, jot them down and share them with your team to sweeten their journey.

We've covered a lot of ground refactoring common tasks. Each problem gave you the opportunity to explore a bit deeper into writing code using the functional style. Take a break; review and reflect on the examples before moving ahead to the next chapter.

Imperative Style	Functional Alternative
Regular for loop	range() or rangeClosed() of IntStream, LongStream, and so on
Irregular for loops	iterate() of Stream, IntStream, and so on
break from a loop	takeWhile()
for-each loop	Stream's of() or Collection's stream()
Nested loop	Stream's flatMap()
if block with continue	Stream's filter()
Accumulation of data	reduce(), collect, or a suitable specialized reduce like sum(), average(), and so on
Get a select number of matching values	limit() with filter()
Get a matching value	findFirst with filter() and optional use of skip() or dropWhile()
Short-circuiting loop with boolean result	anyMatch(), allMatch(), noneMatch()

Wrapping Up

We looked at a number of examples written in the imperative style and refactored them to the functional style. The first step in that journey is to think declaratively and then look for functions to realize the series of transformations into the functional style. Once you get a handle on the steps to take, look for functions (in the JDK) that you can delegate those steps to. Sometimes we'll have to step back and rethink the algorithm before refactoring code to the functional style. With practice, you'll get better and more comfortable and be on your way to reducing accidental complexity in legacy code.

In the next chapter we'll discuss several ways to write better-quality functional style code.

CHAPTER 12

Functional Programming Idioms

Cranking out code is easy, but creating maintainable code takes effort, discipline, diligence, and continuous review and refactoring. That's true for any paradigm, including functional programming.

Developers don't write bad code because they derive pleasure in seeing the team suffer. A few different forces influence poor practices.

Sometimes developers write code that's hard to maintain because they haven't developed a true sense of quality. They might have learned from poor examples and lacked much-needed peer reviews that would help them correct their course. Bad practices sadly may turn into patterns of programming for a team, and, although they suffer the consequences of poor code, they may not be able to recognize and change the habits that have been ingrained in them.

Other times developers write bad code because they may have a weak grasp of the actual, often vague, requirements. In that situation, they may quickly settle on solutions that they believe will deliver results but actually fall short of meeting the overall requirements. As a better understanding of the requirements gradually emerges, the developers have to continually keep fixing the code, which has already turned into cruft, a technical debt that will haunt them for a long time.

In this chapter we'll look at a few dos and don'ts for writing functional style code. We'll start with recommendations on how to properly write lambda expressions, and then we'll look at when to prefer method references instead of lambda expressions. We'll also properly structure functional pipelines, use good parameter names, use type inference, and avoid side effects in functional style code.

Some of the practices that I encourage in this chapter are cosmetic and impact the readability and maintainability of code. The effects of other practices are far-reaching and may affect the correctness of code.

Use the recommendations in this chapter as guidelines to examine your own code. Then use these to guide your team towards creating better quality code that's easier to maintain.

Don't Write Dense Lambda Expressions

It's easy to get carried away when writing code and lose sight of code quality. It's often not our fault. We're trying to understand the requirements, figure out possible solutions, try out different ideas, and sometimes struggle to get things working the way we want. After all, programming involves a series of mini-experiments where we turn a bunch of unknowns into knowns. In doing so, we're relieved to see that the code works, but we often forget the next step in the journey: taking the time to refactor in order to improve the quality of code.

A common poor practice among several developers is to write multiline lambda expressions. Avoid that as much as possible and make sincere efforts to refactor immediately if you find multiline lambda expressions.

Java provides a concise syntax for lambda expressions with a single-line body. It also permits us to write multiple lines for the body by placing them within the bounds of {}. Just because the compiler allows this, it doesn't mean we should allow such coding. Our wisdom should override here.

Functional style code's elegance, readability, and ease of understanding are all benefits that are lost when we write multiline lambda expressions.

Let's take a look at an example that illustrates this issue. Quick, take a glance at the next code and jot down what it does and how much time you take to figure that out:

```java
return LongStream.rangeClosed(1, number)
  .filter(i -> { //Bad Code, don't do this
    long factor = 0;

    for(int j = 1; j < i; j++) {
      if(i % j == 0) {
        factor += j;
      }
    }

    return factor == i;
  })
  .boxed()
  .toList();
```

We're iterating over a range of numbers starting from 1 and picking...what?!

Oh!

That delayed "Oh!" is a sign of poor quality code. The density of code within the lambda expression disrupted the flow and took our eyes away from the processing of the pipeline.

It's reasonable to wonder if the issue with the code is the embedded imperative style code, and if that were refactored to functional style, maybe it would be OK. Let's give that a shot.

```
return LongStream.range(1, number)
  .filter(i -> LongStream.range(1, i) //Not good
    .filter(j -> i % j == 0)
    .sum() == i)
  .boxed()
  .toList();
```

Treat lambda expressions as glue code. Two lines may be too many.

That's less clutter now, but the details within the filter still disrupted the flow. That's not good enough. Let's rework the code to improve the flow:

```
return LongStream.rangeClosed(1, number)
  .filter(i -> sumOfFactors(i) == i)
  .boxed()
  .toList();
```

Within the lambda expression passed to the filter() method, we have a single line of code that invokes a sumOfFactors()—the name of the method quickly reveals the intention, and you can move on to the next step. You can retain focus on the big picture—the flow through the pipeline.

In addition to improving the flow, giving a name for the calculation makes the code modular and helps it to adhere to the Single Level of Abstraction Principle (SLAP). The reader of the code can think about what the sum of factors means without having to read the implementation of the calculation code. There is another benefit of extracting the calculation code into a separate method, sumOfFactors(), instead of embedding it into code that needs the result of its calculation. The calculation code can now be tested and validated directly for correctness without dealing with the code where the result of the calculation was used.

If the lambda expression disrupts the flow of thought or can be extracted into a method for better readability and reasoning, refactor it and move the body to a separate function. Keep the lambda expressions as a one-liner. Make sure that the code doesn't require the readers' excessive concentration or attention.

As a quick exercise, take a moment to revisit the code that computed the Pythagorean triples in Refactoring Nested Loops, on page 199 and refactor the functional style code to make the lambda expression adhere to the guideline we just discussed.

In addition to improving the quality of code, keeping the lambda expressions short may also help to rework them into a method reference, especially if they turn into lambdas that only pass through their parameters. Let's explore that next.

Prefer Method References

Short lambda expressions are great, but they still require human eyes to parse through them to find out what they're doing. If we can replace a lambda expression, where possible, with a method reference, the code becomes ultimately more readable and concise—see Using Method References, on page 25. The method names make the overall functional pipeline clearer from the context than the corresponding lambdas. Using method references makes it easier to look at the code and be confident about its intent, and takes less mental effort to maintain the code.

Prefer method references over lambda expressions where it's possible to replace the latter with the former. The following code uses lambda expressions in each stage of the Stream pipeline:

```
drivers.stream()
  .filter(driver -> driver.getAge() > 21)
  .filter(driver -> driver.isDriversLicenseValid())
  .map(driver -> driver.getPrimaryCar())
  .map(car -> car.getRegistration())
  .forEach(registration -> System.out.println(registration));
```

The lambda expressions are short one-liners, but we can replace the lambdas that merely pass through their parameters with method references. On each line, we have a small change and a resulting small benefit to the reader of the code. But when multiple lines of code are involved, the small benefits add up, as we see in this refactored code:

```
drivers.stream()
  .filter(driver -> driver.getAge() > 21)
  .filter(Driver::isDriversLicenseValid)
  .map(Driver::getPrimaryCar)
  .map(Car::getRegistration)
  .forEach(System.out::println);
```

The method references version is certainly clearer, less noisy, easier to read, and easier to think about, demanding less mental effort compared to the version that uses lambda expressions.

Don't go out of your way to bring in method references. For example, we leave the lambda expression passed to the first filter as is. There is no real benefit to rolling that into a function and then passing a reference to it. But, if a lambda is merely passing through the parameters and can possibly be replaced with a method reference, grab that opportunity.

Properly Structure the Functional Pipeline

In the projects that you've worked on, have you ever seen code written like the following?

```
//Please don't do this
names.stream().filter(name -> name.length() == 4).map(String::toUpperCase)...
```

I ask that question in the classes I teach for professional software developers and sadly I get a rather high percentage of "yes" answers.

Encourage your developers to change that practice. If you place multiple functions (like filter() and map()) on the same line, it increases the cognitive load. It makes the code hard to read and hard to understand. And, if we have to make changes, it takes more effort as well.

Ask your fellow developers to line up dots vertically, like so:

```
names.stream()
  .filter(name -> name.length() == 4)
  .map(String::toUpperCase)
  .forEach(System.out::println);
```

With this structure it's easy to get a good glimpse at the big picture of the overall steps taken by the pipeline. It's also effortless to make changes to any single stage in the pipeline. This structure also makes it a lot easier to add or remove a stage from the pipeline compared to the previous poorly structured code.

Vertically aligning the dots is the preferred convention for Java code, and IDEs have settings that support this structure. Make sure to configure your IDE to follow this structure and use the IDE shortcuts to easily format your code appropriately.

Keep Separate Conditions in Separate Filters

A common question I hear from developers is "should I write multiple filters with one condition each or one filter with multiple conditions?" The short and quick answer is to use multiple filter() calls with one condition each.

Consider the following code:

```
drivers.stream()
    .filter(driver -> driver.getAge() > 21 && driver.isDriversLicenseValid())
    //Please don't code like the previous line
    .map(driver -> driver.getPrimaryCar())
    .map(car -> car.getRegistration())
    .forEach(registration -> System.out.println(registration));
```

The lambda expression passed to the filter() method does two separate checks: if the driver is more than 21 years old and if the driver has a valid driver's license. Two conditions in one filter().

Many programmers are tempted to code that way with the perception that somehow merging the conditions into one will give a significant performance gain; it doesn't. In Intermediate and Terminal Operations, on page 129 we discussed that methods like filter() are intermediate operations, and they aren't executed right away. Internally, the intermediate stages in the functional pipeline are fused together into one operation under the hood and evaluated only when a terminal operation is invoked. Thus, whether we write the conditions into one call to filter() or into multiple calls with one condition each, the real optimization happens under the hood and isn't based on the way we write the function. We don't gain any performance benefit by writing multiple conditions in one lambda expression.

Let's take the previous code and rewrite it using two filter() calls instead of one:

```
drivers.stream()
    .filter(driver -> driver.getAge() > 21)
    .filter(Driver::isDriversLicenseValid)
    .map(Driver::getPrimaryCar)
    .map(Car::getRegistration)
    .forEach(System.out::println);
```

That looks a lot better than the previous version. Also, we managed to use a method reference in the second filter().

The version with multiple filter() calls with one condition each has some serious benefits. First, it doesn't have any issues with performance, so we can set aside that fear. Second, the code is less noisy and much easier to read than the other version. Each line of code is very cohesive, does only one thing, and focuses on one condition. It's much easier to add a new condition—add a filter() —without having to mess with one large condition. If we want to try out different behaviors by changing conditions, it's as trivial as commenting a filter() line. It's also really easy to remove a condition. Finally, keeping the conditions small increases the opportunities to use method references, which can further improve readability.

Let's summarize the reasons to keep the conditions separate:

- The code is as performant as if we combined the conditions
- The code is less noisy
- The code is easier to read
- The code is easier to maintain
- It's easier to use method references to further improve readability
- It provides opportunities for further simplification

The code version with multiple filter() calls with one condition is cohesive, easy to write, easy to read, easy to add or remove conditions, and overall much better compared to the other option, and it is the preferred way.

Provide Good Domain-Specific Parameter Names

We write code once but read and change it many times, sometimes thousands of times. The considerations for the ease and cost of reading the code should outweigh those for writing the code the first time.

You've probably seen your share of poor names for lambda parameters. For some reason, x seems to be one of the most favorite bad names for parameters. Other poor choices seem to include p, k, and so on, with the worst offender being l—is it the number 1 or the letter l, the reader may wonder. It's likely that programmers picked up such practices from an example in a presentation, a book (such as this one), or a blog post. Whereas these short, cryptic names may be suitable for a quick example, unfortunately, such names don't help a team maintain production code.

A team who's in the practice of using meaningless variable names may create code like the following:

```
drivers.stream()
  .filter(x -> x.getAge() > 21) //Please avoid meaningless parameter names
  .filter(x -> x.isDriversLicenseValid())
  .map(x -> x.getPrimaryCar())
  .map(c -> c.getRegistration())
  .forEach(r -> System.out.println(r));
```

I have a theory about how these poor names creep into the code: maybe it's not the programmers who key them in. When they're momentarily distracted, their kitten pounces on the keyboard. How would anyone have the heart to change the variable names so purr-fectly chosen by Kitty?

Poor variables make the code hard to understand, which makes fixing the code rather an unpleasant and frustrating experience at the critical moments of fixing errors.

Resist the urge to give single-letter, meaningless variables. Instead, give domain-specific names for lambda parameters. The goal isn't to give lengthy names—they're as bad as the cryptic ones. Instead, choose a short name that clearly conveys what that variable represents. For example, instead of using x, d, c, and so on, we can write the previous code with descriptive names, like so:

```
drivers.stream()
  .filter(driver -> driver.getAge() > 21)
  .filter(driver -> driver.isDriversLicenseValid())
  .map(driver -> driver.getPrimaryCar())
  .map(car -> car.getRegistration())
  .forEach(registration -> System.out.println(registration));
```

Make giving good names a habit. Help your team refactor code that has poor names for parameters of lambda expressions. Cajole and coach them until they naturally start writing good parameter names. Continue to keep an eye on the names during code reviews.

Use Type Inference for Parameters

Traditionally, in Java we're used to specifying the types of parameters. Starting with version 8, the language has been leaning more toward type inference. The Java compiler is smart enough to determine the type of the lambda expression parameters in most situations. That means less typing on the keyboard but without compromising type safety in code.

Many programmers who've been coding in Java for a long time, and especially those who mostly don't program in other languages as well, are often reluctant to use type inference. They feel comfortable when the types of the lambda expression parameters are specified and get frustrated reading code where the types aren't specified.

You can leverage the type inference capability of Java. The context in which the code is written often provides enough details about the type of the parameters. Combining that with good domain-specific names for the parameters often makes it easier to understand the code.

Suppose a programmer is comfortable writing the following code:

```
...
.filter((Driver x) -> x.getAge() > 21)
...
```

Encourage them to give a better name to the parameter and drop the type. As a bonus, you can drop the parentheses around the parameter as well if the lambda expression takes only one parameter.

```
...
.filter(driver -> driver.getAge() > 21)
...
```

Get used to using type inference for lambda expression parameters and provide domain-specific names for parameter names. If the code reads equally well or better without the type, but with well-chosen parameter names, leave the type out.

Side Effects in Functional Pipelines

A common mistake many programmers make is mutating shared variables from the functional pipeline. That's a big *no-no*.

Purely functional programming languages, like Haskell, don't permit mutability. The compilers of such languages will disallow writing code, let alone lambda expressions that mutate data. Java is a hybrid language and the functional programming capabilities were added almost two decades after the language was created. Thus, the compiler for the most part won't complain if it finds impure lambda expressions—but we should.

A programmer once emailed me a snippet of code that had been working fine, but its behavior had become rather unpredictable after the most recent change they had made. They wanted another pair of eyes to look into the issue. A quick glance through the code revealed the culprit. In the last step of the functional pipeline, in the forEach(), they added the result to a collection defined outside the functional pipeline. The code seemed OK until the last change where they converted the call to stream() to a call to parallelStream() instead. In the multithreaded scenario, the code was running into race conditions and some data was missing from the result.

A lambda expression is impure if it modifies an externally visible variable. It's also impure if it depends on an external variable that may possibly change. In other words, a pure lambda expression does no evil—that is mutate—and also sees no evil.

Parallel execution isn't the only situation that will run into issues with impure lambda expressions. Even sequential execution will cause confusion due to lazy evaluation. Let's dig into this to see the issue in action.

Suppose we have a lambda expression that depends on a field in a class. The field isn't defined final and, furthermore, it's modified in the run() method. Let's take a look at the code:

```java
public class Impure {
  private int factor = 2;

  public void run() {
    var numbers = List.of(1, 2, 3);

    var stream = numbers.stream()
      .map(number -> number * factor);

    factor = 0;

    stream.forEach(System.out::println);
  }
  public static void main(String[] args) {
    new Impure().run();
  }
}
```

In the run() method we iterate over a list of numbers and, using the Stream pipeline, transform the data into a product of the number and the value in the factor field. Then, before the execution of the final step in the stream, we set the value of the factor variable to 0.

Show the code to different colleagues and ask them what the output will be. There is a large chance that the responses may not be consistent. Some may say the output will be the double of the values in the list. Some may say the result will be all zeros. Some may protest that they have no clue. The answer depends on the language and the semantics of the functional pipeline as implemented in that language. Thus, the confusion by some programmers is justified, they're probably polyglot programmers.

The result produced by the previous Java code is:

```
0
0
0
```

The transformation in the lambda expression passed to the map() method isn't executed until the terminal operation, forEach(), is invoked. By that time, the value of the field factor has been modified. Thus the transformation isn't based on the value at the time the control passes over that stage, but it is based on the state at the time of execution. At best this can be confusing and at worst the results can be unpredictable and hard to debug.

Functional programming relies on lazy evaluation for efficiency and makes it incredibly easy to parallelize code. Both lazy evaluation and parallel execution rely on the purity of lambda expressions, with no side effects, for correctness.

Thoroughly review code and make sure lambdas are pure. Purity helps you think about what the code does.

Wrapping Up

In spite of the elegant, concise, and fluent nature of the functional style, some developers often write code that's hard to understand. The result of that is counter to what the paradigm is intended for.

As a fellow developer, take the time to encourage your team to practice good coding habits. In this chapter we discussed multiple things we have to keep an eye on as a team to make sure the functional style code is both less error-prone and easier to understand, read, analyze, and maintain. Show your empathy to fellow developers and follow these idioms to get the most out of this amazing programming paradigm.

In the next chapter we wrap up with a discussion about making good use of the functional style and address some limitations.

CHAPTER 13

Bringing It All Together

We explored Java lambda expressions throughout this book, using them to iterate over collections, achieve better lightweight design, and easily compose and parallelize code. In this final chapter we'll bring it all together. We'll review the practices we have to hone to fully benefit from the functional style, then discuss the performance impact of this style, and conclude with some recommendations on how we can successfully adopt the functional style.

Essential Practices to Succeed with the Functional Style

The functional features in Java don't just change the syntax we type. To benefit fully from these features and create highly concise and lightweight applications, we need to change the designs, the code, and our thinking; it's different from the imperative and object-oriented paradigm we're used to in Java. Let's go over some of the fundamental ways we have to change how we develop applications and the benefits we'll receive in return.

More Declarative, Less Imperative

We have to raise the level of abstraction. Rather than imperatively focusing on the steps to take, we have to think and express declaratively the bigger goals we want to achieve. For example, instead of commanding the computer to step through each element in a collection, we ask it to filter out the elements we want or to map or transform one collection into yet another collection. This can help take the "Tell, Don't Ask" principle further and make the code more concise and expressive.[1]

---

1. http://pragprog.com/articles/tell-dont-ask

For example, let's say we're given a list of stock prices and asked to pick the maximum value. From experience, our first instinct may be to write it imperatively like this:

```
int max = 0;
for(int price : prices) {
  if(max < price) max = price;
}
```

Instead, let's think declaratively. We'll tell the program to pick the max rather than ask it to walk through each step:

```
final int max = prices.stream()
                      .reduce(0, Math::max);
```

The benefits go far beyond having fewer lines of code. We have fewer chances to introduce errors—the code we don't write has the fewest bugs. Having fewer lines of understandable code is simpler than many lines of fluffy code.

Imperative code is primitive and involves more mutability. On the other hand, declarative code raises the level of abstraction and reduces the need for mutable variables. This also lowers the chances of errors in code.

Favor Immutability

Mutable variables are in poor taste, and shared mutable variables are pure evil. We often get confused or overlook changes to variables. As a result, code with more mutable variables tends to have more errors. Code with shared mutable variables is hard to parallelize correctly. One way to reduce errors is simply to avoid mutability where possible, and the functional style makes that easier.

Purely functional languages have only values: write-once variables that can't change after initialization. Since Java doesn't enforce immutability, the onus is on us to favor immutability. When we encounter mutable variables, we can examine the libraries to see if there's a functional-style equivalent that will eliminate them.

Reduce Side Effects

A function with no side effects neither affects nor is affected by anything outside of its bounds. Functions or methods with side effects are hard to understand, hard to maintain, more error-prone, and difficult to parallelize.

If we remove side effects, then as long as the input to a function remains unchanged, the output will always be the same. This makes it easier to understand the code and makes us need fewer test cases to ensure the proper behavior.

Having no side effects is critical for *referential transparency*, which means an invocation or a call to a function can be replaced by its result value without affecting a program's correctness. The functional style greatly favors creating functions with no side effects, and the benefits are far-reaching.

The javac compiler and the JVM just-in-time compiler can easily optimize calls to functions with no side effects. Functions that have side effects impose ordering and restrict optimization. On the other hand, calls to functions with no side effects can be moved around and reordered more freely. For example, in the following figure, F_1 and F_2 are two independent function calls. The compiler can change the order of their sequential execution or even schedule them to run concurrently on multiple cores thanks to their referential transparent behavior.

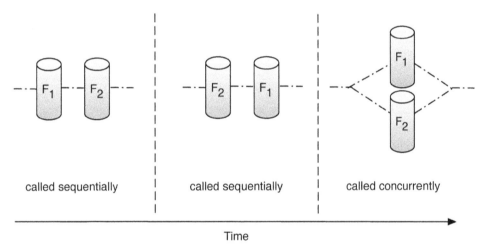

When working with lambda expressions, we should ensure that the code is without side effects. Doing so not only reduces the chance of errors but also helps us easily parallelize the code, as we saw in Taking a Leap to Parallelize, on page 163. It's critical to eliminate side effects if we want to use techniques like the tail-call optimization we saw in Using Tail-Call Optimization, on page 139.

Prefer Expressions over Statements

Both expressions and statements are commands we write in programs to instruct the computer to perform some action or do some work. Statements perform actions but don't return anything, whereas expressions perform actions and return a result. When programming with lambda expressions, we can reap benefits by leaning toward creating expressions more than statements.

First, since statements don't return anything, they have to cause side effects and mutate memory to fulfill their purpose. Expressions, on the other hand, can be designed to favor referential transparency, giving us the benefits we discussed previously.

The other benefit is that, unlike statements, expressions can be composed. This can help us use a powerful pattern in the functional style of programming —function chaining. We can create a chain of functions so the results of computations flow smoothly from one function into the next. The code begins to read like the problem statement, making it easier to follow.

We saw a benefit of this in ...To the Functional Style, on page 161, where we sent a list of stock-ticker symbols through a chain of functions to determine the highest-priced stock and its price. This pattern can also help us create fluent interfaces, as we saw in Creating Fluent Interfaces Using Lambda Expressions, on page 103.

Design with Higher-Order Functions

In Java, one of the biggest changes we have to make is to design with higher-order functions. We're used to passing objects to methods, but now we also have the ability to pass functions as arguments. This gives us more concise code: anywhere we passed anonymous inner classes to single-method interfaces, we can now pass lambda expressions or method references.

For example, to register a simple event handler for a Swing button, we had to jump through hoops before, as in the next example.

```
button.addActionListener(new ActionListener() {
  public void actionPerformed(ActionEvent event) {
    JOptionPane.showMessageDialog(frame, "you clicked!");
  }
});
```

We can trade such clunky code in for more concise code, like this:

```
button.addActionListener(event ->
  JOptionPane.showMessageDialog(frame, "you clicked!"));
```

The ceremony and the clutter are gone, leaving behind just the essence. Not only did we write fewer lines of code here but also needed fewer imports in the code. That's because we no longer have to refer to the ActionListener interface by name, and the reference to ActionEvent is optional since we used type inference.

Once we get used to lambda expressions, they will have a lot of impact on our designs. We can design our methods to receive functional interfaces as parameters. This will enable the callers to pass in either lambda expressions or method references as arguments, which will help us take a lightweight approach to separating concerns from methods and classes, as we discussed in Chapter 5, Designing with Lambda Expressions, on page 85. The common, familiar design patterns are more approachable when we design with lambda expressions; we need fewer lines of code, classes, and interfaces, and far less ceremony to implement our designs.

Performance Concerns

Java has come a long way and is used in a vast number of enterprise applications where performance is critical. It's reasonable to ask whether the functional features will affect performance. The answer is yes, and mostly for the better!

Before we dig into that, let's recall Donald Knuth's wise words: "We should forget about small efficiencies, say about 97% of the time: premature optimization is the root of all evil."[2] With that in mind, we should boldly try out the new style where it makes sense. If the performance we get is adequate for the needs of the application, we can move on. Otherwise, we have to critically evaluate the design and profile the code to figure out the real bottlenecks.

The Java specification provides a great amount of flexibility to facilitate compiler optimizations. In addition, to provide better support for lambda expressions, the JVM bytecode instruction set has been enhanced with invokedynamic pseudocode (see Brian Goetz's JavaOne 2012 presentation "Lambda: A Peek under the Hood")[3] that efficiently handles method call dispatching. This eliminates the need to create anonymous inner classes, and invocations of lambda expressions turn into mere method call invocations—see A Little Sugar to Sweeten, on page 15. This can make calls using lambda expressions fast and also eases the burden on garbage collection. Let's examine the performance improvements we can achieve.

Here's the imperative code to count the number of primes in a collection of numbers.

---

2. http://c2.com/cgi/wiki?PrematureOptimization
3. https://www.youtube.com/watch?v=C_QbkGU_lqY

```
long primesCount = 0;
for(long number : numbers) {
  if(isPrime(number)) primesCount += 1;
}
```

We're using the habitual for loop to invoke a method isPrime() to determine if each number in the collection is prime. If a number is prime, we increment the primesCount mutable variable. Let's measure the time to run this code for a large collection, say 100,000 numbers.

```
0.0250944 seconds
```

That took about 0.02 seconds, but the code is in the style we want to curtail; let's see if the new style we want to adopt will stand up to this performance. Let's refactor that code to our favorite functional style: code that's declarative, is created in favor of immutability, has no side effects, and is composed of higher-order functions chained together.

```
final long primesCount =
  numbers.stream()
        .filter(number -> isPrime(number))
        .count();
```

We transformed the collection into a Stream and then used the filter() method to pick only primes from the collection. Then we got the size of the filtered collection. In essence, we asked the code to filter out just the primes in the collection. Let's see how much time this version takes to run on the same collection the previous version ran on.

```
0.0253816 seconds
```

From the output we see that the performance using lambda expression is about the same; we didn't lose anything, but we've gained quite a bit. It's trivial to parallelize the functional-style version. To parallelize the imperative version, on the other hand, we have to...um...that's a slippery slope we want to avoid.

Let's waste no time. Here's the parallelized functional-style version:

```
final long primesCount =
  numbers.parallelStream()
        .filter(number -> isPrime(number))
        .count();
```

That was hardly any effort. Let's see the gain in speed by running the code.

```
0.00649266 seconds
```

The parallelized version, running on a quad-core processor, took about 0.006 seconds.

Before we run off to celebrate this glorious performance, let's admit that a large number of performance metrics are contrived, and we can't blindly rely on them. If nothing else, this example simply shows that using lambda expressions and the functional style doesn't have to mean poor performance. When creating real code for enterprise applications, we have to keep an eye on performance and address concerns where they arise.

Adopting the Functional Style

Picking up new syntax is relatively easy, but changing the way we design and think takes more effort. Programming in the functional style in Java is a paradigm shift, and we've seen examples that show this change is good. Here are a few ways in which we can make an easy and successful transition to this exciting functional world in Java.

Following a few practices we discussed in Essential Practices to Succeed with the Functional Style, on page 217, will help us get better at functional-style coding. Java is now a mixed-paradigm language with support for imperative, object-oriented, and functional programming. We have to judiciously balance them, but the ability to do so comes from experience, trying out designs, and evaluating the trade-offs.

At the beginning of the transition to this paradigm, it's quite natural to continue to think in the most familiar ways. That's fine; we can implement and quickly refactor the code; "Make it work, then make it better real soon" is a good mantra to follow. With experience, the need for these refactoring efforts will diminish and more functional-style code will flow more naturally.

To get better at what we do, we have to be willing to change our ways. This means we have to fearlessly try out our ideas and then improve them based on feedback from our colleagues. We can benefit a great deal from tactical code reviews, pair-programming sessions, and brown-bag sessions at work. Outside of work, special-interest groups like local Java user groups are great places for us to expand our knowledge. We can participate in local study groups or help organize one if none exist.

Java and lambda expressions have improved and will continue to improve the way we develop software. These powerful features have breathed new life into today's most popular language. It's an exciting time to be a programmer.

Program well, and in style.

Starter Set of Functional Interfaces

The JDK has a number of functional interfaces. Here we review the starter set—the interfaces we frequently encounter and need to get familiar with. All the interfaces we see here are part of the java.util.function package.

Consumer<T>

Description	Represents an operation that will accept an input and returns nothing. For this to be useful, it'll have to cause side effects.
Abstract method	accept()
default method(s)	andThen()
Popular usage	As a parameter to the forEach() method
Primitive specializations	IntConsumer, LongConsumer, DoubleConsumer...

Supplier<T>

Description	A factory that's expected to return either a new instance or a pre-created instance
Abstract method	get()
default method(s)	—
Popular usage	To create lazy infinite Streams and as the parameter to the Optional class's orElseGet() method
Primitive specializations	IntSupplier, LongSupplier, DoubleSupplier...

Predicate<T>

Description	Useful for checking if an input argument satisfies some condition
Abstract method	test()
default method(s)	and(), negate(), and or()
Popular usage	As a parameter to Stream's methods, like filter() and anyMatch()
Primitive specializations	IntPredicate, LongPredicate, DoublePredicate...

Function<T, R>

Description	A transformational interface that represents an operation intended to take in an argument and return an appropriate result
Abstract method	apply()
default method(s)	andThen(), compose()
Popular usage	As a parameter to Stream's map() method
Primitive specializations	IntFunction, LongFunction, DoubleFunction, IntToDoubleFunction, DoubleToIntFunction...

Syntax Overview

We've played with the new syntax for functional interfaces, lambda expressions, method references, and constructor references throughout this book. This appendix is a quick reference for syntax, using sample code selected from various parts of the book.

Defining a Functional Interface

```
@FunctionalInterface
public interface TailCall<T> {

  TailCall<T> apply();

  default boolean isComplete() { return false; }
  //...
}
```

A functional interface must have one abstract—unimplemented—method. It may have zero or more default or implemented methods. It may also have static methods.

Creating No-Parameter Lambda Expressions

```
lazyEvaluator(() -> evaluate(1), () -> evaluate(2));
```

The parentheses () around the empty parameters list are required if the lambda expression takes no parameters. The -> separates the parameters from the body of a lambda expression.

Creating a Single-Parameter Lambda Expression

```
friends.forEach((final String name) -> System.out.println(name));
```

The Java compiler can infer the type of lambda expression based on the context. In some situations where the context isn't adequate for it to infer or we want better clarity, we can specify the type in front of the parameter names.

Inferring a Lambda Expression's Parameter Type

```
friends.forEach((name) -> System.out.println(name));
```

The Java compiler will try to infer the types for parameters if we don't provide them. Using inferred types is less noisy and requires less effort, but if we specify the type for one parameter, we have to specify it for all parameters in a lambda expression.

Dropping Parentheses for a Single-Parameter Inferred Type

```
friends.forEach(name -> System.out.println(name));
```

The parentheses () around the parameter are optional if the lambda expression takes only one parameter and its type is inferred. We could write name -> ... or (name) -> ...; lean toward using the first since it's less noisy.

Creating a Multi-Parameter Lambda Expression

```
friends.stream()
    .reduce((name1, name2) ->
        name1.length() >= name2.length() ? name1 : name2);
```

The parentheses () around the parameter list are required if the lambda expression takes multiple parameters or no parameters.

Calling a Method with Mixed Parameters

```
friends.stream()
    .reduce("Steve", (name1, name2) ->
        name1.length() >= name2.length() ? name1 : name2);
```

Methods can have a mixture of regular classes, primitive types, and functional interfaces as parameters. Any parameter of a method may be a functional interface, and we can send a lambda expression or a method reference as an argument in its place.

Storing a Lambda Expression

```
final Predicate<String> startsWithN = name -> name.startsWith("N");
```

To aid reuse and avoid duplication, we often want to store lambda expressions in variables.

Creating a Multiline Lambda Expression

```
FileWriterEAM.use("eam2.txt", writerEAM -> {
    writerEAM.writeStuff("how");
    writerEAM.writeStuff("sweet");
  });
```

We should keep the lambda expressions short, but it's easy to sneak in a few lines of code. We have to pay penance by using curly braces {}, and the return keyword is required if the lambda expression is expected to return a value.

Returning a Lambda Expression

```
public static Predicate<String> checkIfStartsWith(final String letter) {
  return name -> name.startsWith(letter);
}
```

If a method's return type is a functional interface, we can return a lambda expression from within its implementation.

Returning a Lambda Expression from a Lambda Expression

```
final Function<String, Predicate<String>> startsWithLetter =
  letter -> name -> name.startsWith(letter);
```

We can build lambda expressions that themselves return lambda expressions. The implementation of the Function interface here takes in a String letter and returns a lambda expression that conforms to the Predicate interface.

Lexical Scoping in Closures

```
public static Predicate<String> checkIfStartsWith(final String letter) {
  return name -> name.startsWith(letter);
}
```

From within a lambda expression, we can access variables that are in the enclosing method's scope. For example, the variable letter in the checkIfStartsWith() is accessed within the lambda expression. Lambda expressions that bind to variables in enclosing scopes are called *closures*.

Passing a Method Reference of an Instance Method

```
friends.stream()
       .map(String::toUpperCase);
```

We can replace a lambda expression with a method reference if it directly routes the parameter as a target to a simple method call. The preceding sample code is equivalent to this:

```
friends.stream()
       .map(name -> name.toUpperCase());
```

Passing a Method Reference to a static Method

```
str.chars()
   .filter(Character::isDigit);
```

We can replace a lambda expression with a method reference if it directly routes the parameter as an argument to a static method. The preceding sample code is equivalent to this:

```
str.chars()
   .filter(ch -> Character.isDigit(ch));
```

Passing a Method Reference to a Method on Another Instance

```
str.chars()
   .forEach(System.out::println);
```

We can replace a lambda expression with a method reference if it directly routes the parameter as an argument to a method on another instance; for example, println() on System.out. The preceding sample code is equivalent to this:

```
str.chars()
    .forEach(ch -> System.out.println(ch));
```

Passing a Reference of a Method That Takes Parameters

```
people.stream()
      .sorted(Person::ageDifference)
```

We can replace a lambda expression with a method reference if it directly routes the first parameter as a target of a method call and the remaining parameters as this method's arguments. The preceding sample code is equivalent to this:

```
people.stream()
      .sorted((person1, person2) -> person1.ageDifference(person2))
```

Using a Constructor Reference

```
Supplier<Heavy> supplier = Heavy::new;
```

Instead of invoking a constructor, we can ask the Java compiler to create the calls to the appropriate constructor from the concise constructor-reference syntax. These work much like method references, except they refer to a constructor and result in object instantiation. The preceding sample code is equivalent to this:

```
Supplier<Heavy> supplier = () -> new Heavy();
```

Function Composition

```
symbols.map(StockUtil::getPrice)
      .filter(StockUtil.isPriceLessThan(500))
      .reduce(StockUtil::pickHigh)
      .get();
```

We can compose functions to transform objects through a series of operations like in this example. In the functional style of programming, function composition or chaining is a powerful construct to implement associative operations.

Web Resources

Cutting-stock problem ———————— http://en.wikipedia.org/wiki/Cutting_stock_problem
An optimization problem that can use the memoization technique.

Dependency inversion principle —— http://c2.com/cgi/wiki?DependencyInversionPrinciple
Describes a way to realize extensibility by coupling a class to an abstraction
(interface) rather than to its implementation.

Don't Repeat Yourself ———————— http://c2.com/cgi/wiki?DontRepeatYourself
I'll let the reader refer to that URL, in the spirit of DRY.

***Execute around method* pattern** ——— http://c2.com/cgi/wiki?ExecuteAroundMethod
Describes a pattern to control the flow of logic through pre- and post-opera-
tions.

"Lambda: A Peek under the Hood" —— https://www.youtube.com/watch?v=C_QbkGU_lqY
A presentation by Brian Goetz.

Loan pattern —————————————— https://wiki.scala-lang.org/display/SYGN/Loan
A discussion of the loan pattern in Scala.

MapReduce ———————————— http://research.google.com/archive/mapreduce.html
"MapReduce: Simplified Data Processing on Large Clusters"—a paper by Jeffrey
Dean and Sanjay Ghemawat that discusses this programming model.

Open/closed principle ——————— http://en.wikipedia.org/wiki/Open/closed_principle
Describes Bertrand Meyer's open/closed principle, which states that software
modules must be open for extension, but without having to go through a code
change.

Premature optimization _____ http://c2.com/cgi/wiki?PrematureOptimization
A web page that discusses the perils of premature optimization.

Tell, Don't Ask _____ http://pragprog.com/articles/tell-dont-ask
A column that discusses the "Tell, Don't Ask" principle.

"Test Driving Multithreaded Code" _____ http://tinyurl.com/ab5up2w
Code samples from a presentation on unit testing for thread safety. The direct
URL is https://www.agiledeveloper.com/presentations/TestDrivingMultiThreadedCode.zip.

Web page for this book _____ http://www.pragprog.com/titles/vsjava2e
This book's web page, with full source-code listings.

Bibliography

[AS96]   Harold Abelson and Gerald Jay Sussman. *Structure and Interpretation of Computer Programs*. MIT Press, Cambridge, MA, 2nd, 1996.

[Blo18]   Joshua Bloch. *Effective Java, Third Edition*. Addison-Wesley, Boston, MA, 2018.

[GHJV95]   Erich Gamma, Richard Helm, Ralph Johnson, and John Vlissides. *Design Patterns: Elements of Reusable Object-Oriented Software*. Addison-Wesley, Boston, MA, 1995.

[Goe06]   Brian Goetz. *Java Concurrency in Practice*. Addison-Wesley, Boston, MA, 2006.

[HT00]   Andrew Hunt and David Thomas. *The Pragmatic Programmer: From Journeyman to Master*. Addison-Wesley, Boston, MA, 2000.

[Sub11]   Venkat Subramaniam. *Programming Concurrency on the JVM*. The Pragmatic Bookshelf, Raleigh, NC, 2011.

[Zin01]   William Zinsser. *On Writing Well, 25th Anniversary: The Classic Guide to Writing Nonfiction*. HarperResource, New York, NY, 2001.

Index

Thank you!

We hope you enjoyed this book and that you're already thinking about what you want to learn next. To help make that decision easier, we're offering you this gift.

Head on over to https://pragprog.com right now, and use the coupon code BUYANOTHER2023 to save 30% on your next ebook. Offer is void where prohibited or restricted. This offer does not apply to any edition of the *The Pragmatic Programmer* ebook.

And if you'd like to share your own expertise with the world, why not propose a writing idea to us? After all, many of our best authors started off as our readers, just like you. With up to a 50% royalty, world-class editorial services, and a name you trust, there's nothing to lose. Visit https://pragprog.com/become-an-author/ today to learn more and to get started.

We thank you for your continued support, and we hope to hear from you again soon!

The Pragmatic Bookshelf

Programming Kotlin

Programmers don't just use Kotlin, they love it. Even Google has adopted it as a first-class language for Android development. With Kotlin, you can intermix imperative, functional, and object-oriented styles of programming and benefit from the approach that's most suitable for the problem at hand. Learn to use the many features of this highly concise, fluent, elegant, and expressive statically typed language with easy-to-understand examples. Learn to write maintainable, high-performing JVM and Android applications, create DSLs, program asynchronously, and much more.

Venkat Subramaniam
(460 pages) ISBN: 9781680506358. $51.95
https://pragprog.com/book/vskotlin

Pragmatic Scala

Our industry is moving toward functional programming, but your object-oriented experience is still valuable. Scala combines the power of OO and functional programming, and *Pragmatic Scala* shows you how to work effectively with both. Updated to Scala 2.11, with in-depth coverage of new features such as Akka actors, parallel collections, and tail call optimization, this book will show you how to create stellar applications.

Venkat Subramaniam
(286 pages) ISBN: 9781680500547. $36
https://pragprog.com/book/vsscala2

Functional Programming Patterns in Scala and Clojure

Solve real-life programming problems with a fraction of the code that pure object-oriented programming requires. Use Scala and Clojure to solve in-depth problems and see how familiar object-oriented patterns can become more concise with functional programming and patterns. Your code will be more declarative, with fewer bugs and lower maintenance costs.

Michael Bevilacqua-Linn
(256 pages) ISBN: 9781937785475. $36
https://pragprog.com/book/mbfpp

Agile Web Development with Rails 7

Rails 7 completely redefines what it means to produce fantastic user experiences and provides a way to achieve all the benefits of single-page applications – at a fraction of the complexity. Rails 7 integrates the Hotwire frameworks of Stimulus and Turbo directly as the new defaults, together with that hot newness of import maps. The result is a toolkit so powerful that it allows a single individual to create modern applications upon which they can build a competitive business. The way it used to be.

Sam Ruby
(474 pages) ISBN: 9781680509298. $59.95
https://pragprog.com/book/rails7

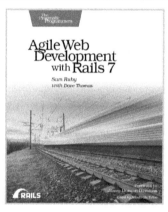

Creating Software with Modern Diagramming Techniques

Diagrams communicate relationships more directly and clearly than words ever can. Using only text-based markup, create meaningful and attractive diagrams to document your domain, visualize user flows, reveal system architecture at any desired level, or refactor your code. With the tools and techniques this book will give you, you'll create a wide variety of diagrams in minutes, share them with others, and revise and update them immediately on the basis of feedback. Adding diagrams to your professional vocabulary will enable you to work through your ideas quickly when working on your own code or discussing a proposal with colleagues.

Ashley Peacock
(156 pages) ISBN: 9781680509830. $29.95
https://pragprog.com/book/apdiag

Mockito Made Clear

Mockito is the most popular framework in the Java world for automating unit testing with dependencies. Learn the Mockito API and how and when to use stubs, mocks, and spies. On a deeper level, discover why the framework does what it does and how it can simplify unit testing in Java. Using Mockito, you'll be able to isolate the code you want to test from the behavior or state of external dependencies without coding details of the dependency. You'll gain insights into the Mockito API, save time when unit testing, and have confidence in your Java programs.

Ken Kousen
(87 pages) ISBN: 9781680509670. $14.99
https://pragprog.com/book/mockito

Designing Data Governance from the Ground Up

Businesses own more data than ever before, but it's of no value if you don't know how to use it. Data governance manages the people, processes, and strategy needed for deploying data projects to production. But doing it well is far from easy: Less than one fourth of business leaders say their organizations are data driven. In *Designing Data Governance from the Ground Up*, you'll build a cross-functional strategy to create roadmaps and stewardship for data-focused projects, embed data governance into your engineering practice, and put processes in place to monitor data after deployment.

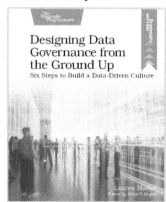

Lauren Maffeo
(100 pages) ISBN: 9781680509809. $29.95
https://pragprog.com/book/lmmlops

Building Table Views with Phoenix LiveView

Data is at the core of every business, but it is useless if nobody can access and analyze it. Learn how to generate business value by making your data accessible with advanced table UIs. This definitive guide teaches you how to bring your data to the fingertips of nontechnical users with advanced features like pagination, sorting, filtering, and infinity scrolling. Build reactive and reuseable table components by leveraging Phoenix LiveView, schemaless changesets, and Ecto query composition. Table UIs are the bread and butter for every web developer, so it is time to learn how to build them right.

Peter Ullrich
(65 pages) ISBN: 9781680509731. $14.99
https://pragprog.com/book/puphoe

Numerical Brain Teasers

Challenge your brain with math! Using nothing more than basic arithmetic and logic, you'll be thrilled as answers slot into place. Whether purely for fun or to test your knowledge, you'll sharpen your problem-solving skills and flex your mental muscles. All you need is logical thought, a little patience, and a clear mind. There are no gotchas here. These puzzles are the perfect introduction to or refresher for math concepts you may have only just learned or long since forgotten. Get ready to have more fun with numbers than you've ever had before.

Erica Sadun
(186 pages) ISBN: 9781680509748. $18.95
https://pragprog.com/book/esbrain

Exploring Graphs with Elixir

Data is everywhere—it's just not very well connected, which makes it super hard to relate dataset to dataset. Using graphs as the underlying glue, you can readily join data together and create navigation paths across diverse sets of data. Add Elixir, with its awesome power of concurrency, and you'll soon be mastering data networks. Learn how different graph models can be accessed and used from within Elixir and how you can build a robust semantics overlay on top of graph data structures. We'll start from the basics and examine the main graph paradigms. Get ready to embrace the world of connected data!

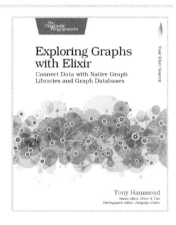

Tony Hammond
(294 pages) ISBN: 9781680508406. $47.95
https://pragprog.com/book/thgraphs

The Pragmatic Bookshelf

The Pragmatic Bookshelf features books written by professional developers for professional developers. The titles continue the well-known Pragmatic Programmer style and continue to garner awards and rave reviews. As development gets more and more difficult, the Pragmatic Programmers will be there with more titles and products to help you stay on top of your game.

Visit Us Online

This Book's Home Page
https://pragprog.com/book/vsjava2e
Source code from this book, errata, and other resources. Come give us feedback, too!

Keep Up-to-Date
https://pragprog.com
Join our announcement mailing list (low volume) or follow us on Twitter @pragprog for new titles, sales, coupons, hot tips, and more.

New and Noteworthy
https://pragprog.com/news
Check out the latest Pragmatic developments, new titles, and other offerings.

Save on the ebook

Save on the ebook versions of this title. Owning the paper version of this book entitles you to purchase the electronic versions at a terrific discount.

PDFs are great for carrying around on your laptop—they are hyperlinked, have color, and are fully searchable. Most titles are also available for the iPhone and iPod touch, Amazon Kindle, and other popular e-book readers.

Send a copy of your receipt to support@pragprog.com and we'll provide you with a discount coupon.

Contact Us

Online Orders:	*https://pragprog.com/catalog*
Customer Service:	*support@pragprog.com*
International Rights:	*translations@pragprog.com*
Academic Use:	*academic@pragprog.com*
Write for Us:	*http://write-for-us.pragprog.com*
Or Call:	+1 800-699-7764

Milton Keynes UK
Ingram Content Group UK Ltd.
UKHW030926270923
429432UK00006B/15